"This excellent book will be a very welcome aid to the many people who daily need to understand and help youngsters who are experiencing serious anxiety. Consistent with much scientific evidence, Dr. Wagner endorses Cognitive-Behavioral Therapy as the treatment method most helpful for anxiety. She explains this treatment method very clearly so that it will be understandable to both parents and teachers. A strength of this book is that it is scientifically sound as well as highly readable for parents and professionals. The tables, forms and tools throughout the book simplify and clarify the treatment techniques for intervention; and those for children are very user friendly. The specific strategies for both normal and problem anxieties should be very helpful for parents and teachers."

Sara S. Sparrow, Ph.D., Professor and Chief Psychologist
Yale University Child Study Center

About the author

Dr. Aureen Pinto Wagner is Clinical Associate Professor of Neurology at the University of Rochester School of Medicine & Dentistry, Director of The Anxiety Wellness Center in Rochester, NY, and member of the Scientific Advisory Board of the International OCD Foundation. Dr. Wagner is a Clinical Child Psychologist whose unique *Worry Hill*® approach to making cognitive-behavioral therapy accessible to youngsters has gained her international recognition. In addition to *Worried No More* and its professional tool kit *Worried No More: Forms and Tools on CD*, Dr. Wagner is the author of three other highly acclaimed books, *Up and Down the Worry Hill: A Children's Book about Obsessive-Compulsive Disorder and its Treatment*, *What to do when your Child has Obsessive-Compulsive Disorder: Strategies and Solutions* and *Treatment of OCD in Children and Adolescents: Professional's Kit*. These three books comprise the only integrated set of resources for children with OCD, their parents and their therapists.

Dr. Wagner received her education at St. Agnes College, the University of Iowa, Yale University Child Study Center and Brown University. Dr. Wagner is a highly engaging and sought-after speaker whose workshops for clinicians, school professionals and parents consistently receive outstanding reviews. Dr. Wagner lives in Rochester, NY with her family.

Aureen Pinto Wagner, Ph.D.

Worried No More

Help and Hope for Anxious Children

Second Edition

Highly effective practical strategies for
parents, school and health care professionals
to help children overcome
worry, school refusal, separation anxiety, social anxiety,
excessive shyness, panic, phobias, disasters and tragedies,
obsessions and compulsions.

A Lighthouse Press book

Copyright ©2002, 2005 by Lighthouse Press, Inc.
All rights reserved.

Library of Congress Control Number 2005904127

Published by
Lighthouse Press, Inc.
35 Ryans Run
Rochester, NY 14624-1160

Toll free US and Canada: 1-888-749-8768
www.Lighthouse-Press.com

WORRY HILL is registered in the U.S. Patent and Trademark Office

Publisher's Cataloging-in-Publication
Wagner, Aureen Pinto.
    Worried no more: help and hope for anxious children
/ Aureen Pinto Wagner. — 2 nd ed.
    p. cm.
    Includes bibliographical references and index.
    "Practical guidance for parents, school personnel and
health care professionals to help children cope with
worry, school refusal, separation anxiety, social
anxiety, excessive shyness, panic, phobias, disasters
and tragedies, obsessions and compulsions.
        ISBN-10: 0-9677347-9-7
        ISBN-13: 978-0-9677347-9-8

    1. Anxiety in children.   I. Title.

    RJ506.A58W34 2005   618.92'8522

Cover photo: Comstock.com
Printed in the United States of America
V22009 Third Printing

To my parents

Baptist and Winifred Pinto,

with love and gratitude.

Acknowledgments

My journey from the inception to the completion of *Worried No More* has been blessed with the wisdom, caring and sharing of many. My foundation in cognitive-behavioral therapy (CBT) is derived from the pioneering work of gifted psychologists and psychiatrists, including Drs. Lee Baer, David Barlow, Aaron Beck, Edna Foa, John Greist, Michael Jenike, Philip Kendall, John March, Isaac Marks and Judith Rapoport. Their seminal contributions have allowed me to share the message of hope and recovery with many children and families who struggle with anxiety.

I am thankful to many who have had a profound influence on me as a clinical psychologist, therapist and writer by virtue of their teaching, mentoring and faith in me. My teachers at St. Agnes College, the University of Iowa and the Yale Child Study Center taught me how to think clearly and rationally, and to pursue rigor, accuracy and efficacy. Greta Francis at Brown University first sparked my interest in treating anxiety. My long time friend and colleague Emily Richardson has been with me through the ups and downs of graduate school and thereafter; her lasting friendship, support and honest critique of my thinking and writing have been invaluable. My colleague, Judy Kelly, a special education expert in a child and adolescent psychiatric clinic, gave me unique insights into the world of the school system. Bette Hartley at the Madison Institute of Medicine was always prompt in her assistance with researching the latest literature.

I am indebted to a loving family: To my husband Scott who has believed in me from the start. His careful scrutiny of countless drafts allowed me to convey my thoughts with greater clarity; to our children Catherine and Ethan, who bring me great joy and delight, and from whom I borrowed the time to work on this book; to my parents, Baptist and Winifred Pinto, for the sacrifices they made to give me the best education possible and to instill in me enduring values of hard work, persistence, and the pursuit of my dreams; to my siblings Adrian and Merlyn whose generosity helped me realize my vision of graduate school, and Jean and Kevin, for their support and encouragement.

Most of all, this book would not have been possible without the children and their families who gave me a window into the world of anxiety. In sharing of their lives, their anguish and their triumphs, I learned what it must be like to live with anxiety every day. I appreciate the opportunity to participate in their recoveries and celebrate their victories.

In the years that I have worked with anxious children and their families, I have been most inspired by their courage. They have been willing to step out of their comfort zone and take the risk of learning and trying new ways to think about and react to anxiety. They have gone against their first instincts to confront and conquer fears. It has been gratifying and edifying to be a part of their journey to mastery of anxiety. It has been heartwarming to see many anxious children shake off the mantle of fear and blossom into the warm, funny, intelligent or creative youngsters they were meant to be.

Putting pen to paper has been a powerful experience. My goal in writing this book has been to bring the simple, safe and successful strategies of cognitive-behavioral therapy to parents, schools and healthcare professionals. I hope that this book will inspire parents and professionals to help anxious children open the gates to a life of freedom from fear.

Table of Contents

Tables and Figures

Chapter 1

Children in the Shadow

It comes as a surprise to many, parents and professionals alike, that anxiety is the most common mental health problem in children and adults. According to the U.S. Surgeon General's Report on Mental Health (1999), 13% of children and adolescents—as many as 1 in 8 youngsters between ages 9 and 17—suffer from an anxiety disorder. The Surgeon General's data described above was collected before the events of 9/11 and the ensuing dawn of an era where safety and security cannot be taken for granted. More recent studies estimate the prevalence of anxiety disorders among youth in the United States to be 12% to 20%. Today, there are more reasons than ever for us and our children to be anxious about danger.

Anxious children are often the *children in the shadow*. They may be in the shadow of children whose more disruptive difficulties claim the immediate attention of parents and teachers. Although anxious children can have problems of similar magnitude, they may be less visible because they often place the burden of suffering on themselves rather than on others. Adults are often unaware of their private anguish. Anxious children may therefore go unrecognized and untreated, leaving them with more challenges to encounter as their anxiety continues to overpower them.

Many anxious children are very capable but may not realize their true potential because anxiety can take over their school, social and family lives. If untreated, anxious children may be at higher risk for academic decline, poor peer relationships, substance abuse and cigarette smoking. They may drop out of school and continue to have difficulties through adolescence. As adults, they may struggle with job difficulties, unsatisfactory personal relationships, depression or substance abuse. The majority of adults with anxiety disorders say that their anxiety began in childhood. Clearly, children don't just outgrow serious anxiety.

The best news in all of this is that there is both help and hope for anxious children. Anxiety is very treatable, and success rates with the right treatment are excellent—as high as 80% in children and adolescents. The strategies in this book are based in cognitive-behavioral therapy (CBT), a highly effective treatment that has been proven in hundreds of research studies with adults and, more recently, with children.

Success rates with the right treatment are as high as 80%

The sooner children with anxiety are identified and treated, the sooner they can get back on track with the business of growing up, learning and being happy. Early intervention, a decision in the hands of parents and professionals, may help prevent a life of trials and tribulations for anxious children. Acting early and wisely can help them take back their childhoods.

My focus in treating anxiety in children and adolescents has been on making scientifically-proven CBT user-friendly for children, parents and professionals. The child-friendly metaphor of the *Worry Hill®* (Wagner, 2000; 2002) conveys the essence of treatment in a language that is easy for children and adolescents to understand. The *Worry Hill* treatment protocol emphasizes building treatment readiness prior to starting treatment, active collaboration between the child, parent and professional in treatment, and fostering self-reliance in recovery. Step-by-step examples, ready-to-use forms and tools for parents and professionals make the techniques clear and easy to understand.

Worried No More is designed to bring simple, safe and successful anxiety management strategies out of the doctor's and therapist's office and into homes and schools. It is written to help the important adults in a child's life—parents and school professionals—teach children to help themselves. It is designed to allow parents, teachers, school psychologists, counselors, doctors and therapists to work in synchrony in the best interest of the child.

Parents and teachers are among the *first contacts* for an anxious child and are therefore crucial to early detection and intervention. They are probably the most influential adults in a child's life. They shape the day-to-day environments in which children function and must continue to function.

Children spend about half their waking hours at home and the other half in school. This amounts to more than 1000 hours a year in school. Parents and teachers are in the unique position of being intimately familiar with the child's day-to-day functioning in ways that doctors and therapists cannot hope to be in their brief and limited contacts with the children they treat. Parents and professionals need to know more about anxiety in children so that they can recognize and help anxious children sooner rather than later.

School is the *real world* for the child. It is the place where children have the opportunity to meet some of the major developmental tasks of childhood — to learn, make friends and have fun. It is the most natural environment that brings together all aspects of a child's growing and maturing needs. Yet, the real world of school can also be the focus of intense performance and socialization pressures for children. There are increasingly high academic standards, extracurricular activities, large volumes of homework and pressure to perform on standardized tests. Children are faced with difficult choices with regard to peer norms concerning substance use and other risky behaviors. The price for making healthy choices may be peer rejection.

Schools and parents also have the potential to be the *first line of defense* in helping anxious youngsters. They are the natural resources most easily available and accessible to the child. Traditionally, mental health treatment has taken place outside the child's natural environment, in the clinician's office. There is now emphasis on the need to move treatment out of the clinician's office and into the context in which children function every day. In fact, schools may be best suited to help children with mild to moderate levels of anxiety. Clinicians need to recognize and harness the potential of parents and school professionals to be active helpers in an anxious child's recovery rather than being passive onlookers. Many children may go without hope if this potential is overlooked.

Parents, schools and clinicians must collaborate and work as a team if children are to receive treatment that is successful in the long-term. Each has a different expertise in shaping the well-being of the child. Each has an equally important and complementary role to play. An effective partnership develops when all players can work together for the child.

Worried No More will systematically walk you from the beginnings of understanding anxiety to learning the specific steps to use at home and at school for mastery of anxiety. Chapters 1 to 8 focus on the nature of anxiety, the differences between normal and problem anxiety, and the fuel that escalates anxiety. The topics covered in these chapters include:

- Normal fears and anxieties
- Age differences in the expression of anxiety
- When does anxiety become a problem?
- Anxiety disorders in children
- Indications of anxiety in school
- Other disorders associated with anxiety
- Warning signs and signals
- What causes anxiety disorders in children?
- The fuel that keeps anxiety going

Chapters 9 to 15 describe treatment and effective strategies for parents, schools and clinicians. The topics covered in these chapters include:

- Effective treatment using cognitive-behavioral therapy
- Medications for anxiety
- What parents can do to help
- What not to do
- An action plan at home
- What schools can do to help
- Collaborations between parents and schools
- An action plan at school
- Building self-reliance in anxious children
- Managing meltdowns and explosiveness
- Engaging reluctant children in treatment
- When and how to find professional help

The techniques offered in this book should not be used as a replacement for guidance, consultation, assessment or treatment by a qualified mental health professional such as a clinical child psychologist, child psychiatrist or social worker. Applying some of the treatment strategies described in this book requires both appropriate training and experience in treating anxious children. Interventions should therefore be implemented either by, or under the supervision of a professional with the requisite training. Some anxious children need additional treatment by a mental health professional.

Clinicians and School Professionals may use the professional tool kit
"Worried No More: Teaching Tools and Forms on CD"
to accompany this book.

Chapter 2

The Many Faces of Anxiety

Anxiety can manifest in many different ways, some of which are not easy to detect. Each child is unique and different; expressions of anxiety can therefore be quite variable. In order to be of help to children with anxiety, it is necessary to be aware of both the obvious and the obscure. The children described below portray some of the faces of anxiety that are in our homes and in our schools. Their names have been changed to protect their privacy.

SARAH

Sarah is 7 and starting second grade. Although bright, warm and popular, she has always been somewhat nervous, timid and hesitant. When Sarah wakes up in the morning, she starts sobbing but is not able to say why she is upset. She clings to her parents and begs to stay home from school. Sarah has been getting to school late, and sometimes does not get there at all. When she is at school, she is tearful, overwhelmed, and embarrassed. She frequently asks what time it is and complains of feeling sick. She is not able to focus on her work, and is restless and preoccupied. She asks to go to the nurse's office to rest. Once there, she asks to call her mother on the phone. When Sarah speaks to her mother, she pleads with her to let her go home.

When Sarah returns home from school, she is exhausted but relieved. She seems to panic if she is alone in any room in her home, and demands to know where her mother is at all times. Sarah seems to be very concerned about family members and asks repeatedly if each one is okay. She is very upset when her mother goes to the grocery store without her, and when her younger brother goes to a neighbor's house to play. Bedtimes are a nightmare of tears, refusal to stay in her bed and repeated awakenings.

CASEY

Casey has just turned 9. A lively, confident and well-liked youngster, he now seems to be very unsure of himself. At home, he cannot decide what to wear, if his bed is made or if he has washed his hands enough. His socks and shoes just don't feel right. He has to eat the same breakfast each morning, and check his book bag several times before school. Often, he barely makes it to the bus on time, even with his mother's prodding and urging. Mornings are very rushed and stressful for Casey and his family.

At school, Casey asks his teacher Mrs. Kelly several times if he is okay, but doesn't seem satisfied with her assurances. He hovers near her and draws her attention to himself frequently, often with the same questions. One question is particularly odd: Casey asks Mrs. Kelly several times if he has said a "bad word" like "idiot" even when he has clearly not. When she tells him he has not, he says he wants to say sorry, just in case he did. He blinks and scrunches up his nose frequently but doesn't seem to notice. Casey is very excited when Mrs. Kelly assigns the class a painting project. But his excitement suddenly fades, and he asks Mrs. Kelly if the paint fumes will make him sick. She reassures him that it is non-toxic paint, but he asks the same question several times. Casey begins drawing but erases his drawing repeatedly. He complains that it is not the way he wants it. He begins to get frustrated, and eventually crumples up the paper and throws it on the floor. When school is done, Casey leaves in tears.

EMILY

Emily is a 12-year-old who has just completed 6th grade. She is a polite, well-behaved, hardworking child and "a joy to have in class." She typically enjoys school, gets good grades and has close friends. Emily has always been compliant and eager to please. Her parents and teachers can count on her to follow the rules. Recently, Emily appears to have lost interest in her work and her friends. She seems distracted, quiet, withdrawn and preoccupied. Her previously diligent and meticulous work is now incomplete and untidy. She seems upset about not doing well, but does not offer any explanations. It's really not like her and the teacher is puzzled.

The teacher knows something is not right because Emily frequently complains of dizziness and nausea. Recently, Emily has left the classroom often because she feels sick.

Emily is having similar difficulties at home. She has always been a bit of a "worrier," fretting about whether she has done her work well, about whether she said or did the right thing, and if she hurt anyone's feelings. Now, she seems to worry constantly about everything—about whether she is sick, if there will be tornados, or if she will let down her dance team by not being good enough. Recently, homework and bedtime have become a battle ground between Emily and her parents. She complains that she is making mistakes, even when her parents verify that she is not, and that she cannot do her work "the way the teacher wants it." She erases her work repeatedly, making it untidy and illegible. Emily and her parents are exhausted each night after these battles. After several visits to the doctor for stomach aches and nausea, Emily's pediatrician has ruled out medical causes for Emily's symptoms.

ALEX

Alex is an energetic, bold and adventurous 14-year-old. Although he is very bright and quick to learn, Alex is not doing well academically. His grades are marginal, and the teacher believes he could easily make top grades if only he would be serious about his work. He has missed school often recently, and sometimes comes in late. Alex can be immature and silly in class, distracting other children and making them laugh when he clowns around. He seems to be clumsy and disorganized, dropping things and reaching to pick them up, and opening and shutting his book bag to get pencils or books. He appears to touch and bump things repeatedly on purpose. He doesn't pay attention to the teacher and seems to forget her instructions in an instant. Alex leaves the classroom frequently to use the bathroom. He can be very irritable and sullen, and "flips out" if the other children touch him or his belongings, even if by accident. Alex recently hit a peer who accidentally bumped into him in the cafeteria line. When staff intervened, Alex ran to the bathroom and refused to come out.

At home, Alex is unpredictable. On some days, he is pleasant and easygoing, but more often than not, he has a meltdown over next to nothing as soon as he walks in the door. He lashes out at his sister in anger, swearing at her and hitting her. Alex's parents say that rewards and punishments don't work for him—he just doesn't care when he's so angry. They feel like they're walking on eggshells for fear of triggering his rage.

JOSEPH

Joseph is a quiet 17-year-old who is easily lost in the crowd. Ever since he was a young child, Joseph was always reluctant to try new activities or go to social gatherings. After years of encouraging and coaxing him to attend soccer games, boy scouts and church youth gatherings, his parents gave up trying because it was easier than the tiresome arguments. At home, Joseph is buried in a book or computer game and likes to be in his room.

At school, Joseph does not appear to have any friends and prefers to keep to himself. He seems to be intensely uncomfortable where there are many students, such as in the cafeteria or the gym. He missed school several times last year after he had the flu, and then seemed reluctant to attend. Joseph says that his classmates look at him as if he is "geeky and weird." The teacher has encouraged him to join in some after-school clubs, but Joseph has responded by becoming angry and asking to be left alone. He often seems sullen and preoccupied, and his classmates seem cautious about approaching him.

Joseph has expressed interest in getting a job to earn money for his computer games. However, he does not initiate any action to make phone calls or request application forms. Joseph's mother finally picked up an application form for him and submitted it to the store after he had completed it. When the call for an interview came, Joseph decided he wasn't interested in the job after all, and didn't go to the interview.

Which of these children is anxious? All of them have an anxiety disorder, even though it may not be obvious at first glance. Sarah and Emily are the more classic anxious children who fit the typecast of anxiety. Casey struggles with doubts that have no basis in reality. Sarah, Emily and Casey are clearly distressed and win the sympathy and support of parents and teachers. On the other hand, Alex comes across as deliberately annoying, silly and defiant. Parents and school professionals may be surprised to hear that Alex has an anxiety disorder. He does not fit the stereotypic profile of the anxious child—meek, mild-mannered and deferent. Joseph pushes away those who try to help him. Teachers and peers have found it easier to leave him alone.

Chapter 3

Anxiety: Normal and Necessary

Each of us knows the experience of anxiety, because it is ubiquitous and universal. We don't usually stop to think about or define it because it is so much a part of our lives. What we know as anxiety is the uneasiness, worry or tension we experience when we expect a threat to our security. The sense of danger may be real or perceived, and it may come from outside or from within us.

Although anxiety is not pleasant, it is actually both valuable and necessary to us for our safety. We need it for *preparation* and *protection* against threat and danger. When faced with peril, we gear ourselves up to react with "fight or flight." We either tackle danger head on or escape from it to protect ourselves. Anxiety has survival value and is both adaptive and necessary for our existence.

> *Anxiety is normal, natural and necessary for our survival*

Anxiety is the result of a person's *judgment* of risk or danger inherent in the situation. What makes one person anxious may not arouse the sense of threat in another. For instance, some children become very anxious when there is a thunderstorm whereas others are unperturbed. Moreover, the level of anxiety experienced by each person in the same situation can be quite different. A warning about an impending hurricane may elicit reactions ranging from relative composure to abject terror among both adults and children. We experience anxiety about a variety of situations on a daily basis. For the most part, our anxiety is aroused by a specific situation, and subsides when the perceived threat no longer exists.

Anxiety has three related components: *cognitive*, *physiological* and *behavioral*, which are thoughts, physical symptoms and behaviors, respectively. These three components are closely related and influence each other. Their expression can vary from person to person.

The *cognitive* component reflects the person's perception and interpretation of a situation. The person's thoughts become focused on bad and undesirable outcomes, and there is dread, trepidation, and worry. *"That test will be too hard. I am going to fail."* The *physiological* symptoms of anxiety may include stomachaches, nausea, headaches, muscle tension, rapid heart rate, palpitations, hot flashes, etc. Some or all of these changes occur when the sympathetic nervous system prepares the body to respond to threat and danger. The *behavioral* element refers to the person's actions in response to anxiety. There may be a wide variety of responses from person to person. Common reactions include pacing, avoidance, reluctance to participate, procrastination, poor concentration, edginess, irritability, asking reassurance, crying, or working harder to prevent the feared situation from happening. A child who is afraid of failing the spelling test may study the spelling words repeatedly for many hours. Another may find it easier to stall and avoid having to deal with the list altogether. Yet another may ask her mother several times for reassurance that she will pass the test.

Normal anxiety is protective, manageable, transient and limited to specific situations. At an optimal level, anxiety is a productive and motivating force. We fare better when we are alert enough to foresee and circumvent hazards, and when we have reasonable apprehension about performance. The child who has normal anxiety about a test will most likely work harder to do well than the child who is nonchalant. The mother who is concerned about her toddler's safety will remove potential harm from his path.

Anxiety that is too low or too high can work against us. At low levels, we may be unperturbed and indifferent and may put ourselves in harm's way by being careless, reckless or taking undue risks. High anxiety results in a near-constant state of tension and hyper vigilance that is exhausting and unsustainable. It is high levels of anxiety are the focus of this book.

NORMAL FEARS AND ANXIETIES

Fears and anxieties among children are normal, common and passing reactions to a host of situations. Approximately 40% of grade school children have fears of separation from a parent. Approximately 33% of children worry about their competence and seek reassurance. About 20% have fears of heights, are shy in new situations and are anxious about public speaking and social acceptance. It is also common to have multiple fears at the same time. In fact, research surveys have shown that as many as 40% of children aged 6 to 12 have seven or more fears. Girls may report more anxiety and fears than boys do at most ages, but this may be an artifact of social expectations. Girls' fears generally pertain to animals, illness and injury, whereas boys' fears center on peer rejection and academic failure.

We go through many "developmental stages" in life from birth onwards— infancy, the toddler years, childhood, adolescence and adulthood. At each stage, we are expected to reach and achieve motor, language, social, emotional and psychological milestones known as "developmental tasks". Infants must learn to feed; toddlers to walk and talk; children to read, write and socialize; adolescents to become independent and prepare for adulthood; and adults to work, to name a few.

> *Anxiety occurs when the demands of development exceed the ability to cope.*

The developmental tasks encountered at any age may become a natural focus of anxiety due to difficulty grasping, managing, negotiating and mastering these tasks, especially when they are new. Anxiety occurs when the demands of the tasks exceed the ability to cope.

Fears and anxieties progress and change during different stages of life. Young children commonly have apprehension about situations that involve safety, security and "growing up." Their fears revolve around issues such as separating from parents, attending school and developing peer relationships. As children develop cognitive and emotional skills, they show increasing awareness of the potential dangers and threats in the environment, and in the ability to anticipate the future. The adolescent's anxious energy is diverted to performance, social evaluation, independence, self-sufficiency, moral and ethical issues. The world in which we live provides children with an endless array of opportunities to be anxious about real or imagined events.

Most childhood fears are outgrown or recede in importance as the child matures and moves to the next developmental stage. Awareness of the normal course of childhood fears allows parents and school personnel to recognize when the child is expressing expected and age-appropriate worries and to discern if there is reasonable cause for concern. It also allows them to be prepared to deal with the child's fears when they arise, and to ease the challenge of outgrowing them.

Normal fears and anxieties at various stages in life manifest as follows:

Table 1: Normal Fears and Anxieties

Stage	*Focus of Anxiety*
Infancy	Stranger anxiety
Toddler years	Separation, sudden, intense, novel
Preschool/kindergarten	Large, harmful, dark, imaginary
Elementary school	Dangers of the world
Middle school	Academic/social competence, natural dangers, death
High school	Abstract, relationships, future

Infancy

Stranger anxiety is the first clearly identifiable anxiety, and occurs around 7 to 9 months of age. It reflects the infant's growing ability to differentiate its mother from other people. The infant recognizes that familiar caregivers provide safety and nurturing, and is unsure and cautious around unfamiliar people. She is wary, keeps a safe distance and displays resistance, crying and clinging when strangers approach. Stranger anxiety decreases after the first year of life.

The toddler years

Separation anxiety emerges at the end of the first year and dissipates within a few months. Separation fears reflect the child's growing attachment to parents, and a sense of belonging. The child is sad when the parent leaves, and fears being left behind; his trust grows when his parents return. By the end of the second year, most children are able to accept the mother's temporary absence, are comforted by others, and engage in play with other children. Young, immature, shy children have more difficulty with separation. In addition to separation fears, toddlers are afraid of intense, sudden or loud noises, and new, large and potentially harmful objects such as large toys or vacuum cleaners.

Preschool and kindergarten years

Separation fears may resurface when the child starts preschool or kindergarten. Yet, the fear at this age may not be so much about separation as it is about the new, unfamiliar and overwhelming environment that children encounter at school. There are many more children and adults to deal with in a large, new place. Children also become afraid of potentially dangerous things such as large dogs, "creepy crawlies," the dark and imaginary characters such as monsters.

Elementary-school years

Children of elementary school age become more aware of the dangers of the world beyond their home and classroom. They are cognitively able to appreciate these dangers, but less equipped to put them in perspective or cope with them effectively. This is coupled with the realization that their parents are not omnipotent and cannot protect them from everything. Newly acquired information pertaining to health and safety may be taken to heart. Grade-school curricula such as "stranger danger" and information provided in health and hygiene classes may be taken to an extreme by the child. Children also become cognizant of events in the media that present alarm and danger, such as missing children or violence. However, in most cases, there is a novelty effect, and the intensity of the fear wears off with time.

Middle-school years

During the middle-school years, the focus of anxiety shifts to school-related events such as academic performance, personal and social competence. Making and keeping friends is a source of significant anxiety at this time. Children become more conscious of their public presentation and image and more sensitive to social scrutiny. Other areas of fear are health-related issues and natural phenomena such as thunderstorms, earthquakes and floods. Death, afterlife, finality and mortality begin to raise questions in the minds of children at this age. They commonly worry about parents or loved ones getting hurt or dying.

Adolescence

Adolescents are less concerned about concrete threats than they are about the more abstract. The focus of adolescent anxiety shifts from external threats to internalized worries. Teenagers have concerns regarding acceptance in peer groups, rejection in social relationships, the future, moral issues, dating competence, career choices and separation from parents. The "separation fears" of adolescents are the polar opposite of childhood separation fears. Whereas younger children don't want to separate, adolescents may be only too impatient to separate!

Adulthood

Adults worry about a multitude of issues such as finances, relationships with significant others, children, job stability, satisfaction, health and personal competence.

Fears common across ages

Fears pertaining to illness, pain, death, medical and dental procedures, doctor visits, natural disasters, wars and traumatic events can occur at all ages. As we are well aware, traumatic and tragic events such as the spate of school shootings, abductions of children by sexual offenders, terrorism and war can induce tremendous anxiety in children, parents and school professionals alike.

Parents, teachers and other school professionals can help children negotiate these fears with greater ease by providing appropriate guidance and support. Many intuitive parenting responses can ease a child's anxieties. These include comforting, providing assurances of safety, preparing children for unfamiliar events with information and explanations, removing uncertainty, and providing opportunities for repetition of new or unfamiliar tasks. When possible and reasonable, it is appropriate to remove the source of the threat. For instance, it is reasonable to shut off the vacuum cleaner that makes the toddler afraid. Yet, in many circumstances, it is neither possible nor appropriate to eliminate the threat. Instead, it is more adaptive for the child to learn how to cope with the anxiety. It is not possible to stop a thunderstorm, provide certainty about safety or guarantee academic or social success. In these situations, it is more helpful to teach the child an appropriate way to deal with the fear. Specific interventions for overcoming fears are discussed in Chapters 9 onwards.

NORMAL RITUALS AND SUPERSTITIONS

The familiar ring of the childhood chant, "Step on a crack, break your mother's back," reminds us of benign and universal childhood beliefs, routines and rituals. In addition to fears and anxieties, it is both normal and common for children to have a host of superstitions, fixed routines and repetitious behaviors. Walking around ladders, keeping fingers crossed, knocking on wood and avoiding black cats—children indulge in some form of these common superstitions at some time or another.

As adults, we are not exempt from routines and rituals either. We may check the doors and windows at night. We may go through toilet and grooming routines in the same invariant sequence every day. These seemingly inconsequential routines and repetitions also have an important role to play in our lives. They allow us to be more organized, efficient and productive. Familiarity allows us to develop a level of automation that permits us to divert our energy to where it is really needed. Normal routines and habits help us thrive, succeed and gain a sense of mastery over our day-to-day environment. In fact, many highly accomplished people are successful because they are 'compulsive' in their work habits. Checking, ordering, repetition and perfectionism make them methodical and thorough.

For children, routines play an even greater role in development, as they provide security, soothing and comfort. The set sequences of bedtime, goodbye, dressing and eating rituals are familiar to all parents. Jenny will only drink from her "favorite" blue cup at breakfast. Three year-old Catherine who is being dressed in haste protests, "But Mommy, we always put my pants on *before* we put on my shirt." About two-thirds of young children may insist on sameness in the daily routine and become agitated if interrupted or disrupted. Routines make the day familiar, comfortable and predictable, easing the child's transitions, uncertainty and fears. They allow the child to develop mastery in learning new tasks, and to sort through an often overwhelming and confusing world. Repetition fosters mastery and learning. Children never seem to tire of reading the same book, watching the same movie or playing the same game an infinite number of times.

As children grow into adolescence, they phase out of early rituals and are drawn into collecting habits, hobbies, and focused interests on specific topics such as sports cards, dinosaurs, electronic games, airplanes or science fiction movie characters. Not only are these pastimes enjoyable and satisfying; they also allow youngsters to assimilate large amounts of knowledge and gain mastery of the world around them.

AGE DIFFERENCES IN EXPRESSION OF ANXIETY

There are notable differences in the expression of anxiety across the lifespan. Understanding these differences is essential for proper assessment and treatment that is flexible and sensitive to a child's age and maturity.

At the young end of the age spectrum, anxiety is expressed very openly and with obvious distress. Infants and toddlers may display anxiety by crying, clinging and refusal to encounter the feared situation by backing away or freezing. Preschoolers and elementary school children may become restless, irritable, agitated, or resistant, and have temper tantrums or hair-triggered "meltdowns." They may check to see if the threat is still present or seek reassurance repeatedly. They may have nightmares or sleep terrors.

With increasing maturity comes the capacity to internalize the anxiety response. Middle-school children may become more worried, withdrawn and shy away, or complain of feeling sick, with frequent stomachaches or other physical symptoms. Older children and adolescents may suffer from excessive worry or insomnia and are more likely to be preoccupied and keep their fears and worries to themselves. Society is generally unreceptive to negative emotions, which are often attributed to a character flaw. Girls are socialized to be pleasant and unassertive and boys are socialized to curtail expression of fear, anxiety and other emotions suggestive of "weakness." Adolescents are also more likely to be reticent and hard to engage, and may even be secretive, because they are either embarrassed or think they will be misunderstood. They are unlikely to divulge anxiety, seek comfort or help from adults, and may attempt to cope on their own.

Among adults, anxiety generally takes the form of worry, rumination, physical discomfort, tension and irritability. Adolescents and adults may resort to numbing behaviors such as substance use or gratifying behaviors such as overeating to relieve anxiety. Sleep difficulties such as insomnia, frequent awakenings, restlessness and disturbed sleep are common to all ages. Frayed tempers and anger outbursts are likewise common when overwhelmed and stressed, regardless of age.

In general, children are less equipped than adolescents and adults to recognize and label anxiety, identify anxious thoughts, connect thoughts, physical sensations and feelings, or name specific triggers. Younger children are often unaware of their feelings or cannot articulate what they feel—they cannot give their anxiety a voice. They may not be able to distinguish between different types of feelings, or to communicate them verbally. They are not inclined towards self-awareness and do not know what makes them scared or nervous. These skills usually develop with age and maturity. Sarah, the youngster in Chapter 2 who has separation anxiety clings, sobs, clings and screams when she is away from family members, but is not able to say what makes her so upset.

It is very important for parents and professionals to know that children express anxiety very differently than adults. As adults, we may often assume that children know what's bothering them and are able to tell us, so that we know how to help. We have to remind ourselves that this skill is developed with age, and does not come intuitively to most children.

One significant implication of age differences in anxiety expression is that anxiety in children often goes unrecognized, undiagnosed, and even misdiagnosed. In fact, because children often express anxiety by having anger outbursts or being defiant, parents, teachers and even healthcare professionals may consider it noncompliance or misbehavior. They may then go down the wrong path in handling the symptoms. More

> *Anxiety in children is often unrecognized, undiagnosed, and even misdiagnosed*

concerning is the fact that an anxious child can receive the wrong kind of treatment. Parents and professionals who do not know the signs and signals of anxiety may therefore respond and react to the child's behavior in ways that are more harmful than helpful.

WHEN DOES ANXIETY BECOME A PROBLEM?

Since anxiety is normal, necessary and appropriate during certain periods in life, the importance of telling normal anxiety apart from problematic anxiety is crucial. Knowing these differences can help greatly towards identifying children who need treatment.

Anxiety becomes a problem when it begins to affect a child's ability to engage in the three main responsibilities of childhood—to learn, to make friends and to have fun. For most children, fears and anxieties come and go with time and age. For some children, anxiety does not follow this expected course, and becomes severe and long lasting.

Parents and school professionals are often confronted with the challenge of deciding whether a child's anxiety is merely normal, expected and will be outgrown in due time, or whether it merits concern and intervention. The distinction and decision process can sometimes be straightforward and at other times be quite complex and challenging. Often, parents don't have a clear benchmark against which to compare their child's behavior, especially in the case of an only child or a first child.

Anxiety extends on a continuum from normal and productive to excessive and detrimental. "Normal" anxiety in a child is that which appears to be age-expected, justifiable and reasonable to the circumstances. Table 2 indicates when anxiety crosses the threshold from normal to problematic. These rules of thumb are based on subjective judgments, which vary from one situation to the next.

Table 2: Indicators of Problem Anxiety

Normal Anxiety	*Problem Anxiety*
Reasonable	Excessive
Productive	Detrimental
Manageable	Uncontrollable
Mobilizing	Paralyzing
Specific	Pervasive
Time-limited	Chronic
Age-matched	Age-mismatched

Anxiety can cross the threshold from normal to problematic when children and adults encounter stress or major life events. For children, the loss of friends, a geographic move, change of schools, challenging academic requirements, tragic events, parental divorce, death or illness may be triggers for problem anxiety. This adjustment-related anxiety may diminish for some children when the stress resolves; for others, anxiety may persist.

THE FOUR D'S OF DISORDER

An anxiety disorder is at the extreme end of the continuum of anxiety. It is a matter of severity rather than differences in symptoms from normal anxiety. Not all anxiety becomes a problem, and not all problem anxiety becomes a disorder. Children can display a wide variety and high number of anxiety *symptoms* without ever developing a *disorder*.

The Four D's are a rule of thumb that parents and professionals can use to decide whether a child's anxiety is reaching the level of a disorder that warrants further assessment or treatment.

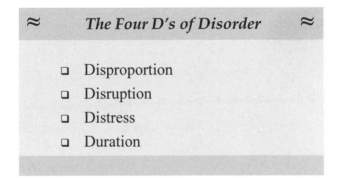

| ≈ | *The Four D's of Disorder* | ≈ |

- ❏ Disproportion
- ❏ Disruption
- ❏ Distress
- ❏ Duration

Disproportion

The anxiety is excessive, unreasonable, and well out of proportion to the situation or trigger. It is far beyond normal expectations for the situation and child's age. The child has an exaggerated sense of threat and danger, in situations where most people would not be concerned. The child is unable to stop or control the worry or fear, regardless of effort.

Disruption

The anxiety interferes substantially with the child's ability to function normally. She is not able to accomplish normal daily routines such as eat, get dressed, go to school, do homework or sleep.

Distress

The child is distraught and easily upset. The anxiety is burdensome and bothersome and the child is unhappy and miserable.

Duration

To meet criteria for a diagnosis of an anxiety disorder, a significant level of anxiety should be consistent over a period of time, typically one month.

Chapter 4

Anxiety Problems and Disorders

Diagnosis is a complex task that requires training, experience and astute clinical judgment. It should only be made by a qualified mental health professional after a thorough evaluation. This chapter is intended to help parents and school professionals become informed and aware of the range of anxiety problems and disorders in children and adolescents, to aid in early detection and referral. Expressions of each type of anxiety at school are also discussed.

The current system for diagnosis of anxiety disorders is the *Diagnostic and Statistical Manual of Mental Disorders, Fourth Edition* (DSM-IV) of the American Psychiatric Association. A diagnosis is made when a certain number or configuration of symptoms for a specific disorder is met. However, we don't come neatly packaged into categories, so making a diagnosis is not as simple as sorting apples from oranges. We are complex human beings, and while we have several similarities that allow us to fall into categories, we also have unique attributes that do not fit into boxes.

Many children with high levels of anxiety do not neatly fit the description of any anxiety disorder; whereas others may fit more than one category. A given diagnosis therefore may not capture all aspects of a child's anxiety. Although the DSM-IV may not be sensitive enough to all expressions of anxiety for children, there is no better system yet. Practically speaking, the treatment of anxiety (discussed in Chapter 9), is focused on specific *symptoms* and behaviors rather than specific diagnoses; therefore, treatment can be delivered effectively even in the absence of a good diagnostic fit.

SEPARATION ANXIETY DISORDER

Separation Anxiety Disorder (SAD) is the most common anxiety disorder among children and affects 2% to 3% of grade-school children. It involves excessive distress over day-to-day separation from parents, home or other familiar situations, and unrealistic fears of harm to loved ones. Seventy-five to eighty percent of the children who refuse to go to school have separation anxiety. Whereas normal separation fears are outgrown by age 5 or 6, SAD usually begins between the ages of 7 and 11. It often occurs fairly abruptly among children who previously had no problems with separation.

SAD is diagnosed only if fears persist, with very extreme reactions, beyond that expected for the child's age. A ten-year-old who cries and clings to a parent, refuses to go to school, or is afraid to stay at a friend's house may be showing signs of SAD. Children with SAD may often "shadow" their parents. They may beg for reassurance when a parent is away even briefly, cower from any opportunity to be separated, and sometimes even follow them from room to room. Sarah, the second-grader you met in Chapter 2, has SAD. She worries that something bad will happen to her or her parents and brother when she is away.

≈   ***Signs and symptoms of Separation Anxiety Disorder***   ≈

- ❑ Extreme, disproportionate distress over separation from loved ones
- ❑ Unwillingness to leave home, attend school, or go on outings
- ❑ Unrealistic worry about harm to self or loved ones
- ❑ Frequent seeking of reassurance about safety of self and loved ones
- ❑ Crying, clinging, tantrum, nausea or vomiting in anticipation of separation
- ❑ Reluctance to be alone, especially at night
- ❑ Nightmares about harm and danger
- ❑ Symptoms for at least four weeks

Indications of SAD in school

School refusal and tardiness are common indicators of SAD. Once in school, a child with SAD may be agitated, restless and nervous, and complain of stomachaches, headaches or nausea. The child may make frequent trips to the nurse's office, and ask to call her parent or to go home. The child may not eat or drink in school, and may ask for repeated reassurance about safety. Usually, the child experiences tremendous relief when the parent takes her home.

GENERALIZED ANXIETY DISORDER

Generalized Anxiety Disorder (GAD) is the most common anxiety disorder among adolescents. It involves uncontrollable worry or rumination over day-to-day events, both trivial and profound, with disproportionate fears of catastrophic consequences. The worry is often accompanied by physical tension, feeling on edge, stomach discomfort and sleep disturbance. Children with GAD are the "worrywarts" who carry the weight of the world on their shoulders. *"But what if...?"* pervades the thoughts of these children and is echoed in their repeated seeking of reassurance from adults. Past conversations, actions, family matters, friendships, school performance, health, the weather, what to wear tomorrow and a host of other issues, none too trivial to worry about, saturate the minds of children with GAD. Their worries are not confined to their own lives but may extend to the world beyond to social and global concerns such as poverty, nuclear war, terrorism or the end of the world.

Children with GAD are often perfectionistic. They fear the disastrous consequences of making mistakes, and have an unwarranted sense of responsibility for preventing bad things from happening. Twelve-year-old Emily, whose story you read in Chapter 2, cannot seem to stop the worrisome thoughts that enter her mind, no matter how hard she tries. She stares at her open books and does no work because she is preoccupied with, *"What if it rains today? Will there be a flood like there was in Grandma's town when the river overflowed? Will we have to leave our homes for safety? My mom and sister are at home — what if they're trapped? When will the rain stop? Perhaps it won't rain — those clouds are drifting away. Is there going to be enough rain this year? Will the farmers' crops be ruined? Will we have a water shortage?"*

≈   ***Signs and symptoms of Generalized Anxiety Disorder***   ≈

- ❏ Unrealistic fears over many routine events
- ❏ Uncontrollable, unstoppable worry
- ❏ Irritability, tension, nausea, aches and pains, poor concentration
- ❏ Difficulty sleeping, fatigue
- ❏ Perfectionism
- ❏ Frequent reassurance and approval seeking
- ❏ Significant interference with daily life activities

Indications of GAD in school

Children and adolescents with GAD may be nervous, easily upset, tense, cautious and generally unable to relax or enjoy themselves in school. They express worries and doubts about numerous issues ranging from the trivial to the critical, and may seek repeated reassurance pertaining to their fears. They may appear burdened and "old beyond their years." Due to a strong drive for perfection, children with GAD are often very conscientious and hardworking. Their perfectionism is often to their disadvantage, because they are rarely convinced that their work is satisfactory. Concern about getting everything right consumes them. As a result, they may spend hours erasing, checking and rechecking assignments, and seeking reassurance about the quality of their work from parents and teachers.

SPECIFIC PHOBIAS

Phobias involve intense fear of one or more specific events or objects such as insects, thunderstorms, heights, elevators, needles, bees, snakes, etc. Although the object of the phobia may be one that poses some threat for most people, the phobic reaction is at the level of panic. For instance, whereas the threat of a bee sting may make most people cautious around bees, a child with a phobia of bees may have an overly dramatic reaction to the mention of bees, refusing to go outdoors even when none are within sight. Unlike other types of anxiety, phobias are very specific and are usually accompanied by strong avoidance of the feared object. Children do not generally display any anxiety or fear if they can avoid the feared situation. They do not have undue anxiety in other situations.

Indications of Specific Phobias in school

Children with phobias do not present as anxious or nervous in routine school settings. Extreme fear, panic or avoidance occurs only if the child encounters the object of his phobia. For instance, a child with a phobia of bees and insects may refuse to go to the playground and become hysterical if she sees bees, but is otherwise unperturbed.

≈ **Signs and symptoms of Specific Phobias** ≈

- ❏ Unreasonable and persistent fear of an identifiable object or situation such as animals, insects, the dark, medical procedures, thunderstorms
- ❏ Anticipation of or exposure to the feared object triggers intense fear
- ❏ Exposure elicits panic, freezing, crying, clinging
- ❏ Strong avoidance or endurance of the feared situation with great distress

SOCIAL ANXIETY/EXCESSIVE SHYNESS

Social anxiety, which may be better recognized by many as excessive shyness, involves intense and paralyzing concern about appearing foolish or doing something to embarrass or humiliate oneself. Children with social anxiety are very self-conscious in social and performance situations, and generally try to avoid them. School, family gatherings, church and public places may elicit fears about being evaluated and ridiculed. Joseph, the 17-year-old in Chapter 2 remains aloof because he is anxious about how he is perceived by his peers.

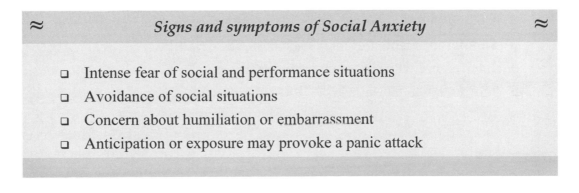

≈ **Signs and symptoms of Social Anxiety** ≈

- ❏ Intense fear of social and performance situations
- ❏ Avoidance of social situations
- ❏ Concern about humiliation or embarrassment
- ❏ Anticipation or exposure may provoke a panic attack

Indications of Social Anxiety in school

In school, children with social anxiety may present as painfully shy, hesitant, passive and intensely uncomfortable when they are in the spotlight. They may interact and converse minimally with peers, and may appear isolated and on the fringes of the group. They may be the ones to sit alone in the cafeteria, and hang back in the shadows on the playground. Relatively routine events such as being called on to read or answer in class may elicit panic-like distress. School situations involving large numbers of peers such as public speaking, gym classes, the cafeteria or playground, are very stressful for children with social anxiety.

OBSESSIVE-COMPULSIVE DISORDER

Obsessive-Compulsive Disorder (OCD) affects 1% to 3% of school age children, and consists of repeated obsessions and compulsions that are distressing and interfere with day-to-day functioning. *Obsessions* are unwanted, unfounded and upsetting thoughts, images or urges that are unrelenting, uncontrollable and unstoppable. They can be bizarre, frightening and disturbing. Children often describe obsessions as "worries" or uncomfortable feelings that things are "not right." *Compulsions*, also known as rituals, are deliberate physical or mental actions that are geared toward relieving the worry and discomfort created by the obsessions. They appear to be senseless habits that are excessive and unreasonable, but are repeated in a rigid and fixed manner. They are far from pleasant, but the person feels driven to repeat them because they relieve anxiety.

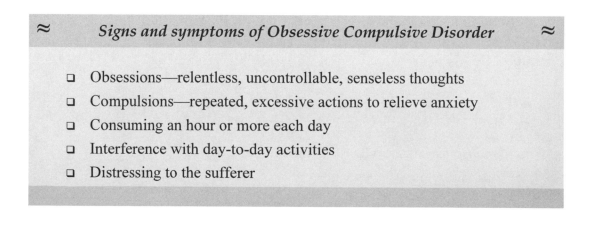

≈   *Signs and symptoms of Obsessive Compulsive Disorder*   ≈

- ❑ Obsessions—relentless, uncontrollable, senseless thoughts
- ❑ Compulsions—repeated, excessive actions to relieve anxiety
- ❑ Consuming an hour or more each day
- ❑ Interference with day-to-day activities
- ❑ Distressing to the sufferer

OCD stands out as a relatively distinct anxiety disorder because obsessions are usually not simply worries about real-life problems. They are often bizarre in content; even when focused on day-to-day issues, OCD worries can reach complex proportions. Children and adults who suffer from OCD are often so embarrassed and ashamed of their fears and rituals that they hide them rather than seek help.

Fears of germs, contamination, harm and danger are frequent childhood obsessions. For example, children may have morbid fears of contracting AIDS or hepatitis from passing by strangers. Strong urges or needs for symmetry, precision and closure (also known as "just right" urges) are also common obsessions, more so among young boys. Children with just right urges may feel intensely uncomfortable and unable to proceed with an activity or action until they achieve a sense of closure. Other obsessive urges include the need to tell, confess, ask, or know things with certainty. Moral dilemmas, religious preoccupations, sexual and forbidden thoughts may plague older children and adolescents with OCD.

Among childhood compulsions, washing and grooming rituals predominate. Other typical rituals include repeating, retracing or redoing actions, touching, tapping, checking, counting, or ordering and arranging things until they feel "just right." Confessing, apologizing, praying, hoarding and seeking repeated reassurance are also common rituals. A child with OCD may spend hours bathing, washing hands, touching objects, arranging or checking things repeatedly. He may develop elaborate rules and sequences for routine activities such as eating, cleaning or dressing, and insist that family members comply with the rules as well. Children with OCD may not be able to articulate their fears or the reasons for their rituals.

Casey, the youngster you met in Chapter 2, has fears of contamination from paint and chemicals, fears of saying "bad words," and "just right" urges. He asks for frequent reassurance and repeats his drawings until he feels that they are "just right." It might surprise you to know that Alex, the youngster who is angry and disruptive, also has OCD. He is afraid of contracting hepatitis if others touch him, but he hides his fears and rituals because he is embarrassed about them. School staff, who are unaware of his OCD, misunderstand the reasons for his behavior.

Indications of OCD in school

OCD is relatively easy to detect when it presents in classic ways such as excessive hand washing. More often than not, OCD is difficult to spot, especially in school, because rituals may be hidden. OCD is harder to recognize when it manifests in reading and writing difficulties, school refusal, habitual tardiness, repetitive movements, touching or counting inconsequential things. OCD can also generate sudden, unexplained distress and excessive reassurance seeking. Surreptitious and unusual behaviors may be an attempt to hide or camouflage embarrassing rituals. Alex is disruptive and disorganized because he attempts to disguise checking and touching rituals by clowning around and being "fidgety." When the boy in the cafeteria bumped into him, Alex panicked because he thought he would get hepatitis and die, unless he washed his hands thoroughly (for an hour). He was both angry and afraid, and ran to the bathroom to cleanse himself immediately.

Parents, school professionals and clinicians can find extensive and in-depth coverage of OCD in children and adolescents in *What to do when your Child has Obsessive-Compulsive Disorder: Strategies and Solutions, Up and Down the Worry Hill: A Children's Book about OCD and its Treatment,* and *Treatment of OCD in Children and Adolescents: A Cognitive-Behavioral Therapy Manual* (see the pages at the end of this book for more information).

PANDAS

Pediatric Autoimmune Neuropsychiatric Disorders Associated with Streptoccocal Infections: In the last decade, researchers at the National Institutes of Mental Health (NIMH) made the dramatic discovery that strep infections may trigger OCD for *a small number* of children. OCD may develop abruptly or be worsened due to a misdirected immune system reaction triggered by strep infections. The antibodies generated by the body's immune system to combat the strep infection begin to mistake the child's body tissues for the strep bacteria. The antibodies may sometimes attack the child's heart or joints and cause rheumatic heart disease or arthritis, or attack parts of the brain. An antibody attack on the basal ganglia in the brain may trigger obsessive-compulsive symptoms or tics.

Before parents get alarmed, it is important to keep this information in perspective. The diagnosis and treatment of PANDAS OCD is still controversial. Strep infections are very common in school-aged children and it is a very small percentage of these children who develop OCD as a result. Why and how some children and develop strep-triggered OCD and not others is unclear, but there is speculation that these children may already have a genetic predisposition to OCD, and the strep infection is a biological stressor that triggers the onset of symptoms.

The *onset* and *course* of PANDAS-triggered OCD is distinct from that of non-PANDAS OCD, although the actual symptoms are similar. The onset of PANDAS OCD is sudden and dramatic. Parents can often pinpoint the exact day the child's symptoms began. The symptoms also subside dramatically when the strep infection is resolved. There are equally sudden remissions and recurrences of symptoms, usually following a strep infection. Further, the symptoms tend to be severe rather than mild. There are also likely to be other personality changes, irritability, moodiness and separation anxiety. In non-PANDAS OCD, the onset and course are typically more gradual and insidious, with severity increasing over a period of time, not abruptly. Symptoms also tend to be prolonged rather than short-lived, and do not remit as quickly or completely.

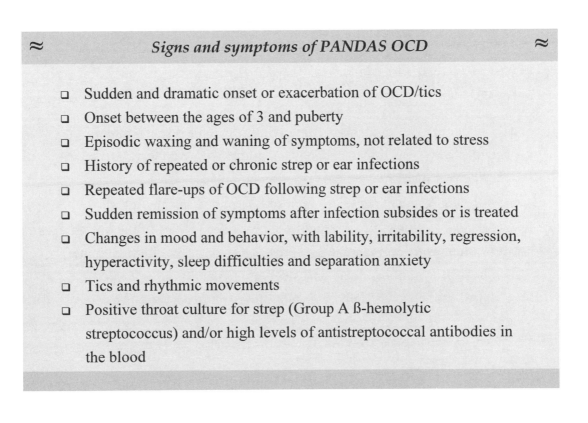

≈ ***Signs and symptoms of PANDAS OCD*** ≈

- ❑ Sudden and dramatic onset or exacerbation of OCD/tics
- ❑ Onset between the ages of 3 and puberty
- ❑ Episodic waxing and waning of symptoms, not related to stress
- ❑ History of repeated or chronic strep or ear infections
- ❑ Repeated flare-ups of OCD following strep or ear infections
- ❑ Sudden remission of symptoms after infection subsides or is treated
- ❑ Changes in mood and behavior, with lability, irritability, regression, hyperactivity, sleep difficulties and separation anxiety
- ❑ Tics and rhythmic movements
- ❑ Positive throat culture for strep (Group A ß-hemolytic streptococcus) and/or high levels of antistreptococcal antibodies in the blood

In some cases, identifying the infection with a throat culture and treating it with a full course of antibiotics may reduce the OCD symptoms. Researchers at the NIMH are studying experimental treatments for very severe cases of PANDAS. Plasmapharesis, which is a filtering of the child's blood to remove strep antibodies, is an invasive procedure requiring a few days hospital stay. The other treatment is intravenous injection of immunoglobulin, which is a blood product and may carry risks of viral transmission. The NIMH has issued caution against the use of these treatments in clinical settings, due to their invasiveness and potential risks.

POST-TRAUMATIC STRESS DISORDER

Post-Traumatic Stress Disorder (PTSD) is an anxiety reaction following exposure to a catastrophe of great magnitude. Unfortunately, children today have been exposed to many tragic events such as the terrorist attacks of 9/11 and war. Other events such as repeated instances of school shootings and abductions of children by sexual predators have had a direct impact on children, parents and school personnel because they have come close to home. PTSD can also occur among children who have endured physical, sexual or emotional abuse, especially if it is chronic.

≈   *Signs and symptoms of Post-Traumatic Stress Disorder*   ≈

❑ Exposure to a traumatic event in which death or serious injury occurred or was threatened, and accompanied by intense fear, terror or helplessness

❑ Reliving of the experience via upsetting memories, thoughts, dreams, feelings of recurrence when exposed to cues of the event

❑ Avoidance of events, objects, situations associated with the trauma

❑ Physical symptoms: Problems sleeping, irritability, exaggerated startle response, difficulty concentrating and hypervigilance

Persons exposed to a disastrous or tragic event can have a range of reactions that are influenced by the proximity of exposure, the direct impact of the trauma, previous exposure to trauma, age and temperament.

Although most people have reactions to tragedies, these reactions generally fade with time. For some, PTSD reactions may develop. Initial reactions may include shock, disbelief, helplessness, and a sense of the surreal. As reality sinks in, a multitude of tumultuous emotions may surface. There may be intense, overwhelming grief, panic, confusion and feelings of unreality. Dreams, nightmares, tension and vigilance are also common PTSD symptoms. If the event was manmade, deliberate or preventable, there may be anger, outrage and urges for justice or vengeance.

Children may have a range of responses to trauma. Some do not fully appreciate the nature of the event, and may have limited interest or passing curiosity. At the other end of the spectrum, some children may develop intense fear, a sense of horror and confusion. Reactions may evolve over a period of time and not happen in a predictable sequence. Children who are prone to anxiety or who have previously experienced trauma may have more severe reactions, even if they are not directly impacted. They may question their safety, and lose trust in adults who were unable to keep them safe. They may express fear that the event will reoccur or will happen directly to them. Separation fears may emerge if children worry that they or their parents will be hurt or killed if the event recurs. They may be confused over the difference between real and imagined events, particularly those in movies and TV shows.

Some children may be easily upset and revert to immature and regressed behaviors such as thumb sucking, bedwetting, clinging or tantrums. Bedtime fears and nightmares may resurface or increase; some may insist on having parents stay with them at night. Older children and adolescents may grasp the larger implications of a tragic event or disaster, and question the possible reasons for the event. They may also experience confusion, sadness, anger, and a need for justice or vengeance. Sometimes, teenagers may appear callous and unconcerned by joking about the events. Although humor is a normal way of coping, it may be carried to insensitive levels.

The duration of PTSD reactions also varies. For most, the impact fades with time and support, and they are able to move on with their lives. For others, the emotional trauma may persist and resurface over time. Over the long term, there may be increased emotional numbness, detachment, and an inability to feel or express feelings. There may also be strong avoidance of situations related to the trauma and its aftermath.

Indications of PTSD in school

Children with PTSD may develop separation anxiety and school refusal. They may not want to go to school because they do not want to have their parents out of sight. In school, they may have headaches or vomiting. They may be preoccupied, irritable, unable to concentrate, agitated, restless and easily upset. They may raise many concerns about safety in generally low-risk situations and ask the same questions over and over again. They may avoid situations that remind them of the trauma, and may become upset or panic when required to encounter such circumstances. Children who were previously quiet and compliant may become loud and aggressive. Those who were friendly and outgoing may become shy and afraid. Children may be clingy and dependent, seeking frequent reassurance. Children who are severely affected by trauma may be disorganized, disoriented and "detached" from happenings around them. School personnel may not understand the child's seemingly inexplicable behavior unless they are aware of the child's traumatic experience. Chapter 15 details the specific ways in which parents and schools can help children cope with trauma, disasters and violence.

PANIC DISORDER

Panic *attacks* occur when anxiety peaks abruptly and is intolerable to the sufferer. A myriad of physical symptoms such as pounding heart, trembling, faintness, dizziness, chest pain, choking sensations, fears of dying, going crazy or being "detached" may occur within the span of a few seconds or minutes. Panic attacks alone do not imply a diagnosis of panic disorder because they can occur in the context of many different anxiety disorders. Children with OCD, SAD, GAD or social anxiety can have panic attacks when they are exposed to triggers for their specific fears.

≈	***Signs and symptoms of Panic Disorder***	≈

- ❑ Repeated, unexpected, "out of the blue" panic attacks
- ❑ Dreaded anticipation of another attack or its outcome
- ❑ Avoidance of perceived triggers of attacks
- ❑ Reluctance to venture outside the home for fear of possible attack and inability to cope

To have panic *disorder*, which is rare in children, the child must have repeated, *unexpected* panic attacks that are unrelated to fears triggered by another condition such as OCD, separation, or generalized anxiety. In panic disorder, there is persistent apprehension in anticipation of an impending panic attack—the fear of fear itself.

Indications of Panic Disorder in school

Children with panic may have intense, seemingly unprovoked and abrupt episodes of overwhelming fear that is focused on their physical symptoms. They may be afraid of dying because they cannot breathe or because they don't know what is happening to them. During a panic attack, a child may cry hysterically and be difficult to soothe.

SCHOOL PHOBIA

The term "school phobia" is a misnomer because it suggests that the child is afraid of school. This is not necessarily the case. The term *school refusal* is a more accurate term because reluctance to attend school may be driven by a dozen different reasons, not all of them anxiety-based (see Table 3, *Possible Reasons for School Refusal*). School refusal describes the behaviors of children who refuse to attend school, those who remain in school with great difficulty or those who visit the nurse's office frequently with complaints about pains or discomfort, crying, and temper tantrums.

School refusal occurs in about 2% of children, most often between the ages of 5 and 11. It is equally common among boys and girls. Although school refusal is often associated with anxiety, a child's school refusal may have nothing to do with school at all. For instance, a child with OCD may refuse to go to school because he cannot find the right pair of socks and he cannot tolerate the discomfort of wearing the wrong socks all day. Sarah, Alex and Joseph, all have school refusal but for different reasons. Sarah has separation anxiety, Alex is unable to get through his OCD cleansing rituals to get to school on time, and Joseph struggles with social anxiety.

School refusal is usually considered different from truancy, because children stay home with their parents' knowledge, and do not display other antisocial behaviors typically associated with truancy. Children who are truant are generally absent from school without their parents' knowledge, and are not usually at their homes during school hours.

Table 3: Possible Reasons for School Refusal

Problem	Related Thought
❑ Separation anxiety	*Something bad will happen to my mother while I'm at school.*
❑ Generalized anxiety	*I'm going to get a B on the spelling test.*
❑ Obsessions and compulsions	*I'll get AIDS and die if the kids touch my things.*
❑ Social anxiety	*No one will talk to me in recess today.*
❑ Panic	*I won't be able to breathe and I'll die because no one will be able to help me.*
❑ Performance anxiety	*I'll get too nervous and forget everything.*
❑ Learning difficulties	*Math is too hard. I'm dumb anyway.*
❑ Medical illness/absences	*I'll never catch up with the other kids.* *I'll have an asthma attack in class.*
❑ Fear of bullying/aggression	*They'll laugh at me on the bus and grab my bag.*
❑ Discipline in the classroom	*The teacher picks on me. She makes me feel stupid.*
❑ Sleep deprivation/fatigue	*I can't get up. I'm too tired to go to school.*
❑ Adjustment to transitions	*High school is way too stressful.*
❑ Oppositional behavior	*I'm angry I couldn't play Nintendo this morning.*
❑ Truancy	*School sucks. I'd rather hang out at the mall.*

WHICH ANXIETY DISORDER IS THIS?

Diagnosis of anxiety disorders can sometimes be relatively straightforward, and at other times quite complex and challenging. There is some similarity and overlap among the signs and symptoms of various anxiety disorders. For instance, reassurance seeking may be a sign of OCD, GAD or SAD. To make matters more complicated, a child may have more than one anxiety disorder at the same time.

One way to differentiate anxiety disorders is to consider the main focus of the fear. For instance, in SAD, the fears are primarily about separation from loved ones, whereas in social anxiety disorder, fears are confined to social situations only. Whereas children with GAD, SAD, or OCD may also be uncomfortable in social situations, this is not the primary focus of their fears. In GAD, fears are pervasive and permeate many aspects of day-to-day life. In panic disorder, the fear is about having another panic attack.

When the content of the fear is common to more than one disorder, the *expression* of the fear is also used to make a differential diagnosis. For example, with regard to the fear of failing a test—a child with GAD will ask for reassurance, whereas a child with OCD may engage in rituals such as touching, tapping or stepping to prevent herself from failing.

The expression of OCD is sometimes easily distinguishable, due to rituals that tend to be grossly excessive and often irrational in their connection to the obsessions. No other anxiety disorder is expressed via compulsions. Although SAD, OCD and GAD share common features with regard to fears of harm coming to loved ones and ritualistic reassurance seeking, only OCD involves compulsions to avert or prevent harm. In OCD there are usually other fears and obsessions, accompanied by rituals. In specific phobias, the fears are limited to one or a few areas. Avoidance is the primary response and there are no rituals to counteract the fears.

Perfectionism is a symptom that is shared by GAD and OCD. However, in contrast to OCD, the themes of GAD worries are everyday concerns, and are typically not bizarre or unusual in nature. In addition, there are no compulsions associated with GAD, with the exception of seeking reassurance, or the repetitive behaviors associated with perfectionism.

Chapter 5

Disorders Associated with Anxiety

Almost 75% to 80% of children diagnosed with an anxiety disorder suffer from another psychiatric disorder, most commonly depression. The Surgeon General's report on mental health states, "*Anxiety and depression frequently co-exist, so much so that patients with combinations of anxiety and depression are the rule rather than the exception.*" The disorders described in this chapter either share similarities with or accompany anxiety disorders.

DEPRESSION

Depression and anxiety share some common symptoms that can make it harder to discern one from the other. These include despondency, withdrawal, sleep problems, nightmares, tension, poor concentration, fatigue, guilt and loss of appetite.

Children with anxiety can be prone to demoralization, discouragement, and hopelessness. For some children, this can reach the severity of a depressive episode. Depression is characterized by more sadness than anxiety. Children with depression are also prone to rumination, but the focus of preoccupations is typically their negative self-worth, which is consistent with their mood. Anxiety can be much harder to treat when it is complicated by depression. Emily, the 12-year-old with GAD is becoming demoralized and depressed because she cannot find a way out of her increasing anxiety.

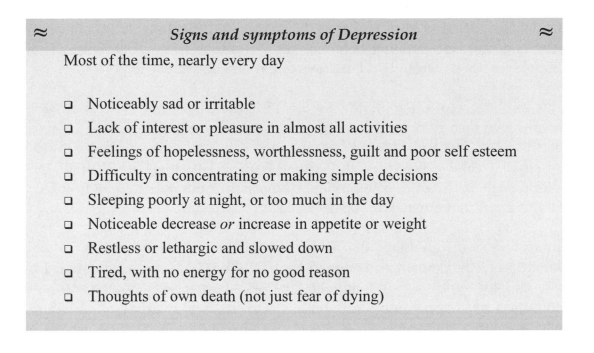

≈ **Signs and symptoms of Depression** ≈

Most of the time, nearly every day

- ❑ Noticeably sad or irritable
- ❑ Lack of interest or pleasure in almost all activities
- ❑ Feelings of hopelessness, worthlessness, guilt and poor self esteem
- ❑ Difficulty in concentrating or making simple decisions
- ❑ Sleeping poorly at night, or too much in the day
- ❑ Noticeable decrease *or* increase in appetite or weight
- ❑ Restless or lethargic and slowed down
- ❑ Tired, with no energy for no good reason
- ❑ Thoughts of own death (not just fear of dying)

TOURETTE SYNDROME

As many as 30% of the children diagnosed with OCD have a tic disorder such as Tourette Syndrome (TS), which consists of multiple involuntary motor and vocal tics (e.g., jerking motions, eye blinks, grunts and sniffs). Conversely, upto 60% of the children who are diagnosed with TS also have OCD. Casey, the boy with OCD in Chapter 2 has a frequent eye blink and has a nose twitch, which are tics.

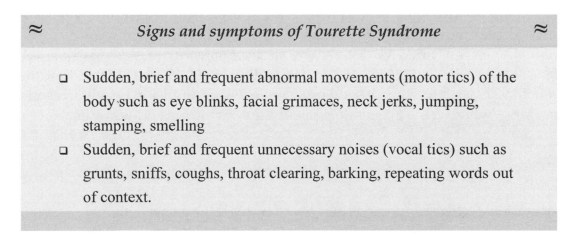

≈ **Signs and symptoms of Tourette Syndrome** ≈

- ❑ Sudden, brief and frequent abnormal movements (motor tics) of the body such as eye blinks, facial grimaces, neck jerks, jumping, stamping, smelling
- ❑ Sudden, brief and frequent unnecessary noises (vocal tics) such as grunts, sniffs, coughs, throat clearing, barking, repeating words out of context.

TS is thought to originate in the same part of the brain as OCD, but it is not clear exactly how they are related to each other. Children who have both

OCD and TS are also more likely to have difficulties with attention, learning and oppositional behavior than children with OCD alone. They may be easily frustrated and anxious due to uncontrollable tics.

It is important to differentiate between TS and OCD, because the treatments for the two disorders are quite different. However, telling OCD and TS apart can be puzzling and difficult because they can look quite similar. Tics can resemble rituals and tics and rituals can occur together. Rituals are particularly difficult to differentiate from *complex tics*, which may involve a sequence of movements or vocalizations.

In order to differentiate tics from compulsions, it is necessary to pay attention to the context and triggers to which the behaviors are related. Tics are usually sudden, rapid, involuntary and purposeless movements and sounds. They happen more randomly, occur in a wide variety of situations, and are not designed to defuse anxiety or obsessions. In contrast, rituals or compulsions are triggered by fear or worry, and are purposeful, deliberate actions designed to counteract anxiety. Children also appear to be more consciously aware of engaging in compulsions than tics. Compulsions are usually more elaborate, follow rigid rules, and occur in specific situations. For instance, if a child turns around 3 times before getting into his bed at night, and not at any other time, it is more likely to be a compulsion. If it were a tic, it would occur more erratically, and not necessarily in the same situation from day to day.

The most telling clues to the difference are evident when children can articulate the thoughts behind their actions. Casey, an insightful 9-year-old, helped me understand how he knew which of his symptoms were rituals and which were tics. *"My brain makes me want to touch things again and again, but when my eyes blink, they just do that on their own."* He was aware that the touching was a more purposeful urge and was a compulsion he felt driven to perform, whereas the eye blink happened automatically and was a tic.

ATTENTION DEFICIT HYPERACTIVITY DISORDER

Attention Deficit Hyperactivity Disorder (ADHD) is well known to both parents and school professionals. It is characterized by inattention, distractibility, impulsivity and high levels of motor activity. Children with anxiety are often mistakenly thought to have ADHD, because they appear inattentive and distracted, and have difficulty with concentration at school.

This is particularly true for children with OCD or GAD. In fact, ADHD is the most common misdiagnosis for anxiety in children.

In reality, children with anxiety have poor attention and concentration because they are preoccupied by worries, obsessions and ruminations, not because they have a deficit in the ability to attend. Rituals or attempts to disguise rituals can be mistaken for hyperactivity. In fact, Alex, the 14 year-old with OCD in Chapter 2 was attempting to cover up checking rituals with clowning antics. His restlessness was mistaken for hyperactivity.

> *ADHD is the most common misdiagnosis for anxiety in children*

The quality of the inattention in anxiety is different from that in ADHD. Children with anxiety are more likely to appear distant, as they are preoccupied with worries that occupy their minds against their will. They may appear burdened, serious in countenance, and unaware of their surroundings. In contrast, the attention of children with ADHD is more likely to shift from one activity to the next in rapid succession, with spirited interest in novelty. The difference between daydreaming and anxious preoccupation is that the former is a pleasant experience, whereas the latter is distressing. It is also important to keep in mind that some children may suffer from *both* anxiety and ADHD.

≈   **Signs and symptoms of ADHD**   ≈

- ❑ Hyperactivity: Frequently fidgets, squirms, is "on the go," leaves seat, talks excessively, has difficulty playing quietly, runs and climbs in inappropriate situations
- ❑ Impulsivity: Frequently interrupts or intrudes on others, blurts out answers out of turn, has difficulty waiting his turn
- ❑ Inattention: Has difficulty staying focused on task, misses details, makes careless mistakes, is disorganized, forgetful, loses materials easily, is unable to follow through or complete tasks, doesn't seem to listen when spoken to, dislikes activities involving concentration and mental effort

AUTISM AND ASPERGER'S SYNDROME

Autism and Asperger's Syndrome are Pervasive Developmental Disorders (PDD), a spectrum of disorders involving deficits in developmental tasks such as socialization and communication. Classic *autism*, which may involve complete lack of language and social interaction, is at the severe end of the PDD spectrum, whereas *Asperger's Syndrome* (AS) is somewhere on the continuum between autism and normal development. Children with AS have deficits primarily in social interaction. Although they develop functional language skills, their conversations are stilted, and they do not appreciate the emotional or reciprocal aspects of social dialogue. Their social interactions may appear awkward, odd or different.

≈   ***Signs and symptoms of Asperger's Syndrome and Autism***   ≈

Apparent by the preschool years:

❑ Awkward, odd or absent social interaction with adults and peers
❑ Lack of initiation of social contact with others
❑ Rigid, intense and inflexible patterns of behavior
❑ Intense preoccupation with limited interests and activities
❑ Repetitive, stereotyped motor mannerisms

In addition, for *autism*:
❑ Delays in, or complete lack of spoken language
❑ Inability to sustain conversations
❑ Solitary play and lack of make-believe play

Children with PDD typically have stereotyped behaviors and very narrowly focused interests that are easy to confuse with obsessions or rituals. For instance, they may become "obsessed" and talk incessantly about specific idiosyncratic topics such as license plates, dinosaurs, maps or insects. They may arrange objects in lines, count items repeatedly, rock back and forth, or flap their arms. In contrast to OCD, these stereotyped behaviors and repetitious habits are comforting and pleasurable to the child with PDD. They are often used to self-soothe when nervous or upset. The child is not aware that the behavior is excessive or unusual, and is not distressed by it.

Children with PDD may also experience tremendous anxiety when faced with transitions and changes in routine, unfamiliar people or surroundings, abstract tasks, unclear expectations, or unexpected physical or social contact. They may lack flexibility and the ability to shift gears when caught off guard. They are often highly sensitive and over-reactive to sensory inputs like noise, touch, or light that are barely noticed by most other children. There are many children who fall in the shades of grey of the PDD spectrum, displaying milder versions of PDD behaviors. To make matters more complex, some children may have OCD in addition to PDD.

TRICHOTILLOMANIA

Trichotillomania (TTM), which involves impulsive hair plucking, is often associated with an increasing sense of tension prior to plucking, and followed by pleasure, gratification or relief afterwards. Subsequently, distress may ensue due to realization of the long-term implications of hair plucking, and guilt may follow due to the perceived loss of control. Hair pulling often tends to occur during times of stress and anxiety, but can also occur when the person is relaxed, distracted or bored. Although TTM and OCD have some similarities, one clear difference between the two is that there is no pleasure, gratification or desire associated with OCD rituals. In addition, hair plucking in TTM is not associated with obsessions or fears.

Other compulsive habits like skin picking and nail biting are also associated with diffuse anxiety, tension and stress. They provide gratification, soothing and the release of tension. Like TTM, skin picking and nail biting are not elicited in response to a specific fear or obsession. They are generally not distressing except for the outcome. Sufferers are often ambivalent about stopping the behavior due to the gratification derived from it.

BODY DYSMORPHIC DISORDER

Body Dysmorphic Disorder (BDD) may affect adolescents and adults. It is an intense preoccupation with a minor real or imagined flaw in appearance, which is perceived as a deformity and magnified to mountainous proportions. It is usually a very specific and restricted part of the body that is the offender, such as a wrinkle, scar, hair, the size or shape of the nose, eyebrow or fingernails. The sufferer is tormented because the flaw is perceived as hideous and unsightly. Her life revolves around checking, comparing, concealing and fixing this defect in appearance. Unlike OCD, BDD preoccupations are restricted to appearance, and there are no associated rituals other than checking and seeking reassurance.

≈   ***Signs and symptoms of Body Dysmorphic Disorder***   ≈

❑ Excessive preoccupation, distress and concern with slight anomalies or imagined defects in appearance

❑ Belief in the defect is stubbornly held and appears out of touch with reality

❑ Frequent checking, concealment, avoidance of defect, or reassurance seeking

❑ Interferes with functioning

EATING DISORDERS

Eating disorders such as anorexia nervosa and bulimia typically develop during the teenage years and most commonly affect girls. The sufferer has a morbid fear of becoming fat and is irrationally preoccupied with being thin. There are many rigid, ritualistic behaviors designed to lose weight, but the obsessive worrying is focused on becoming fat. These children can also have significant anxiety, pressure themselves to excel and meet their high standards, seek perfection, and endure chronic stress as a result.

≈   ***Signs and symptoms of Eating Disorders***   ≈

❑ Significant weight loss due to diet, exercise and desire to lose weight

❑ Intense fear of becoming fat, despite being underweight

❑ Excessive focus on body weight and shape

❑ Frequent episodes of binge eating—large quantity in short time

❑ Weight gain curtailed by vomiting, fasting, misuse of laxatives, or other medications

Eating disorders may resemble OCD. Children with OCD can have many unusual food preferences and rules around eating. However, restricted food intake in OCD is generally due to fear of contamination, not due to fears of gaining weight. Further, other than a preoccupation with weight, there are no obsessions associated with eating disorders.

DELUSIONS, HALLUCINATIONS AND PSYCHOSIS

Delusions and hallucinations are the cardinal symptoms of psychosis, which is usually accompanied by disorganization, confusion, and deterioration in functioning. Delusions are strongly-held beliefs with no basis in reality, and hallucinations are sensory experiences such as hearing voices, seeing visions and tactile sensations that also have no basis in reality. The person with delusions or hallucinations is convinced of their reality, and does not usually view them as unusual, distorted or upsetting. Disorganization, confusion, incoherence, tangential speech and disorientation are also telltale signs of psychosis.

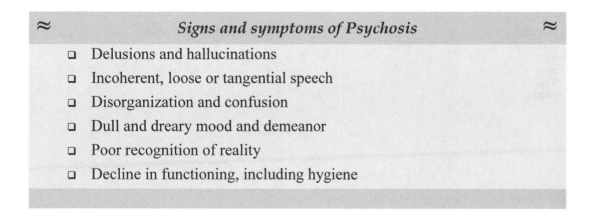

≈	*Signs and symptoms of Psychosis*	≈
❑	Delusions and hallucinations	
❑	Incoherent, loose or tangential speech	
❑	Disorganization and confusion	
❑	Dull and dreary mood and demeanor	
❑	Poor recognition of reality	
❑	Decline in functioning, including hygiene	

The bizarre beliefs of OCD may sometimes be mistaken for psychosis. This is especially so because young children may often refer to their obsessive worries as "the voices in my head" that are "telling me to do these things." The mention of "voices" of course, is very startling and frightening to parents or teachers.

There are distinct differences between the voices of OCD and the voices of psychosis. OCD is generally accompanied by "insight," which means that sufferers know that the thoughts are bizarre or unreal. Children are generally upset by the involuntary and intrusive voices of OCD. In addition, children with OCD usually know that the voices do not make sense, whereas children with psychosis believe their thoughts to be true. However, insight occurs on a continuum, and children, especially young ones, may not always be able to distinguish OCD thoughts from reality (or communicate this in ways we understand). Although children routinely play imaginary games that appear delusional, they will acknowledge imaginary fantasies when queried appropriately.

That much said, it is sometimes truly difficult to sort out the two. Beliefs in anxious fears and obsessions can sometimes reach delusional proportions — referred to as *overvalued ideation* — which can occur both in children and in adults. A child may sometimes not be quite sure whether or not obsessive or anxious fears are "real," or may hold on tenaciously to the belief that they are. On occasion, children and adults may have both OCD *and* psychosis. When children have developmental or language delays, they are not able to communicate well, and may appear to have delusions. Diagnosis may become complicated, and even an experienced clinician may have to take a "time will tell" or "medications will tell" approach. Psychotic symptoms do not respond to treatments that are effective for OCD.

Chapter 6

The Far-Reaching Effects of Anxiety

Life is not pleasant for anxious children. They carry the weight of the world on their shoulders. Many are not able to have the carefree, happy childhoods that we expect children to have. Yet, adults often assume that an anxious child is simply "just the way he is." Not only is anxiety usually a source of considerable suffering for the child, it has far-reaching and long-lasting effects on the child's academic, social, family and occupational life.

The impact of anxiety on children cannot be overstated. About half the children who have an anxiety disorder suffer significant impairment in functioning. Academically, anxiety lowers performance and productivity, and results in much wasted potential. At mild to moderate levels of anxiety, children may be able to compensate because they are often hardworking, persistent and diligent. At severe levels, tardiness, absenteeism, perfectionism, preoccupations, and rituals may result in incomplete work, failure on tests and even the need to repeat grades or be schooled at home. There are high drop out rates among adolescents with anxiety, but these are often attributed to substance abuse and truancy, which may mask untreated anxiety.

Psychologically, children with anxiety can be brutally hard on themselves. Anxious children are often sensitive, caring, empathic, conscientious, industrious and highly moral—perhaps too much so for their own good. They set high expectations for themselves, and are intensely self-critical when they aren't able to meet their standards. They believe that they are letting down parents and teachers, and suffer from poor self-concept. They may be under a great deal of duress due to the time and energy consumed by their worries and attempts to cope. They may be irritable, oppositional, and have panic and temper outbursts. As a result of the stress, they may suffer from secondary depression, hopelessness and possibly suicidal thoughts. Some, especially those with OCD, worry about being "crazy" and carry the added burden of secrecy. In severe situations, they may even be housebound.

Socially, kids lose out on friendships and activities. Who wants to be around a child who is hesitant, apprehensive or afraid to do much of anything? Studies have shown that anxious children have fewer friends, on average, than their non-anxious peers, which may delay the development of normal socialization skills. They may be unable to invite friends over, accept invitations and attend parties, camps or sleepovers. Adolescents may not be able to drive or meet friends in public places like the mall or movie theater.

> *Left untreated, children with anxiety disorders are at higher risk for serious academic underachievement, low social support, underemployment, cigarette smoking, alcohol, and drug abuse.*

Anxious youngsters are easy targets for teasing and aggression because they are timid and unassertive. Bullies can usually get away unscathed when they pick on an anxious child. Good social skills are strongly related to successful school adjustment. Limited peer support and interaction may pave the way for loneliness, depression and withdrawal.

Parents and families feel the disruption of a child's anxiety in many and varied ways. They may have to wear kid gloves around children who are more fragile and vulnerable. Getting through the daily routine of homework, meals, bathing and bedtime may be a nightmare of battles. There may be guilt and confusion about parenting a child with anxiety. Marital conflict may ensue when parenting styles differ, and one parent is more "indulging" and the other "rigid" and "doesn't understand." Siblings resent and rebel against the anxious child occupying center stage in the family. Family events, outings and vacations may be thwarted or end prematurely due to anxiety-related crises. The family may be under chronic and prolonged stress and frustration; there are few opportunities to and relax. The tension and conflict may take a toll on parent-child and parent-to-parent relationships.

A child's anxiety may also permeate the classroom and school environment. Teachers and other school professionals may not always easily recognize or identify anxiety due to variability in symptoms or inexperience with anxiety in children. They may be puzzled or misattribute a child's inattention, resistance or temper outbursts to deliberate and controllable behaviors. The teacher must manage the academic and emotional needs of an entire classroom. A child with anxiety may sometimes require more care, requiring the teacher to balance that child's needs with the needs of all the other children in the class. It is similar to the situation that parents experience, when the needs of an anxious child detract from their ability to give adequate attention to their other children.

A teacher may be presented with many daily dilemmas:
> *How do I know if this child is anxious?*
> *How should I manage a child with anxiety?*
> *How do I know what's the right thing to say?*
> *How do I handle this child in front of peers?*
> *How can I minimize the disruption to the class?*
> *When is it okay to set limits?*
> *How can I help this child without being unfair to my other students?*

The daily challenges presented by an anxious child can become overwhelming and exhausting for teachers with multiple demands on their limited resources. Mental health personnel in the school may face similar challenges. For them, anxious children may be the least needy, compared to other children in their care whose behaviors demand immediate attention.

Anxious children can get easily overwhelmed and unable to cope or problem-solve their way through even typical everyday challenges. They turn to parents and teachers for help, and they get the help they seek. As a result, anxious children often become dependent on adults to help them cope, and do not learn how to manage anxiety on their own. They do not develop self-reliance.

The high level of engagement and energy demanded by these children can quickly become draining for parents and teachers alike. Adults may soon lose sympathy with the child who needs frequent reassurance and support, yet is insatiable in his needs. Consequently, anxious children are often misunderstood. Parents and teachers may think they are deliberately being fussy, annoying, manipulative, attention-seeking or making excuses to avoid expectations. Actually, children with anxiety have a hard time explaining why they behave the way they do. Some are unable to articulate their fears and thoughts. Others may know that they are being illogical and feel embarrassed to disclose their thoughts or fears.

In some cases, a confusing situation may emerge. Children may sail through the day at school, then return home and "fall apart." This may be particularly true for children with OCD and/or TS, who may exert a tremendous amount of energy to inhibit their rituals and tics at school in order to fit in and go unnoticed. The exhaustion of keeping it together at school and the fact that home is a "safe place" results in the child releasing all the pent-up emotions in the confines of home. The child who is quiet and compliant at school is transformed into a belligerent, disagreeable, hysterical mess when she enters the front door of her home. The discrepancy in the child's behaviors at home and at school may leave parents wondering if the child has control and is taking advantage of them. Teachers may speculate that the home environment is "causing" the child's distress. Clearly, neither of these may be true.

Childhood anxiety can continue into adolescence and adulthood. About half the adults with anxiety disorders report that their illness began in childhood. As anxious children progress into adolescence, they may have great difficulty with initiating and or sustaining dating relationships. Anxiety may limit their ability to drive, which may limit their socialization, independence and job opportunities. As anxious adults, they may have problems performing at full caliber in jobs. Many have difficulty initiating or sustaining relationships and suffer from loneliness and unhappiness.

Anxious adolescents and adults may resort to drugs or alcohol to compensate for ineffective coping skills and to mask the pain and discomfort they experience. Depression, suicidal tendencies and medical problems are common. Untreated and chronic stress and anxiety can also lower immune system functioning and increase susceptibility to infectious diseases. People with an anxiety disorder often seek relief for symptoms that mimic physical illnesses. They are three-to-five times more likely to go to the doctor and six times more likely to be hospitalized for psychiatric disorders than non-sufferers.

There is plenty of reason for optimism, despite this gloomy picture. There is effective treatment today. The earlier adults intervene on behalf of anxious youngsters, the sooner children can get their lives back on track.

Chapter 7

Warning Signs and Signals

Parents, school professionals and pediatricians may be the first to see the early signs and signals of childhood anxiety and are therefore the gatekeepers for early intervention. Since anxiety disorders are the most common mental health problem in children, early indicators of anxiety are particularly worthy of attention.

The following clues are suggestive of anxiety, but do not imply a definite case of anxiety in isolation, as many other factors have to be taken into consideration. Neither are the signs and signals described below exclusive markers of anxiety. They may also be clues to other problems for which a child may benefit from intervention.

SIGNS AND SYMPTOMS OF ANXIETY

- ❑ *Out-of-character behaviors*: Behaviors that are described as "not acting his age," or "not like himself," such as sudden, unexpected resistance from an otherwise compliant child. For instance, an 8-year-old who insists on an elaborate bedtime ritual is not acting his age, because such behavior is more fitting for a preschooler or kindergartner. Other uncharacteristic behaviors may include sudden rigidity, stubbornness or undue cautiousness and hesitation.

- ❑ *"What if?"* Asking, *"But what if?"* more than the average child. Questions may pertain to topics from the trivial to the profound, including friends, grades, performance, schedules, routines, family safety, the family pet, natural disasters or the weather.

❑ *Avoidance:* Sudden, strong avoidance and reluctance in situations that were formerly not an issue. Fears of contamination, death or harm may persuade children to avoid all manner of potential triggers of these fears.

❑ *Reassurance seeking*: Incessant and insatiable need for reassurance; repeated explanations and reassurance seem to never to be enough. *"Am I going to be OK? Am I going blind? Am I going to throw up? Can you feel my forehead and see if I have a fever? Are you sure all my homework is in my bag? Is it zippered?"*

❑ *Frequent physical complaints*: Nausea, vomiting, feeling on edge, or many aches and pains for which no medical cause can be found.

❑ *Sleep problems:* Insomnia, nightmares and frequent awakenings, followed by exhaustion and drowsiness during the day. This may be the result of staying up late, absorbed in rituals or obsessions, procrastinating with homework or trying to get it done to perfection.

❑ *Decline in attention, concentration and organization:* Distraction, preoccupation, difficulty focusing or disorganization that appears initially to be willful daydreaming or an attention problem (see Chapter 5 for misdiagnosis of ADHD).

❑ *Perfectionism*: High and unattainable self-imposed standards with regard to schoolwork, behavior or socialization. Repeating tasks endlessly, easy frustration with perceived imperfection, inability to accept parents' or teachers' satisfaction with the quality of the performance.

❑ *Incomplete tasks:* Assignments or tasks that are clearly within the child's capability are not completed due to perfectionism, or other repetitive rituals such as checking, re-reading or counting. Sometimes, a child may get "stuck" and be unable to proceed.

❑ *Reluctance or refusal to go to school*: Reluctance or refusal to attend school due to avoidance of anxiety triggers, inability to cope with expectations, or demands of schoolwork.

❑ ***Easily-triggered distress***: Unusual tearfulness, clinging, fear of being alone in situations that most children of that age do not mind, restlessness, agitation, crying, irritability, hair-trigger "meltdowns," unhappiness, poor self-esteem, depression or withdrawal.

❑ ***Wasted logic***: The child is seemingly impervious to common sense. Logic, reassurance, explanations, and distraction do not appease the child's anxiety.

RED FLAGS FOR OCD

OCD, because of its distinctive nature, may be evident from an additional set of clues.

❑ ***Endless doubt and need for certainty:*** Repeated questions about seemingly trivial issues. *What time does the mail come? What's for dinner tonight? Is the TV show on yet? Was the garage door shut properly?*

❑ ***Intensity, frequency or excessiveness*** of an otherwise normal behavior. Washing hands before every meal and after using the toilet is perfectly normal. Spending several minutes lathering, scrubbing, and rinsing repeatedly, still not assured of their cleanliness, or complaining about feeling dirty is a strong sign of OCD.

❑ ***Slowness and tardiness***: Inordinately long times spent on routine daily tasks such as toileting, eating, getting dressed or doing homework. The child may be chronically late for school, outings or bed due to difficulty completing routines in a timely manner.

❑ ***Unexplained physical changes***: Sore, chapped, red hands may indicate elaborate hand washing in secret. Untidy, slovenly appearance, wearing strange attire or the same clothes repeatedly may indicate "just right" or contamination obsessions. Bleeding gums may be a sign of copious brushing of teeth to get them clean enough. Rash or scabs on legs and arms may be indicators of skin picking. Frequent urinary urges for which no medical problem can be found may be obsessive urges to empty the bladder due to fear of having an "accident."

❑ *Unusual patterns and rule–bound behavior*: Odd behaviors such as walking in specific patterns through doorways, counting tiles or syllables, touching or tapping in symmetry or sitting and standing repeatedly may be "just right" rituals. Frequent checking of the book bag or under the desk and chair may be checking rituals. Opening and shutting lockers, lining up, ordering or arranging items are other signs of rituals. Unusual rules or preferences around food such as inspecting food, arranging food on plate in specific patterns, or rules for eating or drinking in specific sequences may be clues to OCD.

❑ *Circuitous paths:* Taking elaborate pains to circumvent or avoid triggers by taking the laborious route to a place or item when the easy one is obvious and accessible. Opening doors, lockers, desks, or books with elbows or with tissue in hand, holding hands in the air to avoid physical contact, refusal to shake hands or share supplies with others are instances of avoidance of OCD triggers.

❑ *Apologizing and confessing:* Confessing to inconsequential or imagined "misdeeds," asking for forgiveness repeatedly for perceived "bad" thoughts and actions, or praying often.

❑ *Secretiveness:* Clandestine behaviors, attempts at concealment, or lengthy unexplained disappearances into the bathroom or bedroom. Adolescents with OCD may be very secretive, because they are embarrassed and ashamed to disclose senseless worries and rituals.

❑ *Magical thinking*: Excessive and tenacious adherence to magical rules, superstitions and lucky and unlucky phenomena may also be a clue to OCD. For instance, Casey refuses to wear the shirt he was wearing when he caught a cold, because he is afraid he will catch another cold from the shirt (despite it being washed).

❑ *Distress when interrupted:* Becoming unduly distraught or frustrated and having temper outbursts when interrupted in seemingly minor activities or in rituals.

In-depth information about OCD for parents and school professionals is available in *What to do when your Child has OCD: Strategies and Solutions.* Therapists and physicians can learn about treatment in *Treatment of OCD in Children and Adolescents: A Cognitive-Behavioral Therapy Manual* (see the back of this book for more details).

Chapter 8

What Causes Anxiety Disorders?

There is no known cause of anxiety disorders. What is known is that there are several "risk factors" that may contribute to the development of anxiety disorders in children. The precise way in which all the risk factors come together to result in anxiety for a given person is not understood. An inconclusive answer regarding the causes of anxiety can be disappointing to parents, because it is natural to want to know why, and because knowing a cause often points to a direction for treatment.

The good news is that anxiety can be treated without knowing exactly what caused it. Treatment, discussed in Chapter 9, is focused on changing the factors that *exacerbate* or *maintain* anxiety. This chapter provides a brief overview of risk factors, emphasizing the "Fuel for Anxiety," which is most relevant to learning how to take control of anxiety.

GENES AND TEMPERAMENT

Anxious children may come into this world with a genetic *predisposition* or susceptibility towards anxiety. Children or adolescents are more likely to have an anxiety disorder if their parents have anxiety disorders. Rather than inheriting a specific anxiety disorder, what children inherit may be a general tendency to being sensitive, emotional, fearful, high-strung and highly reactive. No "anxiety gene" has been identified, and the mechanism for inheritance is not fully understood.

Psychologist Dr. Lewis Kagan at Harvard University found that about 10% of children have an anxious or fearful temperament from very early in life. He referred to this temperamental style as "behavioral inhibition." Dr. Kagan and his colleagues found that behaviorally inhibited children are easily startled, scared, withdrawn, cry often and cling to familiar adults. They are less likely to explore or try new things. They may be more vigilant to potential threats and more prone to react with alarm. These children have been found to have an over-reactive sympathetic nervous system, and may experience the physiological arousal of anxiety more rapidly and intensely than children who are not behaviorally inhibited. Children who *remain* inhibited throughout childhood appear to be at increased risk for an anxiety disorder compared to those who outgrow the inhibition. Although temperament tends to endure over time, not all children with anxious temperaments will develop anxiety problems or disorders.

> *Genes, temperament and brain chemistry are neither necessary nor sufficient for the development of anxiety disorders*

Brain function and chemistry are also thought to play a role in the development of anxiety disorders, although the specific pathways are far from clear. The basal ganglia of the brain and the neurotransmitter serotonin have been implicated in OCD, and norepinephrine is thought to be involved in GAD. Genes, temperament and brain chemistry are neither necessary nor sufficient for a child to develop an anxiety disorder. The final outcome is a far more complex equation than we understand. For more about risk factors for OCD, see *What to do when your Child has OCD: Strategies and Solutions.*

STRESS

Life experiences, stress and other factors, not all of them known, may interact with genetics and biology to contribute to the final expression of anxiety, just as in many medical conditions such as heart disease or asthma. However, stress does not *cause* anxiety, although for some children and adults stress may *trigger* anxiety. Major life events and milestones such as starting school or moving, or unpleasant events such as conflict in the family can be stressful and increase anxiety. Past experiences with danger, trauma, or failure may also set the stage for the development of anxiety.

Chronic daily hassles and stress may make children feel less safe and confident, more insecure and apprehensive. In today's world, children may face a lot of pressure in school. There are increased homework assignments and pressure to excel on standardized tests that contribute to the school's performance rating. Children with a predisposition towards anxiety may take school requirements and responsibilities more seriously and become anxious when they cannot meet them. Peer pressures towards using drugs, alcohol or cigarettes are more acutely experienced by some than by others.

The "overscheduled" child or adolescent is a major issue in our society today. Youngsters are pushed, by parents, peers, schools and themselves, into simply too many commitments, between academic and extracurricular activities. There are pressures to pursue and excel in every known form of enrichment, from soccer, baseball and swimming, to dance, gymnastics, piano or karate. Often, these activities are less about having fun and more about competing and winning. There is tremendous time pressure to squeeze all these commitments in — these youngsters are on a treadmill. Lessons and practices take up every evening of a child's week, leaving, after homework, little to no "down time" for youngsters to rest, regroup, develop creative play, or simply to decompress.

Youngsters need to have down time to refresh and rejuvenate. Creative minds are born of time to think and explore ideas — the overscheduled child has no time to think because he has barely enough mindshare to give all the activities in which he's involved. Parents and families today are likewise often rushed for time due to excessive commitments. Families need down time too. When families are constantly hurried and harried, there is less time to be proactive, positive or preventive. They are forced to deal with life reactively. These pressures can result in tension and conflict in the family.

The world climate of terrorism and war that we live in may result in fear, dread, apprehension and caution for many. Children are bombarded with the replays of tragic and frightening events repeatedly through the media. Those who are predisposed to anxiety may have more difficulty coping with such stressful happenings.

Chronic health conditions, illnesses, impairments and disabilities may also add stress when they impede the child's ability to keep up academically or fit in with the peer group. Often, children with physical disabilities are easily visible and conspicuous. Children who are frequently ill or have to attend doctor's appointments may be noticed for their frequent school absences. These children may become socially self-conscious and also become targets for teasing and bullying by inconsiderate children.

THE FUEL FOR ANXIETY

There are several factors that fuel or exacerbate anxiety once it occurs—these are the fuelling factors for anxiety. Although it may not be possible to change one's genetics, temperament or major life stressors, the fuelling factors for anxiety are usually malleable. In fact, treatment for anxiety, discussed in Chapter 9, is directed at changing these fueling factors.

The fueling factors for anxiety can influence each other to either accelerate or decelerate anxiety, a process known as *"reciprocal interaction."* Three types of reciprocal interactions that feed the fires of anxiety are *the anxiety triad, the vicious cycle of avoidance*, and *caregiver interactions*.

THE ANXIETY TRIAD

The three components of anxiety, which are cognitive, physiological and behavioral, or thoughts, physical symptoms and behaviors, can interact with each other to fuel an upward spiraling of anxiety. In other words, the ways in which people think about, feel and behave in situations of perceived threat can increase or decrease their anxiety.

Figure 1: The Anxiety Triad

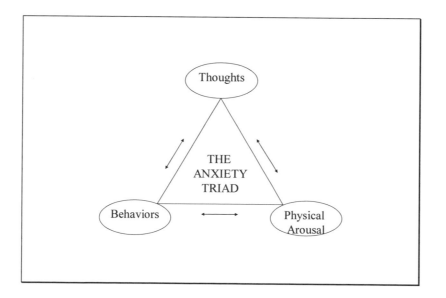

Anxious thoughts

People with anxiety tend to perceive danger and threat more readily and in more situations than non-anxious people; they experience many false alarms. They tend to greatly overestimate the probability of catastrophe, and underestimate their ability to cope and survive. Simply said, they expect the worst. In addition, anxious people seek safety and certainty in situations where they cannot be guaranteed. This lack of certainty makes them feel out of control, and drives them to regain control by being overly cautious, taking no chances, checking, seeking reassurance, or avoiding mistakes at all costs. Chapter 9 describes anxious thoughts in more detail.

> *Anxious people tend to overestimate danger and underestimate their ability to cope with it.*

Physical symptoms

Typical physical signs of anxiety that we all experience include heart pounding, sweating, tension, difficulty breathing, nausea, stomach upset and insomnia or nightmares. These normal physical sensations are the result of arousal of the sympathetic nervous system when we perceive danger or threat. It is possible that people who are prone to high anxiety may have sympathetic nervous systems that are more easily aroused; further, they may be more reactive to normal physical sensations and may interpret them as confirmation of danger and threat.

Behaviors

It is a natural instinct to want to escape or avoid a situation that is dangerous or threatening. People who are highly anxious are more likely to exit the situation as soon as they perceive danger cues in the environment or have uncomfortable physical symptoms. Other anxious behaviors include asking for repeated reassurance and conducting safety checks to make sure everything is safe.

The three pieces of the Anxiety Triad reinforce and strengthen anxiety. People with high levels of anxiety have a high level of vigilance for danger, may be overly sensitive to physical symptoms, and remain poised and ready for easy escape. Anxious thoughts and physical symptoms are converted into anxious self-talk that drives avoidance and escape. Over time, an accumulation of these experiences cements the anxious person's sense of constant danger.

For example, Emily is afraid of failing the spelling test and thinks, *"It's too hard. I can't do it. I'm going to fail"* (thoughts). She feels tense, nervous and has an upset stomach (physical symptoms). She can't focus and rushes through the test (behaviors), making several mistakes on words she knows well. She gets a C on the test, which confirms her initial belief that it was too hard. The next time a test comes up, she is less confident and more anxious, and the entire sequence repeats itself. In due time, she comes to believe that she will fail all tests, and refuses to go to school on test days.

Likewise, Joseph thinks he is unpopular and none of his classmates want to talk to him (thoughts). His stomach feels queasy when he is in the cafeteria line, and he fidgets and averts his gaze (physical symptoms). He is too nervous to speak to anyone. When he gets his tray of food, he hesitates and goes to an empty table rather than one that already has children at it (behaviors). No one comes to sit at his table. Joseph believes that he was right—no one likes him.

THE VICIOUS CYCLE OF AVOIDANCE

Avoidance and escape may be the most powerful of the factors that perpetuate anxiety. When faced with threat, anxious people are more likely to resort to "flight" rather than "fight." Avoidance fuels anxiety through a process known as *negative reinforcement*. Negative reinforcement is often confused with punishment, but is actually a *reward*. It is called negative

> *Avoidance and escape are the most powerful fuel for anxiety*

reinforcement because the behavior (escape) is rewarded by the avoidance of a negative consequence (the discomfort of the anxiety). We learn faster when our behaviors are rewarded.

The *Vicious Cycle of Avoidance* is portrayed in Figure 2. The left slope of the graph shows how anxiety rises when the person has to confront a feared situation (exposure). When anxiety becomes unbearable (panic peak), the person escapes from the situation, and thereby gets immediate relief from the anxiety. This relief is immensely rewarding and reinforces the belief that escape is the only way to overcome the anxiety, because he never takes the time to figure out any other way to cope. The belief that avoidance gives relief is strengthened and reinforced each time the person successfully escapes. As a result, he engages in avoidance or escape more frequently and quickly. However, this relief is only temporary, because when the same situation resurfaces, the person has no other way to cope. This fuels a vicious cycle of anxiety because, in the absence of any other coping mechanism, the person resorts to escape once again. (The downward curve that follows the "panic peak" in Figure 2 is discussed in Chapter 9).

Figure 2: The Vicious Cycle of Avoidance

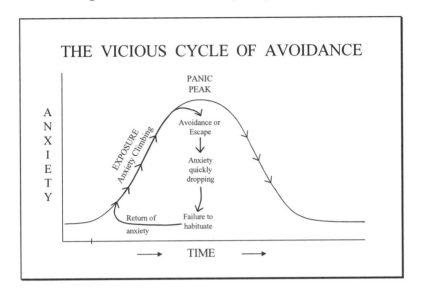

When Sarah asks repeatedly asks for reassurance that her mother is safe, or stays home from school, or when Casey washes his hands repeatedly, they are engaging in escape and avoidance. Sarah asks for reassurance as soon as she starts to worry about her mother. She feels better when her mother or teacher reassure her that all is well. Similarly, Casey makes a beeline for the sink as soon as he is uncomfortable, and feels much better when he washes his hands and gets the germs off them. They may feel better in the moment, but they are actually making their anxiety worse! The immense relief that Sarah and Casey experience strengthens their belief in avoidance as the best way to overcome their fears. They do not give themselves the opportunity to learn that their fears are unwarranted, or that there are other ways to cope. Chapter 9 describes how the anxious person can break the vicious cycle of avoidance.

CAREGIVER INTERACTIONS

Children in today's world may interact everyday not just with parents, but many other care-giving adults as well. This section pertains to all caregivers of children and adolescents, including parents, grandparents, teachers, and child-care providers. "Caregiver" and "parent" are used interchangeably in this book because the primary caregiver for a child is typically a parent.

Reacting and responding appropriately to a child's anxiety can be quite a challenge for caregivers. There is a wide spectrum of reactions to a child's anxiety. While some parents are able to find an approach that helps their child conquer anxiety, many find that intuitive parenting techniques don't seem to work with their children. Parents may stumble through a series of trial and error techniques when customary approaches don't work. Those who are fatigued and frustrated with an unresponsive child may run out of patience. Some may swing from one end of the spectrum to the other, from indulging and handling with kid gloves, to anger and punishment, followed rapidly by feelings of guilt. Parents of anxious children are often relieved to know that they are not alone in this experience.

Although the propensity for anxiety may be inherited, it can be influenced in either direction by the reactions and responses of caregivers. Although parents do not consciously intend to perpetuate a child's anxiety, they may be surprised to learn that some of the ways in which they interact with the child may unwittingly reinforce and strengthen the child's anxiety. The intent of this section is to increase awareness of caregiver interactions that may fuel anxiety. It is not to lay blame on parents for causing anxiety, nor is it to categorize "good" or "bad" parents. Parents mean well and do the best they can in their particular circumstances. It is hard for anyone to be objective when caught up in an emotional situation.

Research studies have shown that parents of anxious children are more likely than parents of non-anxious children to be more protective and closely involved with their children. Understandably, it is hard for parents to watch a child cry, panic or become terrified. Out of caring and concern, parents of anxious children may rush to alleviate their child's distress by "fixing" the problem for the child or enabling their avoidance of the situation. They may be reluctant to do or say anything that will upset their child. They may therefore hesitate to encourage them to try, to leave them when they are upset, or allow them to learn from their experiences.

Anxious children may be more likely to approach problem solving with avoidant solutions. Psychologist Dr. Paula Barrett found that when anxious children were asked to find solutions to hypothetical problem scenarios, they gave higher rates of avoidant responses, compared to oppositional and other non-anxious children. Further, when they were asked to discuss the problem with their parents, the likelihood of an avoidance-oriented solution almost doubled. In contrast, when non-anxious children discussed solutions with their parents, avoidant responses decreased.

In contrast to parents of non-anxious children, parents of anxious children may participate in and even support their child's avoidance rather than confrontation of problems. It is possible that past experience has shown parents that avoidance is the least aversive approach for their child. Parents who have previously encouraged their child to tackle a problem actively may have found the child's protests and fear to be too draining and exhausting. Parents may therefore default to supporting avoidance because their attempts at encouraging other approaches have been futile. For instance, Joseph's parents support Joseph's passive acceptance of teasing and avoidance of all altercations with peers. Their efforts to encourage Joseph to be assertive and defend himself were met with such resistance and anger that they found it easier to resign themselves to his avoidance.

There are three important issues before drawing conclusions about the parents of anxious children. First, not *all* parents of anxious children are over-involved or overprotective. In fact, many are quite appropriate in parenting their anxious children. Second, anxious children may actually *elicit* protective and rescuing behaviors from their parents, resulting in a reciprocal interaction. The child's behavior shapes the parent's behavior, and the parent's behavior in turn shapes the child's behavior. Parent and child continually influence each other to reinforce the anxious response style. Third, parents of anxious children may interact differently with their *non-anxious* children than they do with their anxious child. In other words, the same parents may be less protective and reactive, and offer less assistance to their non-anxious children. These facts indicate that parents do not "cause" anxiety in children.

THE VICIOUS CYCLE FOR PARENTS

Over the course of many years of handling an oversensitive, highly reactive and easily distressed child, caregivers may fall into the trap of anticipating and rushing to the rescue even before the child encounters fear. The parent derives *negative reinforcement* from rescuing the child quickly and thereby avoiding the discomfort of enduring the child's distress. The child learns that the more upset he is, the more likely his parents are to respond. In other words, he is rewarded for being distressed and avoidant. Parents who fall into this vicious cycle thereby inadvertently foster anxious behavior.

Parents of anxious children may also become the spokesperson for the child, guessing and voicing the child's feelings, reactions, thoughts or opinions, and doing many basic and routine tasks for the child. In doing so, they may inadvertently foster dependence, with which the anxious child becomes very comfortable. Soon, the child comes to expect this easy assistance, depending on the parent to be available on demand to soothe and fix the problem. The child may be lost and helpless when the parent isn't on hand to save the situation. A pattern of dependence and lack of self-reliance is established.   The child needs excessive soothing, nurturing and reassurance. Over a period of time, parents move into "auto-assist" mode without realizing it.

This reciprocal interaction is compounded even further when parents are themselves anxious. Anxious parents may be hyper vigilant to threat and danger, react with alarm, become easily upset and fearful, and avoid difficult tasks. Their children witness these behaviors and may learn to be more cautious, make associations with danger, and stay away from perceived threat. In other words, anxious parents may unwittingly model anxious responses and raise the child in an "anxious environment" (an instance of the joint contribution of genetics and environment). Anxious parents may also empathize with their child's plight because they have experienced anxiety themselves. Many anxious parents wish to protect their children from fear-inducing situations. They are more likely to be overprotective and controlling.

When adults are overprotective, allow the child to avoid fearful contexts, and rescue the child from difficult situations, the child loses natural opportunities to break the "vicious cycle of anxiety." He fails to learn productive coping strategies and lags behind in developing self-reliance. In an attempt to care for, protect, and support their child, parents are actually supporting the child's anxiety, not the child. For example, Sarah's parents may hover, provide repeated reassurance, become upset themselves and refuse to leave Sarah until she calms down. They tentatively ask her permission to leave, rather than matter-of-factly set the expectation. "*Are you sure you'll be okay? Do you want me to stay for a little while? Do you want to go to the classroom now? You don't have to if you don't want to."* By doing so, Sarah's parents give her mixed messages, agree with Sarah's perception of danger, validate her fears and reinforce her belief that her fear is justified.

Treatment of anxiety by changing the fueling factors is discussed in Chapter 9. Medication treatment is discussed in Chapter 10.

Chapter 9

Cognitive-Behavioral Therapy for Anxiety

Cognitive-behavioral therapy (CBT), a scientifically-proven treatment, offers both adults and children the skills to overcome anxiety successfully, regardless of how it develops.

CBT is a practical, logical and methodical approach to the mastery of anxiety that has been used successfully for adults with anxiety since the 1960's. It is directed at changing the factors that fuel anxiety, as discussed in Chapter 8. CBT targets the anxiety triad of thoughts, physical symptoms, and avoidance, as well as caregiver interactions with an anxious child.

With CBT, people with anxiety learn a new way of reacting and responding to anxiety. The automatic, spiral of fear or panic, accompanied by escape or avoidance is halted by relearning how to interpret and react to the instinctive reaction of fear. The child learns to think more realistically about fears, to confront them and test their validity, and to become less reactive to physical symptoms and feelings of anxiety. Caregivers play a crucial role in the child's recovery by becoming aware of and adapting their reactions and responses in ways that foster non-anxious behaviors (see Chapter 11). In essence, the idea in CBT is to "take control of anxiety or let it take control of you." Children and their caregivers learn how to break free of the anxiety trap.

> *Take control of anxiety or let it take control of you*

CBT is an active, experiential form of learning, like bicycling or swimming, which are learned by doing, and for which practice is an essential element. If learned early, these skills can serve a lifetime of use. The ultimate goal is to teach the child skills that he can internalize and use to help himself whenever the need arises.

Can young children participate in CBT? For many years, it was generally believed that children were too young and immature to have the skills necessary to participate in CBT. Clinicians complained that children did not comprehend CBT, and that they were often unmotivated or noncompliant. Children are less likely to be future oriented, and therefore less motivated to work for delayed rewards. This is especially true when they have to face high anxiety situations immediately. The safety and security of the present are more tangible than the benefits of the distant future.

Today, we know that young children can participate in CBT just as successfully as adults. It is not as daunting as it may sound. One of the first rigorous studies of CBT with anxious children was published in 1994 by Dr. Philip Kendall at Temple University. Of the anxious children in his study who received a 16-week CBT treatment, 64% improved significantly. In contrast, only 5% of the children on a waiting list who received no treatment improved. The anxious children remained improved even one year after completion of treatment. Other studies have found similar rates of success using CBT with children. Dr. Kendall's pioneering work and subsequent studies make it clear that children respond remarkably well when CBT is adapted to suit their developmental age and maturity. CBT can be used effectively with children as young as 6 years of age.

CBT is an approach to treatment that consists of a variety of techniques, based on common principles. CBT

The goal of CBT is not to remove all anxiety, but to bring it back into the normal range

techniques are grouped in this chapter according to the anxiety-fueling factors they address. The categories are not mutually exclusive and do have some overlap. Good treatment is directed at specific symptoms and behaviors, not at a particular disorder. There are many common symptoms among the anxiety disorders; treatment strategies may therefore similar across different disorders. In treating a particular child, the best approach is to use a combination of suitable techniques, and to tailor the treatment plan to a child's actual symptoms and unique needs.

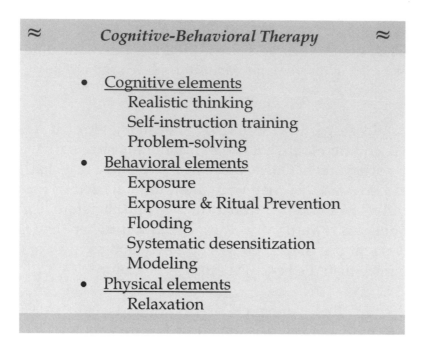

COGNITIVE TECHNIQUES

Central to CBT is the premise that a person's thoughts or beliefs about situations affect his feelings and behavior. Cognitive techniques are aimed at modifying the thoughts that escalate anxiety.

The first step for the anxious child or adult is to understand the relationship between thoughts and feelings. I developed the *Noise at the Window* analogy to clarify this relationship in child-friendly language:

Let's say you heard a noise at your bedroom window at night. If you thought it was a burglar trying to break in, you would probably be afraid. If you thought it was just a branch rustling in the breeze, you might be soothed as you drift off to sleep. If you thought it was a broken hinge, you could be annoyed at yet another thing that needed fixing. The thought of a squirrel at the window could be irritating. If you weren't sure, your curiosity might be aroused. If you just lay in bed and didn't find out what was creating the noise, you would never know what it really was.

In essence, your *feelings* about the noise would depend on your *beliefs* about what was happening. If you did not find out the source of the noise, you would not have tested the reality, and your belief about the sound would merely be an *assumption*. Your feelings then would be dependent on that assumption. As a result, a mistaken belief might result in unwarranted feelings that would bring more angst than necessary. A person with high levels of anxiety is more likely to overestimate danger and threat, and to expect the worst. He is more likely to think the noise at the window is a burglar, and to imagine being attacked and helpless. Further, he is likely to confuse these thoughts and feelings with reality. *"I think it's a burglar, therefore it must be a burglar,"* reflects the anxious person's reliance on his thoughts as the truth. The anxious person reacts to situations with instinctive feelings rather than the reality.

The Noise at the Window	
Thought	*Feeling*
It's a burglar	*Afraid*
It's a branch in the breeze	*Relaxed*
It's a broken hinge	*Annoyed*
It's a squirrel	*Irritated*

In CBT, cognitive strategies are geared towards changing anxious thoughts and self-talk into realistic and productive thoughts and self-talk. Children are first taught to recognize the relationship between their thoughts and feelings. They then learn to make more accurate estimations of danger, recognize their potential to cope and to develop this potential into actual coping. Cognitive strategies that build these skills include *realistic thinking, self-instruction training,* and *problem-solving training,* described below. They are often used in combination, and are most useful when they are used in conjunction with behavioral strategies described under *Behavioral Techniques* in the next section.

Realistic thinking

Realistic thinking involves recognizing that "the noise at the window" could involve many possibilities, not just the burglar. Children and adolescents are often not even aware of their anxious thoughts and self-talk. The first step is to teach children to become aware of their self-talk by playing "psychological detective." Children learn to identify thought patterns that are unrealistic, and then to replace them with accurate thoughts. It is important to note that the goal is *realistic* thinking, not *positive* thinking (which is not necessarily realistic). The skills involved in developing realistic thinking include:

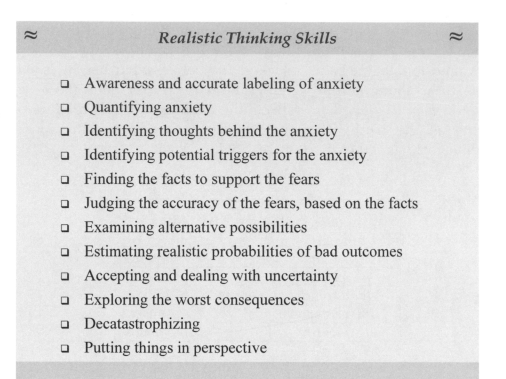

Realistic Thinking Skills

- ❑ Awareness and accurate labeling of anxiety
- ❑ Quantifying anxiety
- ❑ Identifying thoughts behind the anxiety
- ❑ Identifying potential triggers for the anxiety
- ❑ Finding the facts to support the fears
- ❑ Judging the accuracy of the fears, based on the facts
- ❑ Examining alternative possibilities
- ❑ Estimating realistic probabilities of bad outcomes
- ❑ Accepting and dealing with uncertainty
- ❑ Exploring the worst consequences
- ❑ Decatastrophizing
- ❑ Putting things in perspective

The Socratic Method

CBT therapists do not merely tell anxious adults or children how to think realistically. Anyone who has tried to give advice to an anxious person knows that it is usually not well heeded and is therefore ineffective. Instead, CBT therapists rely on the *Socratic questioning* method. The Greek teacher Socrates did not impart his wisdom by just expounding on it. He posed a series of questions to his pupils that challenged them to think through and arrive at the right answers for themselves. The wisdom they gained as a result came from within. Likewise, CBT therapists use thought-provoking questions to guide patients to "figure out" logical, rational and realistic answers *on their own*. The change in thinking patterns is more powerful and enduring when it is internally driven.

Effective Socratic questioning is an art that calls for creativity, flexibility, quick thinking and experience. This is more so when the "pupil" is a child. It is important that the child not feel defensive, evaluated or put on the spot with this technique, as this will raise both anxiety and unwillingness to participate. Children respond surprisingly well to Socratic questioning when used skillfully by an experienced therapist.

The "Fearmometer"

The *Fearmometer* (Figure 3), also known as a Fear Thermometer or Feeling Thermometer, is a very useful tool in CBT. It is used to teach children how to differentiate, quantify and communicate levels of anxiety. Used in conjunction with Socratic questioning, it allows children to rate anxiety or *"Fear Temperature"* on a graduated scale from 1 to 10, where 1 is "No anxiety" and 10 is "Out of Control." It is often used for realistic thinking and primarily for exposure exercises (described in the next section).

Figure 3: The "Fearmometer"

When children are anxious, they often think in an all-or-none manner and do not differentiate between levels of threat or levels of reaction. As a result, they may experience and report severe anxiety regardless of whether the threat is minor or major. For instance, Emily perceives getting an A- on a quiz as just as catastrophic as failing it altogether. Instead of reacting to both situations with panic, Emily needs to learn how to make relative rather than absolute judgments and thereby modulate her response accordingly. Using the *Fearmometer*, Emily differentiates and quantifies her anxiety. She rates getting an A- as a 5 ("Not too good") and failing a test as a 10 ("Out of control").

The use of the *Fearmometer* in gradual exposure is described under *Behavioral Techniques* in the next section of this chapter and in Chapter 13. The Feeling Thermometer is a versatile tool that can also be used to quantify other feelings such as anger or sadness (see *Corrective Learning Experiences* in Chapter 14).

Table 4: Socratic Questions for Realistic Thinking

From Worried Thinking to Calm Thinking*

Socratic question	Skill development
What are you feeling?	Awareness/labeling of anxiety
What is your fear temperature (1-10)?	Quantifying anxiety
What are you worried about?	Identifying cognitions
Why are you worried about it?	Identifying triggers
What are you saying to yourself?	Identifying anxious self-talk
What are the chances it will happen (0-100)?	Anxious estimation of probability
What clues do you have that it will happen? How many times has it happened before? How many times has it not happened to you? How many times has it happened to other kids? How many times has it not happened to other kids?	Testing the fear against evidence
Can you be absolutely sure it won't happen?	Dealing with uncertainty
What else could happen?	Examining alternatives
What are the real chances it will happen?	Estimating realistic probabilities
**What's the worst thing that could happen?	Decatastrophizing
So what if it happens?	Decatastrophizing
Is this as bad as you thought it would be?	Perspective-taking
Have you had worse things happen to you before?	Perspective-taking
What could you do to handle this?	Problem-solving
What helpful things could you say to yourself now?	Coping self-talk, cognitive control
What's your fear temperature now?	Quantifying change in anxiety
What did you learn from thinking through your fear?	Empowerment, taking charge
How did you do and how can you reward yourself?	Self-evaluation/reinforcement

* Relevant questions are written on an index card or notepad for the child to keep handy.
** This question must only be asked in carefully selected situations.

Socratic questions that may be used to generate realistic thinking are presented in Table 4. The questions are neither necessary nor sufficient for a given child; they are merely starting points for the therapist. A skillful therapist will adapt the questions to each child's specific needs. The child's responses to these questions elicit further questions from the therapist, until the child arrives at logical and rational answers.

All too often, children do not stop to consider whether their fears are warranted. They jump to the conclusion that it will be "the end of the world." The Socratic question *"What's the worst thing that could happen?"* (Table 4) helps them stop and consider the worst-case scenario. This question must be used selectively and carefully. It is generally not an appropriate question for children who have fears of parents dying (as in SAD or OCD), or for fears of other disastrous consequences. For these children, questions should focus on the realistic estimation of probabilities. This question is most appropriate for older children and adolescents, and for those whose fears are focused on routine and relatively manageable events such as failing a test at school.

When Emily is asked,

"What's the worst thing that could happen if you fail the spelling test?" she responds, *"Well, that would be just awful."*
"Why would it be so awful?"
"Because everyone will think I'm stupid."
"Who will think you're stupid? What will they say to you?"

Emily thinks about it for a moment and replies,

"Well, I guess my teacher wouldn't think I was stupid because I usually get an A anyway, and my parents know I'm smart. Maybe I'm the only one who'll think I'm stupid. And I know I'm not really stupid."

At the end of this process, Emily arrives at the conclusion that failing a test is not by any means an irrecoverable error.

A key skill for overcoming anxiety is learning how to accept and live with *uncertainty* – the fact that there may not be an answer to the noise at the window. You may never know what it was, and you have no guarantee that it will not return. Anxious persons want reassurances that "bad" outcomes will not happen. Although we can estimate the chances of bad things occurring, we can neither predict nor control them. The fact is that they can and do happen. There are few guarantees in life and the anxious person must learn to come to terms with this reality to overcome anxiety.

An example of Socratic questioning with Sarah, who has school refusal is presented below. The CBT therapist guides Sarah to identify and evaluate her fears using the following Socratic questions:

T (Therapist): *Why is it hard to go to school?*
Sarah: *I want to be near my mom.*
T: *Why is it so important to be near your mom all day?*
Sarah: *Because something might happen to her while I'm at school.*
T: *What do you think could happen to her while you're at school?*
Sarah: *She could die in a car accident or something.*
T: *What makes you think she's in a car accident?*
Sarah: *Sometimes she's late picking me up. I get scared she's been in an accident.*
T: *Has she been late before?*
Sarah: *Yeah, she's been late.*
T: *How many times has she been late in the last month?*
Sarah: *About 4 times.*
T: *Was she in a car accident any of those times?*
Sarah: *Nope, she wasn't.*
T: *Why was she late those 4 times?*
Sarah: *She had to stop at the store to pick up milk once. Another time, there was construction on the road, so it slowed her down. The other two times, she had to finish some work before she left the office.*
T: *Okay, so each time she was late, there was a simple reason for it. How long has your mom been driving, Sara?*
Sarah: *Oh, I don't know, maybe 20 years or something.*
T: *Has she ever been in an accident in those 20 years?*
Sarah: *I guess not. At least, I never heard her say she was, but I hear about accidents on the news, so I worry.*
T: *So she's never been in an accident in 20 years of driving? Would you help me with some math here? Let's see, how many months is 20 years?*
Sarah: *Maybe like 200?*
T: *Close enough! Let's say she's been driving for 200 months. She's never been in an accident for 200 months. So what are the chances she'll be in an accident this month?*
Sarah (realization): *Nothing, I guess. Okay, I get it. She's probably not going to be in an accident now if she hasn't for 20 years.*
T: *And could there be other reasons you could think about when she's late?*
Sarah: *Yes, like the rush hour traffic.*

T: *Right! But you know, we can't be 100% sure she would never be in an accident. We only know that the chances are very, very small. So what do you choose to focus on — the very small chance she'll be in an accident or the very big chances she's not in an accident?*

Sarah: *I guess that she's not in an accident.*

T: *Great, you figured it out! So what could you say to yourself when she's late?*

Sarah: *It's just my mind playing tricks on me again. Mom's probably just late leaving the office today. Or maybe the traffic's slow again. I'll wait for another hour before I let myself worry.*

T: *Now, let's pretend you wanted to be absolutely sure she'd never be in an accident ever. What would you have to do to make sure of that?*

Sarah (laughing): *I guess Mom would have to stay in the house for the rest of her life and never go out again!*

T (laughing): *Let's ask your mom if she'd enjoy being under house arrest like that!*

As you can see from the process of Socratic questioning, Sara deduced that the chances of an accident are miniscule, as her mother has never been in a car accident after 25 years of driving every day. She realizes that her mother has been late getting home on numerous occasions in the past, but never because she was in an accident. She recalls that among many other reasons for her mother being late, slow traffic has been the most frequent. Sarah appreciates the fact that she cannot be absolutely sure that her mother will never be in a car accident. With further questioning, Sarah recognizes that the only way to ensure complete protection for her mother is to keep her under "house arrest." She understands that being confined to the house is neither practical nor enjoyable for her mother or other family members. Sarah arrives at the conclusion that worrying does not protect her mother from an accident in any way.

Another example of the use of Socratic questions is presented in *Facing My Fears* in Chapter 13.

Self-instruction training

Self-instruction training is an alternative to realistic thinking that involves teaching children to replace anxious self-talk with calming self-talk. Young children or those with attention, learning, or intellectual difficulties may lack the insight, ability to introspect, and abstract thinking skills necessary to participate actively in Socratic questioning and realistic thinking. They are not required to evaluate their anxious thoughts using evidence, simply to replace them with calm ones. Self-instruction training is adapted from the work of psychologist Donald Meichenbaum, who developed it to teach self-control skills to impulsive children.

As a first step, the child is taught to recognize anxious self-talk and "catch" it quickly. Then, the child learns to replace negative or danger-oriented talk with self-talk that emphasizes coping ability, decreases worry, boosts self-confidence, and reinforces effort and success. The therapist first models each step and then asks the child to follow suit. Once the child practices these steps, the therapist provides feedback. The child then uses coping statements in imaginary situations, and finally in real-life situations. Following the therapist's example, the child approaches the feared situation while making coping statements. The child then learns how to evaluate his performance and learns how to reward himself.

With the therapists' guidance, Casey learns how to catch himself when he says, "*I thought a bad word, so I'm a bad person.*"

He learns to replace this self-demeaning thought with self-talk such as,
> "*I don't want to think bad words, they just pop into my head. Good thoughts also pop into my head a lot, so I guess I'm not a bad person after all. My doctor says everyone has bad words pop into their heads sometimes, and that doesn't make them a bad person. I'm going to think about something good I did today, instead of thinking of the bad word in my head. I was nice to my sister and shared my cookies with her. There, now that thought makes me feel much better.*"

Problem-solving training

When we are anxious, we think emotionally, not logically. Children with anxiety often become so overcome by their feelings that they are unable to engage in basic problem solving. Problem-solving training involves teaching children a systematic way to solve problems, so that they are manageable rather than out of control. It allows the child to break overwhelming tasks into smaller, manageable steps.

Joseph, who believes that no one wants to be his friend, uses the following sequence of problem-solving steps to think through the situation:

≈	*Steps in Problem-Solving*	≈

- ❑ Define the problem
- ❑ Set limits on its parameters
- ❑ Focus attention to the task at hand
- ❑ Generate all potential solutions
- ❑ Select the most suitable solution
- ❑ Test the solution
- ❑ Evaluate its success

What is the problem? *No one talks to me in the cafeteria.*

What are all the things I can do to handle it? *I guess I could try to be the first to talk, I could just wait until someone talks to me, I could go join a table where kids are talking to each other, or I could stop going to the cafeteria.*

What will happen if I do each of those things? *If I try to talk to someone, they might talk to me or they might blow me off. If I wait for someone to talk to me, they might think I'm a snob and not interested in talking to them. If I sit at a table with other kids, I could say hi and maybe someone will talk to me. If I stop going to the cafeteria, no one will have a chance to talk to me.*

Which way of handling it is the best? *Maybe I'll try to sit at a table with other kids. That doesn't make me as nervous as starting a conversation.*

After Joseph has selected and used a method of handling the problem, he evaluates its effectiveness.

Now that I have tried it, how did I do? *It wasn't so bad after all. It took a lot of guts for me to say hi to the kid next to me, but she smiled and said hi back to me. I guess she didn't think I was nerdy because she didn't ignore me.*

What can I do differently next time? *Maybe I can ask how she's doing.*

BEHAVIORAL TECHNIQUES

Avoidance and escape are probably the most powerful fueling factors for the maintenance of anxiety. Avoidance prevents the anxious person from using the opportunity to confront the fear and learn if it is really as frightening as he thinks it is, or whether he can cope with it. As a result, he will not be able to *overcome* his fear, merely escape it. *Exposure*, the cornerstone of CBT, is the primary strategy for overcoming avoidance.

Exposure

Exposure refers to being exposed to or facing fears to test their reality. It involves purposeful and conscious confrontation of fears, rather than the instinctive tendency to retreat. Exposure allows people to discover that their fears are usually false alarms. When the expected disastrous consequences do not materialize, the person's belief about the fear begins to change.

> *To overcome your fear, you must face your fear*

There is an important difference between *facing* fears and *fighting* fears; facing involves confronting, whereas fighting implies combat and resistance. Children may be confused when they are told to "fight" anxiety because it suggests that they should resist it with all their might. The emotional energy consumed in fighting and resisting may actually intensify anxiety. In a paradoxical way, one has to stop struggling with fears to make them go away. To understand how exposure works, one must first understand *habituation*.

Habituation: Natural and Automatic

Exposure has a lot in common with jumping into a cold swimming pool, turning off the lights at night or walking into a noisy train station. Sounds a bit far-fetched? Not really, because what they have in common is a process known as *habituation*, which is the body's way of accommodating to new sensations. When we initially encounter a sound, heat or cold, light or dark, we experience it in all its magnitude. Over time, the intensity of the sensation fades as our body adapts to it. We experience habituation numerous times every day without so much as a second thought. We get used to cold water, bright lights, the roar of jet planes, and the rumble of trains with little conscious effort.

What most people are surprised to know is that *our bodies can habituate to anxiety*, in much the same way as they get used to the cold water in the pool. We can get used to anxiety until it fades from our awareness. Habituation is a natural biological phenomenon that takes place automatically because our bodies are designed to return to equilibrium. The sympathetic nervous system is responsible for preparing the body to react to threat and danger and the parasympathetic system subsequently restores it to normal resting state. In other words, anxiety simply cannot continue forever, although it may feel that way. If we did not have a built-in mechanism for resetting to equilibrium, how could we handle the cumulative effects of thousands of new threats over time?

We routinely experience habituation to anxiety, although we might not be aware of it. For example, any of us can relate to the anxiety that precedes an important meeting that is potentially unpleasant. We have experienced the desire to avoid it, because it made us uneasy, nervous or tense. Yet, the uneasiness decreased once the meeting was underway. Anxiety habituates rapidly when we confront the anxiety-provoking situation.

Figure 4: Up and Down the Worry Hill

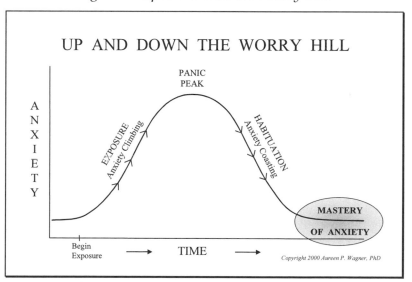

The Worry Hill

Understanding how avoidance, exposure and habituation work is essential to mastery of anxiety. Yet, these are difficult concepts for children to understand. I developed the metaphor of the *Worry Hill* to portray the relationship between exposure and habituation to children and adolescents in child-friendly language. Figure 4 depicts the Worry Hill. The left side of the curve shows how anxiety climbs when exposure takes place. Over time, anxiety reaches a peak, and then automatically begins to decline as habituation sets in. Anxiety is overcome when habituation takes place, on the other side of the *Worry Hill.*

Unfortunately, most people do not know that habituation of anxiety takes place naturally with exposure. It is this lack of awareness and inability to tolerate increasing anxiety that leads the person to escape an anxiety-provoking situation. As described in Chapter 8, escape results in a vicious cycle of anxiety. For habituation to set in, the person must continue with exposure and *remain* in the feared situation until anxiety peaks and begins to decline. Habituation happens if it is allowed to happen. The person must merely wait and let it come to pass. Most people are surprised to find that the anxiety they feel during exposure is generally much less than expected. For many, *anticipatory anxiety,* which is anxiety prior to the exposure, is much greater than anxiety experienced during exposure.

> *Anxiety <u>before</u> exposure may be greater than anxiety <u>during</u> exposure*

Figure 5: The Results of Exposure Therapy

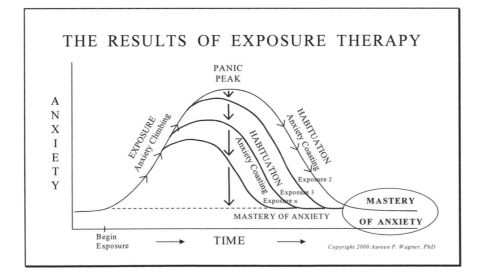

Figure 5 shows what exposure therapy does to anxiety. With each trial of exposure, the peak of anxiety decreases and habituation sets in faster.

Frequent practice results in decreasing anxiety. This process eventually leads to conquest and mastery over anxiety.

Exposure therapy can be conducted in several different ways. *In vivo* exposure is real-life exposure that involves confronting feared situations in their actuality. For example, Sarah confronts her fear of vomiting on the bus by riding the bus everyday. *Imaginal exposure* refers to confronting fears or worries in imagination rather than in real life. This variation of exposure is used when fears or worries cannot be replicated in real life, or when the risk of real-life exposure outweighs the benefits. If Emily is afraid of repeating a grade, it is not sensible to hold her back a grade just to expose her to the fear. Instead, she can confront the fear imaginally. Emily and her CBT therapist create an imaginary scene in which Emily receives her report card and sees that she has failed the test. She imagines her teacher's, parents' and her own reactions to her failure. The imaginal scene should resemble the real-life situation as closely as possible in its real-life details, and must arouse anxiety in order for Emily to experience habituation.

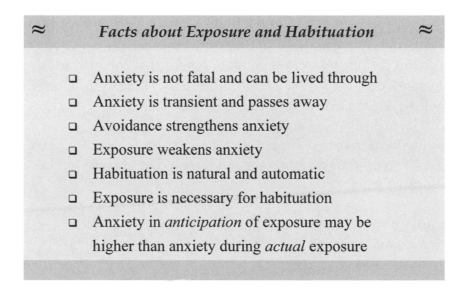

≈ ***Facts about Exposure and Habituation*** ≈

- ❏ Anxiety is not fatal and can be lived through
- ❏ Anxiety is transient and passes away
- ❏ Avoidance strengthens anxiety
- ❏ Exposure weakens anxiety
- ❏ Habituation is natural and automatic
- ❏ Exposure is necessary for habituation
- ❏ Anxiety in *anticipation* of exposure may be higher than anxiety during *actual* exposure

Exposure & Ritual Prevention for OCD

Exposure and *Ritual Prevention* (ERP) is a form of exposure used primarily to treat obsessive-compulsive disorder, where rituals are a form of avoidance and escape from the obsessive fear. Exposure involves confronting the situations or objects that trigger obsessions, and ritual prevention involves refraining from the rituals that relieve the anxiety caused by the obsessions.

Exposure and ritual prevention must be done simultaneously for the best results. The child must *confront and remain in the feared situation* and *not do any rituals* until the anxiety subsides. ERP allows the child to see that his fears do not come true, even when he does not engage in any rituals. This realization, along with habituation, reduces the potency of obsessions.

ERP has been used effectively for adults with OCD for about 40 years, with success rates around 80%. Recent studies of ERP for children with OCD confirm similar success rates for children. More extensive information on how parents, schools and clinicians can help children overcome OCD is available in *What to do when your child has Obsessive-Compulsive Disorder: Strategies and Solutions* (see *Resources* at the end of this book).

Up and Down the Worry Hill: ERP for youngsters with OCD

Children benefit significantly from treatment when they understand the vital concepts of exposure, habituation and anticipatory anxiety. Yet, these are not intuitive concepts. I have developed the metaphor of riding a bicycle *Up and Down the Worry Hill* and the *RIDE* acronym to explain these complex yet key ideas to children and adolescents.

The following is an excerpt from *Up and Down the Worry Hill: A Children's book about OCD and its Treatment* (see *Resources*). Dr. Greene explains ERP to Casey, who has OCD:

"Learning how to stop OCD is like riding your bicycle up and down a hill. At first, facing your fears and stopping your rituals feels like riding up a big "Worry Hill," because it's tough. You have to work very hard to huff and puff up a hill, but if you keep going, you can get to the top of the hill. Once you get to the top, it's easy and fun to coast down the hill. You can only coast down the hill if you first get to the top. Likewise, you can only get past your fears if you face them. You have to stick it out until the bad feeling passes. Then you will see that your fears do not come true. But if you give in to the rituals, it's like riding back down the hill. You don't give yourself a chance to find out that your fears will not come true even when you don't do rituals."

The 4-step *RIDE* acronym (<u>R</u>ename, <u>I</u>nsist, <u>D</u>efy, <u>E</u>njoy), described in Figure 6, simplifies ERP for children and adolescents. It includes both cognitive and behavioral techniques such as externalizing OCD thoughts, taking cognitive control over fear, exposure, and self-reinforcement. The child is coached through the four steps until he learns how to do them for himself. Children are given a picture of the Worry Hill and the steps of the RIDE acronym on an index card or notepad to have handy when needed. The visual and auditory features of the Worry Hill and the RIDE acronym enhance easy comprehension and recall of the process of ERP, even in the midst of anxiety.

The RIDE steps, as applicable to Casey's OCD symptoms (see Chapter 2), are described below. ERP for Casey's fear of germs would involve exercises such as eating breakfast without washing his hands. The exposure for Casey is ingesting food handled directly by his unwashed (contaminated) hands. Ritual prevention involves refraining from washing his hands until well after he is done eating.

Figure 6: RIDE Up and Down the Worry Hill

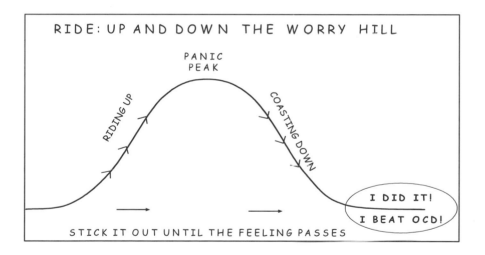

<u>R</u>ename the thought. "It's simply OCD, not me."
<u>I</u>nsist that YOU are in charge! "I'm in charge, not OCD."
<u>D</u>efy OCD, do the OPPOSITE of what it wants.
"I will ride up the Worry Hill and stick it out."
<u>E</u>njoy your victory. "I did it. I can do it again."

Rename the thought: The first step involves recognizing OCD thoughts as unrealistic and distinct from rational thoughts. This step is articulated, *"That's OCD talking, not me."* When Casey recognizes that his OCD thoughts are invalid, he feels absolved of self-blame and shame.

Insist that *YOU* are in charge! The second step helps Casey awaken to the power of choice. It fosters a dramatic shift in attitude from passive acquiescence to active assertion. Instead of complying with OCD's commands, he refuses to be controlled by the senseless thoughts. He decides to take active control over his thoughts and actions. Statements like, *"I am in charge, not OCD"* exemplify this step.

Defy OCD, do the *OPPOSITE* of what it wants. This step involves ERP, which requires a change in behavior. Understanding the metaphor of *The Worry Hill* allows Casey to accept that exposure and habituation must take place in order for OCD to be overcome. He learns that the more he confronts OCD, the easier it will be to overcome it.

When Casey puts the food in his mouth, his anxiety initially increases and may build to a panic-like level. He finds the increasing anxiety intolerable. However, as he continues to eat the food, his anxiety peaks and then automatically begins to decline, because habituation sets in. Casey talks himself through ERP with statements such as,

> *"I'm going to ride up the Worry Hill now. It's going to be tough going up the hill, but if I stick it out, I'll get to the top of the hill. Once I'm at the top, it will be easy to coast down the hill. I won't quit until the bad feeling passes. I won't give in to the rituals."*

Enjoy your success, reward yourself: The final step allows the child to review his success and to take due credit for his effort and courage. Casey learns to give himself positive feedback and to internalize success. *"I did it! It can do it again. Now I deserve to be good to myself."*

Casey realizes that exposure isn't as upsetting as he thought it might be. Once he has actually eaten food with unwashed hands, he doesn't feel quite as worried about getting sick. He is surprised and proud of his accomplishment. He practices this ERP exercise frequently. Each time, he finds it a lot easier to eat without washing his hands. His anxiety habituates faster. As Casey continues his E/RP exercises, his obsession about germs begins to fade into oblivion.

Another obsession that haunts Casey is the fear that paint fumes will poison him. Exposure for these obsessions involves deliberately using non-toxic finger paints to color a picture (exposure), and resisting the urge to ask for reassurance or wash his hands (ritual prevention). In these and other situations, Casey habituates easily to the anxiety, and is able to overcome the obsessive fears and urges.

Alex, the adolescent with OCD in Chapter 2, has obsessions about being contaminated by touch. To prevent contamination, he avoids any physical contact with others, and washes copiously if someone touches him. ERP for Alex involves letting others—his parents, the therapist and a friend—touch him on purpose with *unwashed* hands (exposure) and refraining from showering or changing his clothes (ritual prevention) until the anxiety subsides (habituation).

Worry exposure

This form of exposure involves deliberately and consciously allowing oneself to worry without resisting the worry thoughts. We are all familiar with the experience of trying to stop thinking about "a tune in my head," which appears to make it more prominent. Likewise, the effort to suppress worries actually intensifies them because it prevents habituation. Emily is encouraged to allow herself to deliberately worry about failing, instead of her usual strategy of saying, *"Oh no, I don't want to fail...what if I fail?"* Allowing herself to worry on purpose without restriction will result in habituation and Emily will be unable to absorb any further worry. The worry and it will become meaningless and boring. This process also helps Emily to take control of her worry rather than feel helpless about it. Worry exposure is followed by in vivo exposure when possible and practical. It involves testing the reality of the worries by deliberately making them happen and dealing with the outcomes. For example, Emily is encouraged to make a deliberate spelling error to see how catastrophic it really is.

Gradual exposure

The thought of exposure can be initially daunting and counterintuitive to children. Gradual exposure involves gradually moving in small sequential steps from the least feared situations to the most anxiety-provoking situations (see Table 5). It is the most suitable form of exposure for children and adolescents. Starting with low anxiety situations allows the child to try out exposure with manageable distress and to experience success fairly easily. Success early in the process helps the child see that exposure can be effective, and builds confidence and motivation. Quick feedback is necessary because children need immediate results. Many children have limited ability to defer feedback to the future. Gradual exposure can be applied to both in-vivo and imaginal situations.

The *Fearmometer* (see Figure 3) is also a handy tool during gradual exposure. It is used to rate fears from the least to the most threatening, in order to create a gradual exposure hierarchy. For example, Emily rates her fear of repeating a grade as a 10 on the *Fearmometer*. A gradual exposure hierarchy involving less intense fears of the same nature is developed. The lowest item on Emily's hierarchy, with a rating of 2, is missing two words on the spelling test. Getting a B on the spelling test is a 5, failing the test is a 7 and failing a series of tests is an 8. Using gradual exposure, Emily first confronts her lowest fear, which is to spell two words incorrectly on the spelling test. She then progresses to tackling her fear of getting a B before handling her worst fear, which is repeating the grade. The *Fearmometer* allows Emily to track the level of anxiety she experiences before and during exposure tasks, and to identify when habituation has taken place. It also gives her a tangible index of progress over time. Additional examples of gradual exposure hierarchies are in Chapter 13.

Table 5: Steps in Gradual Exposure

Steps in Gradual Exposure
1. Identify fears
2. Rate the severity of each fear using the *Fearmometer*
3. Rank order fears on a hierarchy from least to most severe
4. Select the fear lowest on the hierarchy
5. Begin exposure to the selected fear
6. Prevent avoidance or escape
7. Wait until habituation occurs
8. Select the next lowest fear and repeat steps 5 to 7

Systematic Desensitization

Systematic desensitization is based on the theory that anxiety is incompatible with relaxation; hence, if a person is relaxed, he is incapable of being anxious simultaneously. It is known as the theory of *reciprocal inhibition*—relaxation and anxiety are mutually exclusive and inhibit each other. Systematic desensitization involves gradual imaginal exposure to the anxiety-provoking object or situation while the person is relaxed. The treatment involves teaching systematic relaxation skills before exposure is conducted. Fears are subsequently confronted in real life when possible, using the same steps. Systematic desensitization is typically used to treat phobias such as fears of heights, airplanes and closed spaces.

Modeling

Children learn a tremendous amount by watching and imitating others. Modeling involves having an anxious child observe another adult or child approach and cope with a feared situation. The model may be a therapist, parent or other child who is instructed in the required steps. The model guides the anxious child through each step in the situation by doing it first. Modeling is often used to treat phobias and social anxiety. It is particularly suitable for young children who need an actual demonstration of how to go about confronting a fear or applying a skill. For instance, if a child has a fear of dogs, the model approaches the dog step by step, while speaking out loud about signs that show that the dog is friendly, extends her hand, and eventually pats the dog. The child watches the model, learns to recognize cues for a friendly dog, follows each step, and sees that the dog does not bite when patted.

PHYSICAL TECHNIQUES

For many children, the tension, stomach discomfort, aches, pains, breathing difficulties and pounding heart that are so much a part of their anxiety are quite scary. This is especially true for children with GAD or panic attacks, who experience a loss of control over the intense physical sensations in their bodies. Overcoming anxiety also involves learning how to turn down the "volume control knob" of the physical symptoms of anxiety. Relaxation techniques are most commonly used to address physiological arousal, the third component of anxiety.

Relaxation

Learning how to relax the body's muscle system allows the child to take active control over terminating the escalation of physical symptoms. More importantly, it gives the child voluntary control over an involuntary state of tension. When children are relaxed, they are calmer, have better concentration, and sleep more restfully.

The simplest approaches to relaxation involve learning deep breathing techniques while making coping statements. Sometimes, children are encouraged to visualize pleasant, calming, relaxing scenes when they feel tense and uptight. Another variation is to learn how to count calmly while breathing in measured amounts.

Progressive muscle relaxation is a more systematic and involved procedure for relaxing the major muscle groups in the body. The child learns how to isolate and tense selected muscle groups such as those of the forearms, legs, thighs, abdomen, neck and shoulder or face. When the muscle group is tensed, the child focuses on the intense feelings of the tensed muscle in order to develop a conscious awareness of tension. The child then releases the tension abruptly and focuses on the feelings of relaxation. The goal is to give children a heightened awareness of the differences between tension and relaxation. Dr. Phillip Kendall, in his CBT program for anxious children, uses the analogies of a stiff robot and a limp rag doll to help children understand the difference between tension and relaxation. In a time of anxiety, the child purposefully relaxes all her muscles, thereby slowing and ending the escalation of anxiety. Over time, the child learns how to "bring on" relaxation with very little effort.

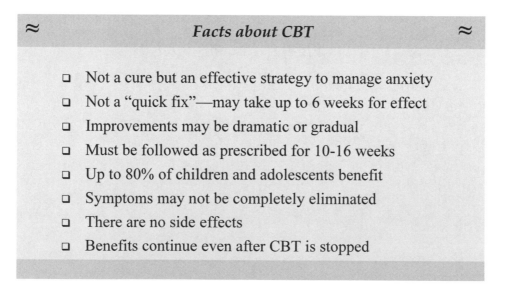

≈   ***Facts about CBT***   ≈

- ❏ Not a cure but an effective strategy to manage anxiety
- ❏ Not a "quick fix"—may take up to 6 weeks for effect
- ❏ Improvements may be dramatic or gradual
- ❏ Must be followed as prescribed for 10-16 weeks
- ❏ Up to 80% of children and adolescents benefit
- ❏ Symptoms may not be completely eliminated
- ❏ There are no side effects
- ❏ Benefits continue even after CBT is stopped

It is important to remember that relaxation is the most commonly used, yet least effective of the CBT techniques when used in isolation. Relaxation in and of itself is insufficient for the treatment of anxiety. It is exposure that is the most critical element of effective treatment. Relaxation can sometimes make it easier for a child to participate in exposure by lowering the level of physiological arousal. However, relaxation skills are not mastered in an instant. They require repeated practice, persistence and commitment. Many children need incentives to overcome the awkwardness they initially experience with relaxation procedures.

REBUILDING SOCIAL SKILLS

Anxious children can vary tremendously in their social skills, competence and acceptance. Some have good social skills and relationships. Others may have difficulty in the interaction skills necessary to initiate and maintain conversations, develop and keep friendships, or seek help in a timely and appropriate manner. Joseph, the 17-year-old teenager who has no friends may benefit from *Social Skills Training* (SST) in addition to CBT. Some anxious children portray a demeanor that reflects meekness, timidity and passivity, rather than one of confidence and self-reliance, as evident in eye contact, posture, volume, facial expression and clarity of communication. Often, even those children who have good social skills become socially isolated because all their energy is put into surviving high levels of anxiety.

Youngsters who are socially accepted by their peers tend to have effective social skills and are better adjusted overall than children who are rejected or neglected by peers. Social rejection has been found to predict emotional and social problems in adolescence and adulthood. Children who are rejected by peers are excluded from normal socialization opportunities that allow them to develop social, emotional and cognitive skills. As a result, their social skills suffer, perpetuating further social isolation.

Anxious children are more likely to be socially *neglected* than rejected; they are more likely to go unnoticed by peers rather than actively disliked or shunned. They may have low rates of social interaction, especially if they are socially anxious. They limit and avoid participation in social activities, and tend to have fewer friendships. Having friendships that are close and supportive can ease the effects of the day-to-day stresses that children face. Close friends provide empathy, acceptance, help and companionship.

SST is a structured coaching approach that may be used as an additional and complementary treatment to CBT. It helps children develop social skills that are important to earning peer acceptance, developing and maintaining friendships, taking initiative, being assertive, seeking help appropriately, and protecting themselves from teasing. Anxious children are often easy targets for teasing and bullying because they do not present a formidable response to the aggressor.

Historically, SST programs have been geared towards children whose social interactions are ineffective because they are impulsive, intrusive, and unpopular. Recently, Dr. Ronald Rapee and his colleagues have incorporated SST as part of their treatment program for anxious children. Another widely used SST program for children of different ages is that developed by Drs. Goldstein and McGinnis. Detailed instructions for structured SST are provided by these authors (see *Resources*).

SST programs for children generally have five components: *coaching* or instruction, *behavioral rehearsal*, *corrective feedback*, *practice*, and *reinforcement*. Not all anxious children need SST; therefore, the first step is to identify those children who are in need of social skill development. The second step is to identify specific problem areas. When a specific skill deficit is identified, the child is coached or instructed in the skill, its importance or necessity, appropriate and inappropriate contexts for its use, and correct and incorrect approaches to using the skill. The social skills therapist or "trainer" demonstrates and models the skill.

The third step in an SST program is to provide opportunities for the child to rehearse the skill with the trainer. A variety of hypothetical situations are role-played to allow the child to practice applying the skill. The trainer then provides corrective feedback, focusing both on aspects of the child's performance that were correct and those that need further development. Further practice and feedback allows the child to fine tune the skills for a range of contexts. Finally, the child is ready to use the social skills in real life situations. Using homework assignments, the child is required to apply the skills in natural settings such as the playground, the classroom, or with parents and teachers. Throughout the program, praise, encouragement and rewards are used to maximize the motivation, compliance and persistence of children. Trainers who can make the program invigorating and relevant to children's day-to-day real-life experiences usually find children to be more engaged and compliant.

SST is often conducted in groups of 4-6 children, because peers learn a lot from each other. They are particularly appropriate in school settings and can be moderated by school counselors, psychologists or social workers.

Group sessions allow children to role model for each other, provide feedback, encouragement, and more opportunities for practice. SST groups are led by a therapist who moderates the appropriateness of peer behaviors within the group.

Parents and teachers can also enhance a child's socials skills by using "peer pairing" or "buddy" approaches whereby an anxious child is paired with a non-anxious child who has the characteristics of a good role model. The buddies are assigned to work together on projects or leisure activities. This pairing provides opportunities for the anxious child to learn how to negotiate academic and social tasks from the buddy without rejection or ridicule. Arranging cooperative peer activities in the classroom or playground also fosters social inclusion and emulation of social skills. Parents can increase opportunities for social interactions in the child's natural environment by encouraging their child to participate in interactive and cooperative extra-curricular activities such as youth groups, team sports, dance or band. The important role that parents can play in helping their children overcome anxiety is discussed in Chapter 11.

In summary, helping children gain mastery over anxiety involves teaching them to:

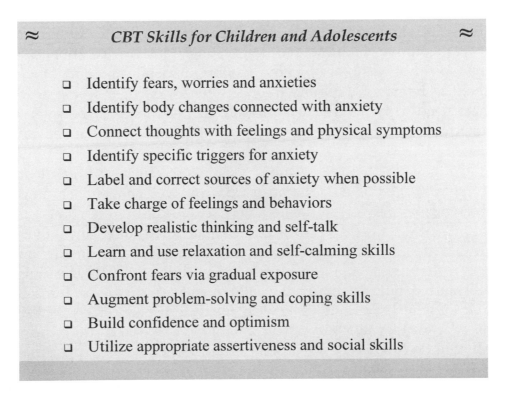

≈ **CBT Skills for Children and Adolescents** ≈

- ❑ Identify fears, worries and anxieties
- ❑ Identify body changes connected with anxiety
- ❑ Connect thoughts with feelings and physical symptoms
- ❑ Identify specific triggers for anxiety
- ❑ Label and correct sources of anxiety when possible
- ❑ Take charge of feelings and behaviors
- ❑ Develop realistic thinking and self-talk
- ❑ Learn and use relaxation and self-calming skills
- ❑ Confront fears via gradual exposure
- ❑ Augment problem-solving and coping skills
- ❑ Build confidence and optimism
- ❑ Utilize appropriate assertiveness and social skills

BUILDING TREATMENT READINESS

Over the many years that I have treated hundreds of anxious children and adolescents and their families, I have learned first-hand that *readiness* is an essential precursor to treatment that is too frequently overlooked. My approach to CBT therefore emphasizes cultivating treatment readiness prior to beginning therapy.

Typically, families seeking help for a child's anxiety are frequently in crisis. There is a sense of urgency and high expectancy for quick success when children are unable to function and parents are at their wits' end. The therapist is often confronted with the child and family's suffering and wants to help as quickly as possible. Exposure is the cornerstone of treatment, but jumping into exposure hastily almost always backfires, because neither the child nor the family is ready for what exposure entails.

Clinicians with insufficient training or experience may unwittingly launch into ERP prematurely, before the child is equipped with the proper understanding or tools to cope with the initial rise in anxiety during exposure. The child may then become afraid and unwilling to go through with exposure. When such false starts occur, children, parents and even therapists are inclined to abandon treatment, and conclude that it is a "failure." False starts in treatment are often attributed to the "unmotivated" child, a pejorative connotation, suggesting laziness or nonchalance. Children do not generally enjoy having anxiety, and are therefore motivated to be rid of the burden anxiety places on their lives. However, they also need to be ready to participate in treatment. To be *ready*, they need to be able to channel the *desire* to get well into the *action* to get well.

> *Readiness for treatment involves the ability to channel the <u>desire</u> to get well into the <u>action</u> to get well.*

Why is readiness so crucial to treatment? It's because CBT involves actively learning and using a new set of skills to overcome anxiety. It is very similar to learning any other new skill such as riding a bicycle — no one can ride a bicycle for a child. Adults can help the child get started, but eventually, the child must learn to ride for himself and he will do it when he's ready. Likewise, the child needs to face his fears for himself to learn that they are unwarranted. No one else can do it for him. He will only do it when he's ready; ironically, when he feels pressured, he is less likely to be ready. Carefully and thoughtfully preparing the child and family for treatment is an important investment with huge dividends.

The chances of success in CBT are likely to be increased when the child and family are ready for treatment.

Building readiness is a planned and systematic process involving active four steps: Stabilization, communication, persuasion and collaboration.

1. Stabilization of the crisis

A child who is overwhelmed and struggling to function each day simply may not have the wherewithal to consider CBT. Just getting through each day with anxiety may consume all his energy. Overzealous implementation of CBT at this time merely adds to the child's sense of burden. Stabilization involves providing the child with respite from the dual challenges of anxiety and everyday living through flexible expectations and temporary accommodations at home and at school. I encourage families to function in "survival mode," to set priorities and cut back on discretionary commitments in order to conserve time and energy for treatment. In some instances, the child may need medication to reduce the severity of symptoms prior to engaging in CBT.

Families need stabilization too because calm, supportive and allied families are better equipped for the demands of CBT. Parents who are highly distressed need support, stress-management, and conflict resolution techniques to regain equilibrium before they can support their child during CBT. A "no blame, no shame" approach helps reduce hostility, guilt and polarization in the family.

2. Communication

Perhaps the most critical part of treatment readiness is helping children and families understand the vicious cycle of avoidance, and the key concepts of exposure, habituation and anticipatory anxiety. Anxiety is overcome by confronting fears (exposure) to learn that they are false alarms, experiencing habituation (getting used to the anxiety, much like you get used to the cold water in the swimming pool) and understanding that confronting fears seems harder before you do it than when you actually do it (anticipatory anxiety).

The *Worry Hill* protocol places significant emphasis on the child's comprehension, acceptance and temporal experience of anticipatory anxiety, exposure and habituation as the tools that make exposure easier for the child. Children who comprehend the relationship between avoidance, exposure, and habituation are more likely to engage effectively in treatment. Exposure may be both counterintuitive and daunting at first glance; a child who is afraid does not exactly want to hear that he must face his fear and endure more anxiety. When children don't understand why and how exposure works, they are unnecessarily intimidated by it. When they do understand, they are more willing to tolerate the initial anxiety that occurs during exposure because they know and expect that it will increase before it subsides.

"No magic, no mystery, no secrets, no surprises." I demystify treatment and remove uncertainty and apprehension at the outset by telling children and families that I am straightforward and open throughout the treatment. I convey the key treatment concepts in child-friendly language via the metaphor of riding a bicycle *Up and Down the Worry Hill.* The *Worry Hill* represents a universal metaphor because almost any child, adolescent or adult can relate to the idea of riding a bicycle up a hill.

3. Persuasion

Effective persuasion involves helping children see the *necessity* for change, the *possibility* for change, and the *power* to change. Children are more readily persuaded when they have an accurate understanding of anxiety and CBT. The child must be helped to see the benefits of overcoming anxiety; this convinces him of the necessity for change. When he learns that anxiety can be successfully overcome, and that many others have done it, he sees the possibility for change.

I tell children stories of other children with anxiety and how they rode up the *Worry Hill.* Children love these stories, which helps them realize that they are not alone and that others have gone before them. Hearing success stories gets families through despair by providing hope. Children also need to have perspective on how difficult exposure may be. I say, "Exposure may be hard, but probably not any harder than your life with anxiety is right now. In fact, it is often harder to think about exposure than it is to actually do it. Besides, the hard work of exposure at least gives you a chance to get rid of anxiety; the work you put into anxiety right now only makes it worse."

Finally, the child must know that he has the power to change. He must understand that he can take charge and take control of anxiety instead of letting it control him. The recognition that he has the power to change can be a liberating experience for the child.

4. Collaboration

Collaboration makes the child a vital partner in treatment. The child, parent and therapist have different but complementary roles to play in the child's treatment. The therapist's role is to guide the child's treatment, the child's role is to RIDE and the parent's role is to rally for and support the child in learning how to master anxiety. Parents are empowered to play a critical role in the child's treatment.

Proactively defining each of these roles before treatment begins can expedite progress by preempting the conflict and frustration that can ensue from misunderstanding. It also corrects the misattribution of power to the therapist. The child and family need to know that the therapist is not the one who will "fix" the child's anxiety—it is the child who holds the power. I assure the child, "I will not force you to face your fears. You and I will discuss together what you will do when you're ready." Most children relax immediately and are more willing to listen and participate when they don't have to be on guard.

Children rarely refuse to participate in treatment when they understand what it entails and are given the freedom of choice. The child is more likely to be invested in his recovery and to take ownership of it when he perceives that he has control. When a child declines to participate despite proper preparation, it may be a good indicator that the child is truly not ready for CBT and therefore unlikely to benefit from it. The reasons for treatment reluctance must be examined (see Chapter 14), and other options such as medication may need to be considered. For some children, CBT may have to be deferred temporarily and attempted later when they are older, more mature or more willing.

Chapter 10

Medications for Anxiety in Children

Experts generally agree that, when possible, anxiety in children must first be treated with CBT. However, this is sometimes not possible for a variety of reasons. Medications are sometimes the only option available to treat anxiety. Some children do not participate in CBT even if it is available and others may need both CBT and medications for the most benefit. When medication is used, it must be part of an overall treatment strategy that addresses the child's social and academic functioning as well. It is important that treatment should not just focus on decreasing anxiety, but also improve family and school functioning. This chapter provides a brief overview of medications for anxiety. More coverage is available in Dr. Wilen's book, *Straight Talk about Psychiatric Medications for Kids* and in *What to do when your child has OCD: Strategies and Solutions* (see *Resources*).

Although a wide variety of medications are used for anxiety in children, there are few rigorous scientific studies to document their effectiveness. The medications used to treat OCD (the SSRI's) have the strongest research backing. Clinical knowledge and case reports indicate that medications can reduce the symptoms of anxiety effectively for some children. Often, a combination of CBT and medications is most effective. A multi-site medication study funded by the National Institutes of Mental Health was published in April 2001. Findings indicated that 76% of a group of children with anxiety disorder diagnoses such as GAD, SAD and Social Anxiety who were treated with fluvoxamine (an SSRI) improved, compared to only 29% of those who were given a placebo (sugar pill). Although physicians often prescribe fluvoxamine for children, this was the first systematic study of its effectiveness. Medication treatment decisions for children are often based on information borrowed from studies of medication among adults.

Table 6: Medications for Anxiety

Class of medication*	Used to treat	Generic names**	Brand names
Selective Serotonin Reuptake Inhibitors Antidepressants 2-6 weeks for effect Newer medications Less side effects than tricyclics	OCD GAD SAD Social anxiety Selective mutism Panic Anxiety and depression	Citalopram Escitalopram Fluoxetine Fluvoxamine Paroxetine Sertraline	Celexa Lexapro Prozac Luvox Paxil Zoloft
Tricyclic antidepressants 2-6 weeks for effect Cardiovascular effects Dangerous if overdosed	SAD Panic Depression OCD	Clomipramine Imipramine Nortriptyline	Anafranil Tofranil Pamelor
Azapirone Anxiolytic Few side effects Low abuse potential 2-4 weeks for effect	GAD SAD Panic attacks Social anxiety Depression	Buspirone	Buspar
Benzodiazepines Anxiolytics Fast-acting Sedating Potentially habit-forming	GAD SAD Panic attacks Social anxiety Severe, acute anxiety/distress	Alprazolam Clonazapam Clorazepate Diazepam Lorazepam	Xanax Klonopin Tranxene Valium Ativan
Other antidepressants Newest medications	SAD Panic Depression Sleep problems	Mirtazapine Nefazodone Trazadone Venlafaxine	Remeron Serzone Desyrel Effexor

GAD=Generalized Anxiety Disorder   SAD=Separation Anxiety Disorder
OCD= Obsessive-Compulsive Disorder

* This overview of medications is for informational purposes only and is not intended to replace professional guidance. Recommendations about specific medications and dosages must be made by a qualified physician after an evaluation.

** There is no one-to-one correspondence between medications and the anxiety conditions listed.

The medications for anxiety fall into two broad categories: the *antidepressants* and the *benzodiazepines* (see Table 6). There is also one medication known as *buspirone* that does not fall into these two groups and is a unique antianxiety compound.

Antidepressants fall into three broad categories. These include the *tricyclic antidepressants* (TCA's), the *Selective Serotonin Reuptake Inhibitors* (SSRI's) and atypical antidepressants. The SSRI's are currently the medications of choice for treatment of anxiety in children and adults. The tricyclics and atypical antidepressants are less commonly used to treat childhood anxiety. Most antidepressant medications have to be taken regularly for at least 2-3 weeks before any effect is seen.

Benzodiazepines are anxiolytics or anxiety-reducing agents. They generally have a relatively rapid effect on anxiety. Although generally safe, side effects are a concern, with sedation the most frequent complaint. Disinhibition and aggression can also occur, most frequently in children with existing behavioral problems. The SSRI's are better tolerated and have fewer side effects than the TCA's. Buspirone has a favorable side effect profile in that it is nonsedating and nondisinhibiting. It is less rapid in effect than the benzodiazepines.

WHEN SHOULD MEDICATION BE CONSIDERED?

In general, experts agree that medications should be used when the child's anxiety has not been responsive to properly delivered CBT or when CBT is not available. Some children with anxiety do not need medication, and experience significant success with CBT alone. On the other hand, some children are unable to participate in CBT, or need medication in addition to CBT. Although many parents are reluctant to place their young children on medications, it is important to be open to considering the option that benefits the child the most.

Medication decisions should be preceded by a thorough diagnostic assessment by a licensed physician, ideally a child psychiatrist, and by thoughtful deliberation of whether the benefits for a given child outweigh the drawbacks. Medication should also be closely monitored by a physician. (See Chapter 14 for information on finding a physician). Table 7 presents some reasons to contemplate the use of medication.

Table 7: Reasons to Consider Medication for Anxiety

≈   *Reasons to Consider Medications for Anxiety*   ≈
❏ The child lacks the maturity to comprehend or participate in CBT.
❏ The child's symptoms are overwhelmingly severe and he is not able to control them sufficiently to engage in CBT.
❏ The child is unable to function, go to school, or leave the house.
❏ The child's suffers from depression, Tourette Syndrome, ADHD, rages, aggression or other conditions in addition to anxiety.
❏ The child has suicidal thoughts or intentions.
❏ The child is unable to muster the motivation, insight, commitment, willingness, time or energy to engage in CBT.
❏ The child is motivated but needs the extra help to get "unstuck."
❏ The level of stress, conflict or distress in the child's family interferes with the family's ability to support the child in CBT.
❏ The child has already had a course of *proper* CBT and still has bothersome symptoms. (The CBT must involve *exposure* by a trained therapist).
❏ The child's suffering and the impact of the anxiety are so great that the aftermath of *not* placing him on medication may be far more severe and permanent than the drawbacks of medications.

Medication may pose a real advantage for children who are too distraught and overwhelmed to engage in CBT. It can give some children the necessary boost to make it easier to do CBT—like training wheels on a bicycle make it easier to learn how to ride. It makes some children more open to CBT because it "takes the edge off" the severity of their symptoms. Anxiety medication may make children calmer, more relaxed and therefore more amenable to CBT. Taking medication only requires the child to take pills diligently and attend regular follow-up visits with the doctor.

It is important to remember that although medications can be extremely effective in eliminating or reducing anxiety symptoms, they do not *cure* anxiety. Once medications are stopped, anxiety symptoms usually return. That is why it is important, whenever possible, to pursue CBT, because it gives the child the skills to cope with anxiety. The chances of recurrence of anxiety may be reduced when medications are combined with CBT.

ARE MEDICATIONS SAFE?

The SSRI's typically generate minimal to no side effects. The most common side effects include headache, stomachache, nausea or sleep difficulties. All physical symptoms should be discussed with the doctor both before and after starting the medication.

In October 2004, the Food and Drug Administration (FDA) issued a warning that antidepressant medications, including SSRIs, may increase suicidal ideation and suicidal behaviors in a small number of children and adolescents. The FDA reviewed 24 studies of 9 antidepressant medications (SSRIs and others) involving over 4,400 children and adolescents with major depressive disorder, OCD, or other psychiatric disorders. The analyses revealed that the 4% of patients treated with an antidepressant had risk of suicidal ideation and suicidal behaviors, compared to 2% of patients who were treated with a placebo (sugar pill). No suicides occurred in any of the studies. There was some evidence that suicidal ideation and behaviors occurred most often at the beginning of treatment or at the time of a dosage change. However, this evidence was far from definitive.

The FDA warning does not prohibit the use of SSRI's in children and adolescents. It alerts patients and families to the risk of suicidal thoughts and behavior, but notes that this risk must be balanced with clinical need.

Parents can play an important role in monitoring the child's behaviors and moods when on medication. Changes in behavior such as agitation, restlessness, irritability or other changes in the child's behavior or personality should be noted. Parents might find it helpful to make note of the child's behaviors and moods before starting medication, and then maintain a daily diary of changes for the first two weeks on medication and subsequently a weekly update. Caregivers should ask the child or adolescent if he/she is having suicidal thoughts. Parents should contact the child's doctor if any of these or other concerns arise. The medication dose may need to be lowered, or the medication may need to be discontinued. Medications should not be stopped abruptly or without the doctor's supervision since this may worsen symptoms. Monitoring should occur throughout treatment.

Chapter 11

What Parents Can Do to Help

As discussed in Chapter 8, parents of anxious children are often perplexed about how to help their child, because nothing seems to work. They are often eager to get some direction in successful parenting strategies and to expand their repertoire of skills. This chapter focuses on caregiver interactions that foster non-anxious behavior. The intent of this chapter is to help parents and other caregivers fine-tune their own expertise in handling the child's anxiety. It offers parents an opportunity to benefit from strategies that are known to be successful with anxious children.

Children fare better in conquering anxiety when their parents and other caregivers encourage and promote non-anxious behavior. The importance of parents in helping children with anxiety cannot be understated. Dr. Ronald Rapee found that when parents of anxious children participated actively in treatment and learned child-management strategies, improvement rates for the children were 84%. In contrast, only 57% of the children whose parents were not included in treatment improved.

Parents who use effective strategies increase self-confidence in their parenting skills. Improved confidence benefits the child through parental consistency, firmness and calmness. Although parents have been the focus of research studies on child management, the concepts described here are just as relevant for grandparents, extended family caregivers, teachers, and other school professionals. Caregivers must be consistent in their approach to the child. If they are not, they may inadvertently undermine each other to the detriment of the child.

Not all parents need to adapt their ways of handling their anxious child. Parents need to apply the strategies described here as they deem suitable to their own needs. Some parents may find some or all the principles described here familiar, although they may have conceptualized them differently. Some parents may just need a refresher or a few pointers to refine their parenting behaviors. Others realize that they have been sidetracked into unwittingly supporting and "enabling" their child's anxiety. Although they know what they need to do, their attempts to extricate themselves have been draining and futile. Some parents may need the help of a therapist to get them back on track.

The parenting strategies described here are based in CBT, as described in Chapter 9. Although these strategies are geared towards anxious children, they are useful even with non-anxious children. The goal of this parenting approach is to help anxious children break free of the powerlessness they experience when weighted with worry, and to blossom and grow, take charge and become self-confident and self-reliant.

The first step for parents who wish to enhance their effectiveness in handling an anxious child is to increase their self-awareness and insight into their "parenting style." They will profit more from honest self-appraisal and a willingness to accept alternative viewpoints and attempt new strategies. Caregivers can then focus on their readiness to change patterns of interaction that foster anxiety in children. They may recognize automatic reactions and responses that need to change if the child is to master anxiety. It takes courage, commitment and risk-taking to change familiar and comfortable ways. It is the same courage, commitment and risk-taking that is asked of anxious children when they have to confront their anxiety. Parenting behaviors for anxious children fall within six areas:

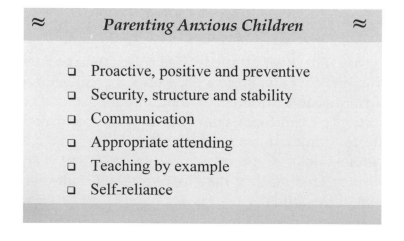

≈   *Parenting Anxious Children*   ≈

- ❑ Proactive, positive and preventive
- ❑ Security, structure and stability
- ❑ Communication
- ❑ Appropriate attending
- ❑ Teaching by example
- ❑ Self-reliance

THE 3 P'S: PROACTIVE, POSITIVE AND PREVENTIVE

The 3 P's, a constructive and child-friendly framework for interacting with children, are described below.

Proactive

Most often, parents try to figure out how best to handle the child's anxiety *after* the fact. They are *reactive* rather than *proactive*. Children do not tend to think or plan ahead for situations that make them anxious. As a result, they may approach the same situations in the same ineffective way each time, seeming not to have learned from previous experience. High anxiety may occur when the child is caught unaware or thrown off by an unexpected situation. Ironically, as adults, we often do likewise, not benefiting from hindsight or using it to our advantage for the future.

Being *proactive* rather than *reactive* calls for having an action plan *before* the crisis develops. It involves becoming more aware, thinking ahead and being prepared to formulate helpful responses to the anxious child. Providing clear expectations, preparing a child for new situations, giving appropriate and reasonable information, and discussing with the child potential problem-solving options, choices and the consequences that follow them are part and parcel of proactive parenting.

For instance, Sarah is excited about the holiday family party at her school, and especially excited that her mother will be there with her. However, when she walks in the door at school, she freezes and seems suddenly paralyzed when she encounters all the people and the noise. She clings to her mother's side and refuses to join her classmates who seem to be having a good time. Her mother patiently encourages, coaxes, pleads and finally scolds her and shakes her off with irritation. Sarah becomes upset and starts crying. Sarah's mother is frustrated and perplexed that what started out as a happy, fun event turned into an unpleasant one.

This situation gives Sarah's mother the opportunity to develop a proactive plan for similar situations in the future. The next time a party comes up, Sarah's mother sits down with Sarah the day *before* the party to make a proactive plan. She discusses with Sarah what the party is about, who might be there, and what events might take place. She asks Sarah how she feels about the party, and they discuss the fun aspects as well as the initial nervousness that Sarah might experience. She asks Sarah what might help her get through the nervousness so that she can enjoy the party. Sarah suggests that perhaps she could stay with her mother for about five minutes, until she gets used to all the things going on. She suggests that she will then look for a friend and then leave her mother to play with her friend. Sarah and her mother agree that if Sarah feels nervous later, they can arrange to meet near the big clock by the piano. Sarah's mother suggests that Sarah can make a choice—go to the party and have a good time, or go to the party and be miserable.

Sarah opts to have a good time, and seems at ease after having a plan to rely on. Sarah's mother revisits their discussion the morning of, and just before they leave for the party. Sarah knows the plan and is confident. They walk in the door and sure enough, Sarah does exactly what she planned—in a matter of minutes she finds a friend and her mother barely sees her for the rest of the evening!

It worked. Sarah had a successful experience. She conquered her fear. Being proactive rather than reactive allowed Sarah and her family to enjoy the evening, rather than have it turn into a disaster. However, had Sarah's mother not had a proactive plan, Sarah's anxiety in social situations would have repeated itself many times over. Soon, Sarah's mother would stop taking her to parties because it was so unpleasant, and both Sarah and her mother would have had a failure experience.

Positive

Positive interactions don't come naturally in times of stress and crisis. Anxiety in a child can result in many unpleasant exchanges and conflict. It is natural to notice and remember all the difficult times. The child's strengths, talents and positive qualities are often lost in the focus on anxiety. Repeated negative interactions can affect the long-term relationship between parent and child.

The anxious child needs to know that he is fundamentally a good person despite his difficulties. It is important to divert and convert some of the energy and time spent in negative interactions into positive experiences. Parents and teachers must make a concerted effort to cultivate and nurture the child's self-esteem by providing opportunities to utilize his good qualities and make him feel more useful. For example, Alex, the 14-year-old with OCD can make others laugh. Parents and teachers can channel his natural aptitude for comedy by inviting him to provide cheer to peers and family members at times when it is needed and welcomed, rather than when it is distracting and detrimental. By doing so, Alex begins to see himself as useful and accepted, rather than always in trouble.

Positive interactions require a planned, proactive effort. *YAMA* time—*You and Me Alone* time—with the child is one way to create a dedicated time to build back the positive relationship with the child. Anxious children are often highly dependent and needy for nurturing from caregivers. "Filling up the gas tank" proactively by nurturing the child proactively may reduce the excessive nurturing the child seeks out at inappropriate times.

YAMA time involves committing at least 15-30 minutes a day (and preferably more) to quality time with the child. It's a time to relax and "yammer" about nothing in particular. The goal of *YAMA* time is to build rapport, comfort and trust by being together to listen and share. *YAMA* time involves a

> *YAMA*
> *You And Me Alone:*
> *Positive time with*
> *your child*

commitment to spend positive time proactively, not just when the child needs help. *YAMA* time should be planned so that it is consistently and regularly available and is private and uninterrupted. There should be no competing demands on parents during *YAMA* time, and the focus should be positive, with no discussion of problems.

Young children are generally very pleased to have special one-on-one time with a parent or parents. Sarah's parents spend 30 minutes with her after dinner, just chatting about the course of the day, playing board games, going for a bicycle ride or getting ice-cream. When they don't, Sarah hovers around them all evening, seeking attention in a myriad of ways. At bedtime, she cannot fall asleep and asks her mother to stay in the room with her. Ideally, YAMA time should be spent doing what the child enjoys, and focusing on strengths and positive attributes. Although adolescents may not be as enthusiastic about spending time with their parents, parents can find ways to engage them by spending time learning about their adolescent interests, such as a computer game, the internet or music.

Where can parents find the time to devote to *YAMA* time with the child? It's a busy world, and families have many time constraints and other commitments. The reality is that parents or teachers will spend time with the anxious and needy child *one way or the other*—is it not better to choose to spend it positively rather than negatively? For many families, the amount of time devoted to *YAMA* time represents a minute fraction of the time spent in distasteful interactions.

It is also important to build a library of good childhood memories because anxiety can lead to significant bad memories for the family. There are vivid recollections of the time when the child was in such a state of panic that the family vacation was ruined, or trips to the grocery store were endured with dread. Families should be able to look back and remember not just "lost" childhood years, but many positive memories as well. Parents are encouraged go out of their way to seek and create positive family rituals and good memories. In Emily's family, one night each week is the "Chef's Special" night. Family members take turns planning the dinner menu and preparing the meal. The family enjoys this activity tremendously and reminisces often about the successes and mishaps of this event. Alex's father spends YAMA time with him by inviting him to join in his carpentry projects. Alex enjoys using the power tools and helping his father build and create items for the home.

Preventive

Being preventive involves anticipating and averting unnecessary triggers for the child's anxiety. Stress challenges the body both physically and emotionally, because the body's energy and resources are spent in handling the stress. As a result, we are more vulnerable when stressed, and our threshold for anxiety or frustration may be noticeably lower. The most common daily stressors are hunger, fatigue and lack of sleep. Alex walks in the door from school and screams at his sister because he is tired and hungry — keeping his OCD under wrap all day at school has taken every ounce of energy he has. He has none left to tolerate his sister's aggravations. Emily did not get to bed until midnight, doing her homework perfectly. She is crabby and tearful in the morning, and cannot decide what to wear or what to eat for breakfast.

Being preventive requires staying one step ahead of the situation, catching it early and nipping it in the bud before it turns into a full-blown crisis. Being alert for everyday stress and pressure can help parents prevent unnecessary crises, creating more positive experiences for the family. Alex's parents have a hearty snack ready for him when he gets home. He then gets 30 minutes of "down time" alone where he can play basketball outside his home. He is much more civil to his sister if she leaves him alone for the first half hour. Emily and her mother select her school clothes the night before, and sometimes an entire week ahead of time. She has only two choices for breakfast, and her mother chooses if she cannot make a quick decision.

Parents and teachers are also encouraged to keep a check on their own emotions that add fuel to the fire. Many unnecessary and futile power battles and arguments can be easily avoided with some conscious forethought (see *Corrective Learning Experiences* in Chapter 14).

THE 3 S'S: SECURITY, STRUCTURE AND STABILITY

Security, structure and stability provide the essential backdrop for children to grow and flourish.

Security

Children experience security when they encounter unconditional love, nurturing and respect from their parents, *in spite of* their difficulties. When children feel loved and nurtured, they trust their parents. A trusting relationship lays the foundation for parental authority. Children are more likely to want to please their parents and to accept parental rules, expectations and injunctions when there is mutual trust and respect. They are also more ready to learn from their mistakes when they feel safe enough to make them.

Yet, there is a difference between nurturing the child and nurturing his anxiety. It is natural and intuitive for parents to nurture their children and to assure them of their safety. When a child is frightened, scared or nervous, parents are naturally inclined to want to relieve their distress. Parents of anxious children often find themselves in this situation. However, as most of them are well aware, the child's need for reassurance can be like a bottomless pit. Unlike most children, anxious children are not easily reassured or calmed. Parents may therefore get caught in providing unrealistic reassurance or false guarantees which fuel anxiety by providing an avenue for the child to escape from dealing with the fear. Providing reassurance is therefore a tricky proposition—it is necessary in appropriate amounts, but parents must draw the line when it begins to defeat its purpose. Specific techniques for reassurance seeking are provided in Chapters 13 and 15.

Anxious children may feel more vulnerable and may be more sensitive to perceived rejection. It is important to remove justification for their concerns by reaffirming their security and eliminating messages of rejection. Every child has a right to safety and respect at home and in the classroom. Dismissing, humiliating or embarrassing an anxious child is not respectful of him as a person. When frustrated, exhausted and angry, it does not take much to say or do things that will be regretted later. If Tyler's parents make threats in anger about leaving, walking out, or never coming back, he is likely to feel insecure; the doubt in the back of his may mind remain even after empty threats are retracted. It is the responsibility of parents, teachers and school personnel to ensure that realistic or implied threats to a child's physical or emotional safety are removed.

Structure

Structure refers to having a systematic framework of expectations, rules and routines within which the child and family operate. Children are unbounded when structure is insufficient, and may operate beyond the boundaries of safety and security. Parents are encouraged to develop fair, reasonable, and consistent expectations and rules for all members of the family. The expectations must be suitable to the child's age, developmental capabilities and temperament. Children need to be able to understand their parents' expectations for them and to have the ability to meet them. Structure provides dependability, clarity and predictability, which enhance the child's sense of stability.

Kind but firm limits help children feel safe and secure

It is as important to set limits for the anxious child as it is for others in the family. Although children protest restrictions and rules, setting *kind but firm* limits on inappropriate behavior is necessary. It teaches children that not everything they desire is necessarily available or good for them. It gives them the opportunity to learn how to cope with disappointment. It tells them that their parents are in charge and that there are safe and sturdy boundaries within which they can operate.

Parents and other caregivers who wear kid gloves around an anxious child need to recognize that rearranging the world to appease the child is neither realistic nor sustainable. Above all, it does the child a disservice. He will lose valuable opportunities to develop the skills he needs to cope as an adult. For example, Sarah insists that her mother not go to the grocery store without her during school hours. Despite Sarah's protests, her mother does not oblige her, because Sarah's request is neither practical nor sensible. She kindly but firmly explains to Sarah that she must go about her business while Sarah is at school.

Stability

Stability is most affected by consistency, which is crucial to effective parenting. Parents must be reliable and predictable in the ways in which they handle situations from one time to the next. Consistency gives the child a sense of stability because the rules of his world are steady and constant, not erratic. There should also be consistency between the child's parents and between parents and teachers.

Say it, mean it and do it is a guiding principle of consistency with children. It is easy to react in haste or in anger, and to make threats of punishment or promise rewards for good behavior. But parents and teachers must choose their words carefully, because they need to honor them. Changing one's mind, retracting promises and being casual about adhering to what was said are perplexing to children because they are mixed messages.

> *Say it, mean it and do it!*

Parents and caregivers lose their credibility when they do not keep their word. It is natural to be overly punitive when angry, and to say angry words that are later regretted. Children do not follow directions when they know that threats or rewards are simply empty words. It is best not to threaten punishment when angry but to defer it until calm. Letting the child know that consequences will be decided later is more effective.

When parents are inconsistent, their children typically push the limits to suit their own preferences. For example, if Sarah's mother sometimes is firm in requiring Sarah to stay at school and at other times buckles under pressure and comes to pick her up before school is done, Sarah is never quite sure what to expect of her mother. If Sarah is like any other child, she will make every effort to get her mother to behave in the manner that *she* prefers, i.e., take her home from school. On the other hand, if Sarah's mother is consistent and firm on the issue everyday, Sarah will eventually resign herself to the fact that her mother means what she says. Likewise, if Sarah's father and mother adopt the same stance, they will be more helpful to Sarah than if they have discrepant responses. If Sarah's father says, "Let her stay at home today, she's so upset," he undercuts Sarah's mother's efforts to get her to school. If the teacher allows Sarah to leave the school very readily, he is also being inconsistent with Sarah's mother's goals. For more on consistency between parents and school personnel, see Chapter 12.

Appropriate Attending

Children's behaviors can be shaped or molded by the attention and feedback they receive from adults. The more attention children receive for their behavior, the more likely they are to repeat it. There are helpful and unhelpful forms of attention and it is crucial for parents and teachers to know the difference, to ensure that they channel their efforts towards the child's desirable behaviors.

Parents can find it hard to be objective when caught up in a child's anxiety. They are more prone to notice their child's negative and anxious behaviors and miss the times when the child is engaging in non-anxious behaviors. Yet, even anxious children are sometimes courageous, self-reliant and adventurous. The small but progressive steps the child has taken may pale in comparison to the magnitude of the anxious behaviors. Yet, small steps lead to big changes. These small steps can be shaped into large gains by noticing them and giving them the right kind of attention. The different forms of attention we give children are described below.

Planned attention

Planned attention involves making an active, deliberate effort to recognize, acknowledge, praise and encourage any behavior that is in the right direction, regardless of how minor it is. Whereas most parents and teachers are not averse to praising children, some may be frugal with praise because they view the child's appropriate behaviors as routine expectations rather than achievements. Planned attention involves selectively and deliberately noticing the times the child is making efforts to take risks, approach feared situations, persist in the face of fear, or to be self-reliant and resourceful. Praise nurtures children and builds their self-concept. Eventually, children learn to recognize their own desirable behaviors and take credit for them. They become self-reliant in giving themselves positive feedback and building their self-concept.

Planned inattention

One way to decrease inappropriate or undesirable behavior is to ignore it, especially when it is minor and is unlikely to result in harmful consequences. Caregivers often have a "knee jerk" tendency to respond to every negative behavior. Not every behavior is worthy of the effort it takes to respond; further, giving it attention may actually strengthen the behavior. Alex's peers laugh when he clowns around; his teacher reprimands him—his peers and teacher are giving him attention, and he is likely to clown around when he gets a chance.

Planned inattention constitutes a conscious decision to take no notice of selected undesirable behaviors such as whining and attention-getting behaviors. The intent of ignoring is to reduce attention and thereby extinguish unwanted behavior; it is not to be unpleasant to the child. Ignoring Alex, as long as his behavior is not highly disruptive, will deprive him of the attention he is seeking. On the other hand, scolding him reinforces him because he is trying to attract attention. It is important that a strategy for ignoring should be planned ahead of time, so that it is not an act of haste or anger.

Planned rewards

Rewards do not make anxiety go away, but work as incentives to make the challenges of confronting and overcoming fears more palatable. They increase the child's motivation and persistence. The incentive to face fears must exceed the incentive to maintain the status quo.

It takes a lot of effort for a child to face situations that are frightening. It is important that children be rewarded for *effort* rather than actual success. This ensures that it is the child's *behavior* in the right direction rather than the outcome that is of importance. Outcomes are not always successful, for a variety of reasons, but a child's effort to succeed is what counts most. Children like rewards, which keep their

Children should be rewarded for effort rather than for success

enthusiasm and willingness steady. Joseph's parents reward him for making the effort to pick up the phone and dial the right number, and Sarah's parents reward her for trying to sleep in her own bed.

Rewards may be *material, social* or *activity* focused. Material rewards include toys, food, clothing and other possessions. Social rewards involve time with other family members or friends. Activity rewards include a trip to the pool or dinner at a favorite restaurant. Younger children need immediate and more tangible rewards, as their ability to delay gratification may be minimal. They also respond well to sticker or star charts and tokens that can be traded for rewards. Older children prefer privileges such as later bedtimes or curfews, additional computer or phone time, or an outing to the mall with friends. Adolescents can be involved in negotiating privileges and in "contracting" for rewards in exchange for meeting responsibilities.

Social rewards are preferable to material rewards because they also provide increased positive interaction time within family or friends. Children may enjoy rewards such as a bicycle ride with dad, a board game with mom, ice cream for the family or playing at the neighbor's. Rewards should be practical, feasible and proportionate to the achievement. Parents who reward excessively and disproportionately to the context must be watchful that they are not compensating for their own anxiety or guilt. For instance, it would not be helpful for Joseph's father to buy him an expensive gadget to make up for having yelled at Joseph.

Unplanned rewards

Caregivers may be surprised to know that they may inadvertently reward a child's anxious behavior even when they don't intend to do so. Unplanned rewards occur when the child receives extra comfort, nurturing or benefits for avoiding or escaping a feared situation. If Alex is allowed to watch TV or play Nintendo when he refuses to go to school, he is being rewarded for missing school. Likewise, when Casey is given reassurance repeatedly, he is rewarded with undue attention. Parents and teachers must make an effort to become aware of unplanned rewards, set limits and eliminate them. When Alex misses school and stays home, he must remain in an environment that resembles school as closely as possible. He must do his schoolwork at home, and there should be no computer, TV, sleeping or talking on the telephone. Casey must only be reassured as much as is necessary and normal.

COMMUNICATION

Children with anxiety may be easily overaroused, overreactive and prone to panic. In an effort to soothe, placate, reassure, or preempt a potential meltdown, parents may communicate *excessively* with their anxious child. They may repeat themselves, give more elaborate explanations and escalate their efforts to reason with or present logic to the child.

Emotion overpowers logic and reason. Like anyone else, a distraught child is not swayed by rational thought. Logical messages are wasted on an upset child. The child's apparent imperviousness to reason is intensely baffling and frustrating to the parent, who perceives it as stubborn or willfully rejecting. This leads the parent to intensify the attempts to convince the child. The more the parent intercedes, the less opportunity the child has to think and problem-solve for himself. The child is further overwhelmed with a barrage of over-stimulation that he cannot tolerate. When Alex is in a panic because he has been contaminated, he is not receptive to lengthy explanations about his safety. His mind is "shut down" and cannot process any further stimulation. He adds insult to injury when he yells out, "*Shut up all of you!*" Parents and school staff are offended by his rudeness, which they perceive as unprovoked, because they do not know that he has OCD. They react to him with punishment. See *Corrective Learning Experiences* in Chapter 14 for a strategy to help Alex handle his fears and anger.

Communication with an overly aroused or distraught child should be minimal. When a child is agitated, it is best to wait until he calms down before engaging in conversation, or reasoning. Nothing positive that can be achieved when the child is over-stimulated. In fact, continuing to reason with the child in that state simply adds fuel to the fire.

> *Emotion and logic may be mutually exclusive*

The *Fearmometer* or Feeling Thermometer (see Chapter 9) comes in handy to help children and caregivers communicate simply and effectively when upset. Parents or teachers can *proactively* discuss with the child the point on the *Fearmometer* at which he can detect early cues that he is getting upset, such as 3 or 4, as well as the "point of no return," usually an 8 or 9. Once these two points have been identified, caregivers know that they can encourage the child to use previously agreed to calming strategies when the early cues are apparent. They also know that intervening with a child who is an 8 or 9 on the *Fearmometer* is a lost cause, and it is best to allow the storm to pass.

Once the child has calmed, adults talk with the child about the incident. One brief and clear explanation should suffice. Children need to be given "quiet" time to ponder and digest the information that is given to them.

TEACHING BY EXAMPLE

Children can also learn how to cope with anxiety from the models they observe — parents, teachers and other caregivers. Children witness the manner in which their parents cope when distressed, overwhelmed or afraid. They can read subtle, non-verbal anxiety cues from parents. Parents who approach the ups and downs of life with reasonable calm and realistic confidence provide valuable role modeling for their children. In many situations, a child's anxiety may be a reflection of the parents' anxiety. A parent who repeatedly asks, "*Are you sure you'll be okay?*" may give the child reason to doubt her safety. It is easy to become accustomed to reacting in automatic ways without thinking. Parents who want to be positive examples may have to first increase self-awareness of their own reflexive responses to danger and threat. Providing messages of confidence in the child's abilities by saying, "*I know it's hard, but you're strong, and I know you can do it!*" will go a long way towards building the child's belief in himself.

Parents can teach and model normal anxiety and help the child recognize the difference between normal and excessive worry. They can teach the child to recognize the connection between thoughts, feelings, behaviors and physical symptoms, labels for feelings, and how to accept and live with uncertainty. Parents are encouraged to use the same anxiety-management techniques their child is learning. If tense or stressed, parents may need to contain and change their own thought, self-talk and behavior patterns before attempting to help their child with his. When parents take control over their feelings and actions, they model the same for their child.

Parents and teachers also need to take space and disengage when they are pushed to their limits by the needs of an anxious child. By taking space in an appropriate way, parents can model the right response to being overwhelmed. Instead of saying, "*I'm getting out of here. I've had it with you,*" which confirms the child's view of himself as unworthy, the parent says, "*I'm feeling too stressed now. I need to take a break so I can calm down and think clearly and be more helpful to both of us.*" Parents can also use the *Fearmometer* as a barometer of their own anger or frustration. It allows parents to be aware of their feelings and to make a graceful exit before they succumb to regrettable words or actions.

Parents who struggle with their own high levels of anxiety are encouraged to seek treatment for themselves. Research has shown that parents who obtain treatment for their own anxiety may help their children make greater improvements. CBT and medication are effective treatment options for adults with anxiety. If there are high levels of conflict in the family, it may also be necessary to seek treatment to address those issues.

SELF-RELIANCE

Finally, the most critical piece for the child in learning how to overcome anxiety is to become self-reliant and resilient. Anxious children need to develop self-reliance in negotiating day-to-day challenges. It would all be for naught if, after the initial guidance of a therapist and caregivers, the child does not eventually learn how to manage anxiety for herself, without adult assistance. Ultimately, the most valuable help a parent can give an anxious child is not to help him through the anxiety, but to teach him to help himself.

Parents may provide hasty and excessive assistance to an anxious child in a sincere attempt to protect the child. Ironically, the assistance that is intended to help the

> *The best help for the anxious child comes not from helping him but teaching him to help himself*

child prevents him from learning how to help himself. The child comes to expect the rescue by well-intentioned adults and depends on support in avoiding fears. It merely strengthens the child's anxiety. Children who take reasonable risks, persist in the face of mild to moderate anxiety, and are resourceful in coping tend to be less anxious.

The goals of teaching self-reliance are to help the child build a repertoire of skills that he or she can draw on whenever they are needed, rather than depend on an adult. Self-reliance allows the child to internalize strategies for coping, initiate and sustain problem-solving and instill self-confidence.

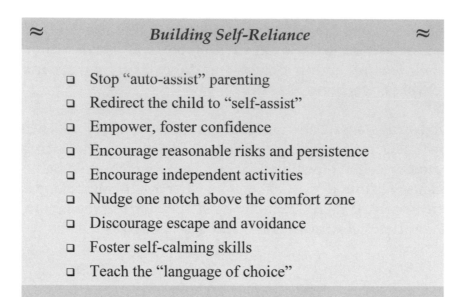

Building Self-Reliance

- ❏ Stop "auto-assist" parenting
- ❏ Redirect the child to "self-assist"
- ❏ Empower, foster confidence
- ❏ Encourage reasonable risks and persistence
- ❏ Encourage independent activities
- ❏ Nudge one notch above the comfort zone
- ❏ Discourage escape and avoidance
- ❏ Foster self-calming skills
- ❏ Teach the "language of choice"

Parents and teachers must play an active role in encouraging and reinforcing the development of self-reliance. They can foster risk taking, encourage the child to "stick it out," and teach the child that not all dangers are bad; simultaneously, they need to discourage escape and avoidance of feared situations. Parents and teachers must consistently give the child the message that he can cope on his own, and that the consequences are not as disastrous as he perceives. It is important to actively seek and provide planned opportunities for the child to overcome fear, and to encourage independent activities.

A good rule of thumb is to nudge just one notch above the child's comfort zone at any given point in time, and gradually nudge upwards. Success experiences with small steps foster the child's self-confidence and belief in

Nudge one notch above the comfort zone

his own capabilities. When challenged and hesitant, reminding the child of his skills, resources and previous successes, no matter how small, may bolster self-confidence. Casey is reluctant to go to a friend's house to play because his mother won't be readily accessible. In order to foster self-reliance, Casey's parents encourage and reward him for playing in the back yard with a friend, and then for going to the neighbor's house to play. They invite his friends over, and suggest that the children go for a bike ride down the street. They praise his efforts and reward him generously for his courage in being independent.

Many anxious children lag behind in the ability to self-soothe when they get overly upset. Over years of seeking reassurance and nurturing from parents and teachers when upset, they may come to depend on adults to soothe and calm them. As a result, they do not develop skills to self-calm. This skill is a very important one in the quest for mastery over anxiety. Children should therefore be gently redirected to learn ways to self-soothe. This is best done via proactive problem-solving when the child is calm. For instance, the child can learn to *take space*, which means that he voluntarily removes himself from a situation that makes him lose emotional control. Using the Feeling Thermometer, he identifies the point at which he can leave the room, go to a designated space or stop a given interaction until he has "chilled out." Then he can return to the situation and participate in a productive way.

Taking space teaches children to take control over their emotions rather than allow them to control them. Children should also be encouraged to generate other calming activities

> *Anxious children need to learn how to self-soothe*

that they can use when upset, such as music, kicking a soccer ball, jumping on a trampoline or going for a bicycle ride. These activities can be written on a card and kept handy for the child to have easy access when needed.

Fostering self-reliance also includes allowing the child to take care of his own daily needs and to speak for himself when necessary. Joseph, who has social anxiety, is interested in a job opportunity at the local store, but is highly anxious about making a phone call to inquire about it. He wants his mother to make the phone call in his behalf. Although it would be intuitive for Joseph's mother to help him by making the phone call, it would do Joseph a disservice in the long run because he would be deprived of the opportunity to overcome his irrational fear. It would be far more helpful to Joseph if his mother fostered self-reliance by encouraging him to do it for himself. She could help by coaching him, role-playing and rehearsing making the call. He could practice by making other phone calls that may not be as intimidating, such as ordering pizza, or calling his father's workplace. Eventually, he would work his way up to making the call about the job he wants.

Many anxious children need to be instructed in appropriate help-seeking behaviors to replace excessive dependence or anxious reassurance seeking. Caregivers need to recognize that repeated questions of the same nature reflect anxiety and cannot be quelled by simply answering again and again.

Children can be redirected to deduce logical answers via Socratic questioning (see Table 3 in Chapter 9), instead of just being handed the answers. Parents may also find it effective to give one reasonable response and then ask the child to answer the question for himself.

Casey, who has OCD, used to be a bold and adventuresome child, but now seems to doubt himself constantly. When at home and school, Casey asks for reassurance frequently. When Casey asks his mother and teacher repeatedly if he has inhaled poisonous paint fumes or said a "bad word," they give him one thorough explanation:

"No, Casey, the paints don't have fumes. Look, it's written here that they are non-toxic, which means that they are not poisonous and will not harm you or anyone else. Even if you breathed deeply near them, they would not poison you."

Subsequently, when Casey asks, *"Will I die if I breathe in the paint fumes?"* his mother and teacher do not repeat the same information. Instead, they ask Casey to answer for himself. *"Casey, tell me what I just explained to you a minute ago."* Setting such limits fosters self-reliance. Casey needs to learn to answer his fear-related questions himself instead of relying on others to do so. A gradual hierarchy for reassurance seeking is presented in Figure 15 in Chapter 13. More techniques are presented in Chapter 15.

Finally, the child must learn the language of choice. He must be empowered to choose his response to feared situations. Children with anxiety may come to depend on adults to fix their anxiety, and may come to see themselves as helpless victims. Acting assertively to reject anxiety and to confront fears does not come intuitively to them. They need more coaching and teaching, but they are very good at learning. When anxious, the parent or teacher can remind the child of his newly-learned skills by asking, *"Which do you choose? Will you choose to be afraid or will you choose to go find out if your fear is true or not? You can choose. You don't have to just accept your fear."* Children can be gently reminded to use their realistic thinking skills, *"How can you change that worry thought? What calm thoughts can you have?"*

Teach the language of choice

Children and parents also need to work together to develop active, assertive and effective problem-solving skills. Parents and child may need to actively practice and use more effective problem-solving methods, such as those discussed in Chapter 9.

UNHELPFUL REACTIONS AND RESPONSES

Chastising, embarrassing and humiliating a child, particularly in front of family or peers is damaging to the child's fragile self-esteem. The child is less likely to be confident about his abilities to overcome fear if he is belittled. Saying, "*Just get over it,*" "*Why don't you just stop?*" or "*If you tried harder, it would be fine,*" suggest that the child has ready control over anxiety, and is simply being lazy or uncooperative. If possible, the child would certainly stop, because anxiety is not an enjoyable experience.

It is sometimes tempting to use humor to deflect a tense situation. While humor can be a welcome diversion, it must be used very judiciously. Humor is only helpful if the *child* finds it amusing. It is necessary to stop and think carefully about light comments. Sarcasm or jibes should be avoided at all costs. Many anxious children are already sensitive and know that their fears are absurd and ridiculous. Humor at their expense will make them feel angry and humiliated.

As discussed earlier, "enabling" responses such as excessive reassurance, supporting avoidance, and participation in the child's rituals or worries may strengthen the child's anxiety. Yet, it is not advisable to make abrupt and surprise changes in the way in which the parent or teacher reacts to and handles the child's anxiety. It is best to plan ahead, involve the child in discussion of the need for the change and enlist the child's agreement and participation. Changes must occur gradually and progressively with the child's full knowledge, and preferably consent.

Chapter 12

What Schools Can Do to Help

Schools strive to provide an environment that optimizes the child's learning potential, academic achievement, social interaction and overall adjustment. Anxiety can interfere with the child's ability to achieve these goals. In today's world, anxiety appears to be everywhere, and appears to permeate the classrooms, the hallways and the cafeteria. Children and adolescents may experience significant academic and performance pressures with the climate of high-stakes testing, greater social and peer pressures towards drugs, smoking and other unsafe behaviors, and greater time constraints with the volume of academic and extracurricular demands on their day.

Schools can play a pivotal role in helping anxious children achieve the primary goals of education and preventing the potential long-term repercussions of anxiety. Parents and schools can together act in the best interest of the child and can achieve their goals when they work within a framework that is *proactive, positive and preventive*—the 3 P's, as described in the previous chapter.

Schools include a wide variety of professionals such as teachers, administrators, counselors, social workers, special education teachers, school psychologists, nurses, occupational, and speech and language therapists. Although there is overlap in the training, skills and roles of various school professionals, each has unique responsibilities. The application of the following interventions vary depending on the particular role of a given school member. It is the responsibility of school personnel and pupil services teams to delegate the functions described below as appropriately as possible.

School professionals can contribute to helping anxious children in many different ways. The contributions described below are derived from the principles of CBT and child management that have been described in Chapters 9 and 11. This chapter extends those principles to the school setting. Chapter 13 details an action plan for helping the anxious child.

≈   ***What Schools Can Do to Help***   ≈

- ❑ Education and training
- ❑ Early detection
- ❑ Establishment of partnerships
    - Level I—Child-home-school
    - Level II—Child-home-school-community
- ❑ Assessment
- ❑ Consultation and appropriate referral
- ❑ Provision of a safe environment
- ❑ Management of anxiety in school
    - Phase I—Stabilization
    - Phase II—School-based intervention
- ❑ Prevention

EDUCATION AND TRAINING

School professionals may vary considerably in their knowledge and awareness of anxiety disorders. Some of the disparity is due to role differentiation, training focus and experience among teachers, counselors, school psychologists, aides and other school staff. There is also wide variation from school to school and district to district. Even school staff with similar roles may have individual differences in training, experience and interest in anxiety disorders.

Some school professionals may not perceive anxiety as a significant problem that warrants their attention. They may attribute a child's difficulties to inertia, lack of motivation, negative attention-seeking or manipulation. Alex, the youngster with OCD who clowns around and is sometimes belligerent, is clearly not the prototype of anxiety. He is often misunderstood as oppositional or defiant. Tyler, the high-school student with social anxiety is perceived as surly and disengaged, rather than anxious. The first step is to provide education and training to all school staff that would allow them to:

≈   *Education and Training*   ≈

- ❑ Increase awareness of anxiety disorders, their symptoms, course and treatment.
- ❑ Recognize anxiety disorders as legitimate disorders rather than willful misbehavior.
- ❑ Recognize the differences between normal and problematic anxiety, and differentiate passing phases from lasting concerns
- ❑ Identify specific criteria to determine the need for intervention.
- ❑ Increase awareness of the immediate and long-term negative effects of anxiety on children, families, teachers and peers.
- ❑ Increase acceptance and tolerance and reduce misunderstanding and mishandling of children with anxiety.
- ❑ Use appropriate skills and strategies to manage anxiety in school.
- ❑ Educate students with the goal of increasing acceptance and reducing teasing.
- ❑ Educate parents of children with anxiety.

Proactive education and training would involve including anxiety disorders in the continuing education or staff development curriculum. Experts in anxiety disorders may be invited to provide advanced education and training.

EARLY DETECTION

School professionals are a key resource in the early recognition of anxiety problems. They may be the first to identify anxiety in a child, before parents or pediatricians. Some forms of anxiety are fairly easy to spot; others can be subtle or hidden by the child. This is especially true for OCD, because children who are embarrassed may go to great lengths to conceal their rituals or fears. It is critical not to let anxious children *remain in the shadow*, taking a back seat to those whose behaviors are more disruptive to the classroom. A child's problems should not be ignored, no matter how small they might appear. No anxiety, normal or excessive, should be discounted.

Teachers, counselors, school psychologists and other school staff work with hundreds of children over a period of time. They accumulate many thousands of hours of interactions and experience with students. Teachers and other classroom staff are privy to a view of the child in a variety of activities, settings and interactions. Over time, they develop a keen sense of what's normal and what's not for a given age or circumstance. Parents rarely have as many comparison points as school personnel do. School staff may therefore have the opportunity to be the first to recognize when a child may need help.

Knowing the early warning signs and signals of anxiety (see Chapter 7) can guide school staff in recognizing children who might need further evaluation or intervention. Yet, sometimes, school professionals may not be aware of a child's anxiety, even if the anxiety is fueled by school-related demands. Many anxious children are overly responsible and conscientious. They compensate for anxiety by working very hard to function properly in school and therefore remain under the radar screen. When they return home, they may "fall apart" because they are exhausted from all the energy consumed by maintaining decorum at school. They have tremendous anxiety at home over homework. Such situations are not uncommon at all. Home is usually the safest place for a child to express pent-up negative emotions freely and to regress. School personnel need to recognize and accept that the discrepancy between the child's behaviors at school and at home is not necessarily a reflection of parenting practices or inadequacies.

ESTABLISHMENT OF PARTNERSHIPS

Children spend roughly half their waking hours in school and the other half with family. Parents and teachers are therefore primary influences in their lives. It only makes good sense that parents and teachers complement each other in their management approaches. As discussed in Chapters 8 and 10, parents' and teachers' responses to anxious children can either fuel or calm anxiety in children. It is therefore critical for parents and schools to work together so that progress made in one place is not undone in the other. A cohesive collaboration can occur when all partners interact with each with "no blame and no shame."

The success of a partnership depends on at least two other elements: *consistency* and *communication*. Consistency among school staff and between school staff and parents in understanding and handling the child's anxiety is just as important as it is between parents in the home. If parents and schools are at odds with each other, they effectively undermine each other's efforts. This may create confusion for the child, prolong his difficulties, and compromise overall outcome. Parents and schools therefore have a *responsibility* to work together in the best interest of the child.

> No blame,
> no shame

Like consistency, effective communication is essential to the success of a partnership. Communication can make or break a good relationship between parents and schools. In today's busy world, there is little discretionary time for either parents or school staff to communicate in person or even by telephone. However, it is also the era of the internet, and many families and schools use email to communicate. Although email will not suffice for more in-depth or interactive discussions, it does offer the advantage of lowering the barrier for brief communications. Further, email is particularly handy when it is not possible to make contact in real time because the schedules of teachers and parents don't match up.

Partnerships may be conceptualized at two different levels:

Level I partnership – Child, home and school

A Level I partnership includes the child, parent(s) and school professionals. Partnership with the child in question is implicit. Although parents and school staff may develop and implement cognitive-behavioral interventions, they are merely *instrumental* in helping the child master anxiety, and cannot actually do it for the child. No one but the child can eventually learn how to overcome his anxiety. The anxious child is therefore a necessary and vital partner. The specific nature of involvement of the child will vary depending on age and developmental maturity. Younger children are typically less involved in developing and planning interventions, whereas adolescents may set their own goals, with less direct involvement of parents and school staff. Specific strategies for involving children in the partnership are presented in *Cultivating Treatment Readiness* in Chapter 13, and *Engaging Reluctant Children* in Chapter 14.

An equally important aspect of the Level I partnership is the *internal* collaboration among school personnel—teachers, school psychologists, counselors, social workers, special education teachers, speech and language therapists or the pupil services team—who might work with the child.

Schools and parents can collaborate to develop a plan for consistent management of the child's anxiety between the home and school. Collaboration is facilitated when a *Case Manager* or equivalent person within the school is entrusted with the task of organizing and overseeing the child's educational and emotional needs at school. The Case Manager may be the teacher, counselor, nurse, school psychologist or social worker and is responsible for ensuring that the child receives appropriate care at school. The Case Manager acts as the "point person" through whom all communication is channeled. A systematic plan for communication is necessary to keep all relevant persons informed so that they can be consistent in their perceptions of and responses to the anxious child. The easier access there is to the Case Manager, the less chance of communication gaps and mishaps.

Given the ease with which advanced information is accessible today, parents are now far more knowledgeable about their child's condition and needs than they have ever been. School staff should not be surprised if parents seek them out to tell them what their child needs in school. Rather than being passive participants, parents are often eager to work actively with schools to develop shared goals and outcomes for their children.

Level II partnership – Child, home, school and community

On many occasions, the school and parents may need the involvement of healthcare professionals in the community to meet the child's needs. Level II involves an *external* partnership with pediatricians and mental health providers such as child psychologists, child psychiatrists or social workers. It may include one or more providers as relevant to the child's needs.

The child's pediatrician is often the first caregiver in the community to whom parents turn when their child is having difficulty. The pediatrician can help prepare parents for normal developmental stages, differentiate normal from excessive behaviors and provide parenting guidelines and strategies. The pediatrician can also evaluate and diagnose the child's condition, and rule out other medical reasons for symptoms or complications. Treatment of severe and complicated anxiety symptoms calls for the specific expertise of a mental health provider.

Community partners provide treatment and support to the child and parents that may be beyond the scope of the school. Treatment with a mental health provider may extend to areas such as family relationships and personal issues that are not relevant in school. They help orchestrate perceptions of the child across settings, establish realistic and meaningful treatment goals, reduce overlap and promote efficient sharing of information. Many children are treated by community providers without the knowledge of the school.

In addition to direct treatment, community partners can provide consultation to school staff in developing and implementing school-based interventions. They can provide continuing education and training experiences to school personnel in general mental health issues, as well as specific training in anxiety and its treatment.

Partnerships don't always work easily. Problems that may arise in partnerships along with suggested solutions are discussed in *Barriers to Effective Partnerships* in Chapter 14.

ASSESSMENT

A good treatment plan is based on a careful, objective and comprehensive assessment of the needs and strengths of the child and how they impact the child's ability to learn, make friends and function in school. There's a lot more to a child than anxiety, so it is necessary to have a balanced assessment that focuses on the child's skills and resources, not just on problems and limitations. A child's strengths, social and psychological competence can be tremendous resources that can be tapped on the road to recovery. An important goal of good assessment is to have a baseline of behaviors against which to compare progress during and after treatment.

The teacher or parent may often be the starting point for the assessment process. The child is referred to the "Pupil Services Team" or equivalent group, who make decisions about the nature and extent of an appropriate assessment. All qualified school professionals may contribute to the assessment of the child in their respective areas of expertise via observations of the child's behavior and interactions.

School psychologists have specialized training to provide systematic and structured evaluations. Assessment tools include interviews, psychological tests, self-report questionnaires and parent and teacher rating instruments. A carefully selected assessment battery will allow the psychologist to determine the cognitive, behavioral and physiological components of anxiety, evaluate stress and adjustment issues, and determine impact on academic achievement and social functioning. The assessment must also examine the need for school-based or community services. The results of the assessment and appropriate recommendations are then shared with the parents and other members of the partnership. See Chapter 13 for more details on assessment of anxiety.

CONSULTATION AND REFERRAL

Once the assessment is completed, qualified school staff can provide consultation to parents, other school staff, and to community providers as indicated. They may discuss the findings of school-based assessments, and provide recommendations for an appropriate intervention plan.

The main purpose of schools is to provide education, not mental health treatment. Therefore, a very important function of school staff is to differentiate between what intervention services are appropriate and feasible for the school to provide and what services are best provided by mental health professionals.

Schools must therefore make appropriate and timely referrals to community healthcare providers. A child with anxiety should always be referred to his or her pediatrician for an evaluation to rule out medical reasons for the child's anxiety or physical symptoms, and to obtain the pediatrician's impressions and recommendations. Disorders such as OCD are fairly complex to treat and are best referred to a community mental health provider. Receiving therapy from a mental health provider is not a sign of weakness of character. Parents and schools need to work together to eliminate the stigma associated with mental health care. Sometimes, even when no specific treatment is indicated, consultation with a mental health professional may be useful to obtain specific recommendations on how best to help reduce the child's anxiety. Table 8 offers guidelines for referral to mental health clinicians.

Table 8: Guidelines for Referral to Mental Health Clinicians

≈ **Guidelines for Referral to Mental Health Clinicians** ≈
❑ There are no qualified school personnel to conduct an assessment or school based intervention.
❑ Anxiety reaches the level of severity of a disorder.
❑ The child's symptoms are complex and involve multiple diagnoses.
❑ The child has suicidal thoughts or intentions.
❑ Anxiety affects the child's functioning outside school.
❑ School-based interventions are not helping the child.
❑ The child's needs extend beyond the scope of the school's resources.
❑ The focus of intervention may need to extend to family members.
❑ Treatment necessitates family disengagement from the child's symptoms and subsequent healthy reengagement.
❑ Interventions at school may compromise the privacy of the family.

PROVISION OF A SAFE ENVIRONMENT

Schools have a responsibility to ensure an atmosphere of *Safety and Respect* that is conducive to learning for all children within their walls. *Safety and Respect for all* refers to a healthy and safe school environment where children should not have to endure ridicule or humiliation for any disability. Teachers should model respectful behaviors, and convey the sense that each child is fundamentally a good person, despite his difficulties. Children with anxiety (and other problems) should feel emotionally safe to make mistakes that are driven by their difficulties. If they do not, the effort they put into suppressing their disability is emotionally draining and detracts from their ability to attend to schoolwork. A child's worries or fears should never be dismissed or belittled. They may appear senseless or unwarranted, but they are still real to the child. Children with anxiety often recognize the incongruity between their fears and reality but simply do not have the skills to refocus and manage their anxiety.

Safety and Respect for all

Safety and respect grow from an appreciation of diversity and individual differences. Schools can foster understanding, tolerance and appreciation of anxiety and its impact on children. They can work to increase awareness and educate peers about anxiety by making it a part of the regular curriculum. Age-appropriate descriptions, books, videos and talks by parents or local experts are helpful. Introducing children's books such as *Up and Down the Worry Hill* (see *Resources*) and other books about anxiety disorders helps children understand what it might be like to have anxiety. Peers can be educated without compromising a child's confidentiality by providing information in general terms. If an anxious child's difficulties raise questions from classmates, school staff may seek permission from the child and parent to educate peers.

Anxious children often have low self-esteem and poor peer relations. They may even be isolated. It is important to make a conscious effort to be inclusive in class activities, and to make opportunities for shy, reluctant children to participate in ways that build their self-confidence. Classroom activities should be structured so that a child is not inadvertently left out or isolated. Classroom environments should be challenging and interesting with predictable routines, rules and expectations. Classroom practices or school policies that exacerbate anxiety should be closely examined and remedied. Punitive discipline, uncontrolled peer teasing or aggression, limited positive interactions and a high level of negative interchanges in the classroom must be eliminated. Anxious children should be assigned to teachers who have knowledge of anxiety and have a *kind but firm* approach. Anxious children benefit from having a safe space to calm down when they are having difficulty (see *Corrective Learning Experiences* in Chapter 11) and from having a classroom "buddy" who assists the child through the course of the day with support, and encouragement.

Anxious children are easy targets for bullies. It is estimated that 15 to 20% of students are bullied each year. Bullying may be the most prevalent form of violence in schools and can have very damaging consequences. Adult attitudes about bullying and teasing have often been that it is "just the way kids will always be" and victims need to learn how to "deal with it." In recent years, our attention has been drawn to tragic school shootings that were perpetrated by teenagers who were bullied and ostracized, and who described their actions as retaliation against the humiliations to which they were subjected. Although these are extreme instances, they should help us realize that victims of teasing suffer tremendously, and are not always able to "deal with it and move on."

Many schools have adopted a "zero tolerance" rule for bullying and aggression. School staff should be vigilant for teasing, and set limits quickly and consistently. However, peer group norms may be a far more powerful tool in the war against bullying than are school policies. That is because clandestine teasing in the hallways, bathrooms and locker rooms occurs regardless of the school's policies. Building awareness of the harmful effects of bullying, changing peer group norms, attitudes and acceptance of bullying, and increasing peer empathy for victims are helpful strategies. Role playing specific disabilities or playing the victim for a day can greatly increase children's sensitivity and empathy. Children become more receptive when they can simulate and "walk in the shoes" of victims. Reframing bullying as a sign of immaturity, weakness or cowardice rather than heroism can go a long way towards protecting innocent children. Bullying thrives because it can remain hidden and unreported. Changing the culture of disdain for those who tell on bullies is just as important.

Anxious children also need to learn how to express anger, anxiety, and other negative feelings safely and acceptably. Peers and teachers should also not be subject to the aggression or anger of an anxious child. Angry episodes and lashing out should be targeted for a *Corrective Learning Experience* (see Chapter 14).

MANAGEMENT OF ANXIETY IN SCHOOL

The process of deciding whether, when and how to intervene with an anxious child can be complex. School-based interventions may be conceptualized as having two phases:

Phase I: Consistent with the *Readiness for Treatment* approach described in Chapter 9, the goal of Phase I is to stabilize the child's anxiety sufficiently to allow him to continue to learn in school. It is an immediate and short-term response to facilitate academic progress until treatment can be implemented.

Phase II: The goal of Phase II is to provide interventions that will offer the child the skills to master anxiety in the long–term.

Phase I is really a means to an end, a stepping stone to Phase II, when the child learns how to manage his own anxiety.

Phase I – Stabilization

Stabilization involves setting realistic expectations about what a child can accomplish in a time of crisis. Even though the child needs to learn how to overcome anxiety, he may not be ready to do so in a time of great distress. Stabilizing the crisis is essential to treatment readiness. An anxious child does not yet have the skills to de-escalate anxiety; until he does, the responsibility for defusing the situation rests with the adults in his life. When a child is having great emotional difficulty, the responses of parents and teachers can either be calming or add to the child's arousal. Being rigid, inflexible and insistent on rules adds to the child's sense of being overwhelmed and unable to cope. It is not possible to reason with a distraught child; it is only possible to increase or decrease his distress.

Crises should be anticipated and a crisis management plan should be developed proactively. It may be necessary to adapt classroom expectations to allow the anxious child to achieve success on the most essential tasks— getting an education and getting well. When the child's academic functioning slides, the stress of trying to catch up can be overwhelming.

Accommodations and adaptations to the curriculum, instructional methods and the pace of delivery can provide relief from routine expectations and reduce the child's responsibilities to the essential. They make it easier for the child to do what's most important. For example, when Emily struggles to write perfectly, it may be helpful to excuse her from writing in cursive or writing at all. She may be permitted use of the computer or audiotapes to get the work done. In the big scheme of things, what is important is that Emily learns the given material, regardless of how she learns it.

Accommodations allow the setting of goals that the child can achieve and not fail. Anxious children need the experience of mastery, not further failure. Children should not be punished for behaviors that are clearly driven by anxiety. For instance, when Casey is late for class because he has a 2-hour long grooming ritual each morning, he will not benefit from being punished for being late, because OCD is not changed merely by punishment. Rather, being excused temporarily while he is learning how to overcome OCD is a more helpful response. Accommodations are generally temporary; some or all may be discontinued when treatment begins to take effect. However, they may need to be continued for a child whose symptoms are not responsive to treatment, or for a chronically ill child.

Accommodations may raise questions for school staff and parents alike.
Isn't it the easy way out?
Don't accommodations promote avoidance of fears?
Are they not counter to treatment success?
Is it not unfair to other students?
Isn't it a bad precedent?
When is it okay to set limits?
What if the child is simply being manipulative to get attention or less work?
Are accommodations justified for this child's behavior?

The controversy stems from the manner in which adults assess the *intent* behind the child's behavior. When a child has an impairment that is clearly due to a medical problem, adults do not question the need for accommodations, because the child has a genuine problem over which he has no control—it is not feigned. However, a child's emotional or behavioral problems are often viewed as controllable if only there were sufficient motivation and effort on the part of the child (and parents). When adults perceive the child's intent in the situation to be self-serving or manipulative, they are less likely to be sympathetic or accommodating.

Anxiety disorders, like asthma or diabetes, are legitimate illnesses that impair coping and functioning. It would be unethical to deprive a child with diabetes of snacks as needed. Depriving a child with anxiety of the aids and supports he needs to function is similar to withholding snacks from a diabetic child. Children with anxiety don't derive any pleasure from their condition, and are not doing it just to be difficult. They are genuinely scared and do not have effective coping skills.

> *There is a difference between fair and equal*

There is a difference between *fair* and *equal*. The belief that all children are equal in their needs is a myth. Each child is unique and different, and not identical to any other. Fairness refers to meeting each child's unique needs, whereas equality refers to treating every child in the same way, regardless of needs. A child with a reading disability is given remedial assistance. The additional help is fair, but certainly not equal. Likewise, the accommodations made for an anxious child are *fair but not equal.*

Can children with anxiety be manipulative to get more attention or do less work? Yes, they can be just as manipulative as children without anxiety. The fact is that children are inherently self-focused and self-serving in nature, and therefore have the propensity to work a situation to their advantage. If it works for them, why not do so? That's what happens when Sarah stays home from school due to fears of being away from her mother. When she's home, and there are no limits or structure, she ends up watching TV and playing all day. She earns an unplanned reward (see Chapter 11). Sarah enjoys that a lot more than going to school, so she is less motivated to attend school. However, that does not negate the fact that Sara suffers legitimately from separation anxiety. Clearly, legitimate illnesses and manipulative behavior in children are not mutually exclusive. The child with asthma or diabetes can just as easily use her illness to her advantage when it is convenient. It is up to parents and teachers to discern legitimate difficulty from manipulation and to stop inadvertently rewarding manipulative behavior.

The danger of being rigid and inflexible about school and classroom policies is that the anxious child may begin to see school as an intensely aversive experience, and may lose all interest and motivation to participate. There are many anxious children who are misdiagnosed and mis-treated, who continue to spiral downwards when schools are inflexible, and eventually drop out of school. Schools are encouraged to make reasonable and justifiable accommodations before the child gives up altogether.

The *Individuals with Disabilities Education Act* (IDEA) and *Section 504* of the *Rehabilitation Act of 1973* mandate a *Free and Appropriate Education* (FAPE) in the *Least Restrictive Environment* (LRE) that meets the child's academic, social and psychological needs. Children with anxiety disorders have a right to appropriate school-based services. Although many children with anxiety do not need to be classified to receive services, some children meet criteria under the IDEA or Section 504, which have specific guidelines and procedures associated with their activation. Thorough coverage of these provisions is beyond the scope of this book. Parents who wish to learn more can find books and online help in the *Resources* at the end of this book.

Phase II – School-based intervention

When stabilization has been achieved, the focus can shift effectively to interventions that help the child overcome anxiety. Qualified school professionals with training and experience in CBT for anxiety (such as school psychologists, counselors and social workers) may design and implement school-based interventions with input from parents and other staff. Interventions may consist of basic cognitive strategies, exposures, relaxation, and child management strategies. School staff can design a systematic and realistic plan with achievable goals that will be implemented collaboratively by school staff and parents. This plan must filter down to all staff involved. Some interventions will take place in the counseling office, some in the classroom and some at home.

The following guidelines for school-based interventions are derived from CBT (see Chapters 9 and 11). Specific CBT interventions are presented in Chapters 13 and 15.

- Interventions must be planned, not developed in haste.
- Treatment plans must be practical and feasible at school.
- Treatment must address the cognitive, physical and behavioral aspects of anxiety.
- Treatment goals must be specific, manageable, discrete and progressive.
- Exposure-based interventions should be conducted gradually.

Adolescents with anxiety should be provided with opportunities for career exploration, the development of vocational skills, and transition to the world beyond school in which they will need to function.

PREVENTION

Schools can also contribute to reducing anxiety proactively. The goal of preventive efforts is to build resilience, promote wellness, and create a climate of proactive and positive handling of stress. A *primary* prevention approach involves educating all children about dealing with anxiety, regardless of their anxious tendencies. *Secondary* prevention involves identifying children who may be prone to anxiety and teaching them anxiety-reduction skills proactively. *Tertiary* prevention efforts are aimed at children who already have problematic anxiety. They attempt to reduce the length and severity of recurrences or increase the time between relapses.

Primary prevention may involve development of a school-wide curriculum to promote healthy coping with stress and anxiety. Stress management, problem solving, coping and mental health issues may be incorporated into health classes, just as other illnesses are. Children can be taught about different types of emotions and reactions to stress and transition. The initiation of appropriate and adaptive help-seeking behaviors should be emphasized. Preventive education helps remove misperceptions of anxiety as a "weakness," reduces the stigma associated with mental illness and increases peer acceptance and appropriate help-seeking behavior.

Primary prevention efforts can also be geared towards parents. The parent-teacher association may sponsor workshops for parents of all students in the school district. Parent workshops presented by a professional with expertise in childhood anxiety can help parents understand the nature of anxiety, the differences between normal and problem anxiety, the principles of CBT and effective child-management practices to foster non-anxious behavior in children. Parents are often eager and receptive to learning more effective ways of helping their children manage everyday stress and anxiety.

Secondary prevention identifies children who have tendencies towards anxiety or who are at risk for developing anxiety disorders. Teachers may identify children who meet given criteria for anxious behaviors. Children may also be screened during health classes using a simple screening measure such as the Multidimensional Anxiety Scale for Children (MASC; see *References*). Children who have been identified as anxiety-prone can participate in a group training on various stress and coping topics, including anxiety. The goals of training include removing blame and shame, validating feelings and fostering appropriate problem solving. Coping skills training may include role-play using imaginary scenarios, modeling, and problem solving, followed by practice in real life. Parents may participate in some sessions, so that they are aware of the skills their children are learning. Parents are encouraged to use the techniques themselves and to reinforce and apply them at home with their children.

Parent support groups can also further the benefits of secondary prevention. Parents of anxious children who have been through treatment may help parents whose children have been recently identified. The former share their experiences so that new parents know what to expect, how to cope and where to find appropriate help. They also derive support from knowing they are not alone in their struggles, and hope from seeing families with successful outcomes. A counselor or psychologist may facilitate the support group.

Tertiary prevention efforts are aimed at children who have already displayed problem anxiety. These prevention efforts primarily involve being proactive in anticipating potential crises, identifying triggers and preparing the child and the classroom for future episodes of anxiety, using a CBT approach.

A few cautions about prevention efforts are in order. First, children should be taught that anxiety has a protective function and is entirely appropriate and necessary for safety in some contexts. For instance, it is good for a child to be alert and vigilant when walking in an unsafe neighborhood. Second, it is important that children not become over-sensitized to threat, danger and symptoms of anxiety by virtue of learning about them in a prevention program. Third, it is important to have an adequate referral base of community clinicians to whom children may be referred if treatment is indicated. (See *Consultation and Referral* in this chapter and Chapter 14).

Prevention programs should therefore be carefully planned, constructed and supervised by personnel with expertise in anxiety disorders. Consultation or supervision by a community expert is recommended. Mental health experts in anxiety could be brought into the schools on a periodic or as-needed basis to facilitate this goal. Preventive interventions require substantial organization and funding. Schools must therefore view anxiety as a significant issue that justifies the added effort and expense. Schools may participate in developing and supporting public policy efforts to facilitate early recognition and intervention for anxious children, and in making efforts to secure funds for training and consultation.

Chapter 13

An Action Plan at School

This chapter presents a systematic and goal-directed method for parents and schools to come together to implement an effective action plan to help the anxious child at school.

The nine steps described below are designed to enhance efficiency and effectiveness of intervention. Application of these steps for the children described in Chapter 2 is illustrated at the end of this chapter.

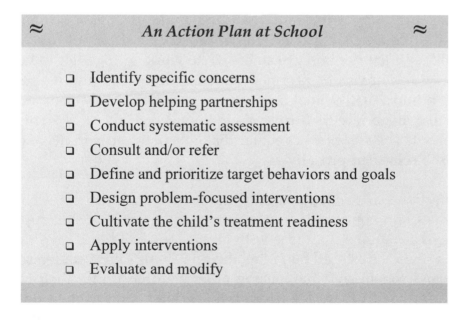

≈   *An Action Plan at School*   ≈

- ❏ Identify specific concerns
- ❏ Develop helping partnerships
- ❏ Conduct systematic assessment
- ❏ Consult and/or refer
- ❏ Define and prioritize target behaviors and goals
- ❏ Design problem-focused interventions
- ❏ Cultivate the child's treatment readiness
- ❏ Apply interventions
- ❏ Evaluate and modify

IDENTIFY SPECIFIC CONCERNS

The process of helping the anxious child begins when a parent or teacher expresses concern regarding a child's behavior. It is important to focus that concern into a precise description of specific behaviors that the child is exhibiting, and the specific conditions in which they occur. Details of when the problem behaviors occur, in what context, and how and when they interfere with the child's ability to acquire academic skills and maintain social relationships are necessary. Broad, global or vague descriptions obscure the ability to develop a targeted intervention plan.

DEVELOP PARTNERSHIPS

School staff can make active efforts to initiate and establish effective partnerships from the start. The teacher and pupil services team determine which members of the school staff participate in the partnership and identifies a "Case Manager" to coordinate and oversee assessment, intervention and communication. The team identifies ways to enable easy access and exchange of information between the parents and the school, and establishes timelines for informing parents and involved school staff.

Effective communication and consistency are essential to a productive partnership. The partnership is fostered by meeting with parents in a timely manner, being supportive and receptive, inviting and welcoming their input and discussing the partnership approach. Most parents are aware of their child's difficulties and are amenable to working together to help their children. Many are well informed and may know far more about their child's condition than school staff may expect. Some may need education and reading materials to further their knowledge about anxiety and its management. The system for regular dialogue between parents and school staff must be clarified proactively.

In an effective partnership, parents and school staff respect each other's perspectives and contributions. Teachers must appreciate the scope of the problems that parents may face with an anxious child and give them due credit for their efforts at handling them. Parents must understand that teachers and school staff have many other children under their care, and reinforce and credit them for effort, time and devotion to their own child. Parents and teachers may also have different perspectives on the child's difficulties. Parents may perceive the child's difficulties as triggered by school or classroom practices. On the other hand, teachers may view the same child as "a joy to have in class." Teachers may have no clue that this child was struggling with homework into the wee hours of the night.

School staff can anticipate and eliminate potential difficulties in the partnership in advance. Some parents may be anxious and stressed; others unaware or defensive. Parents should be approached thoughtfully, objectively, and without judgment. A *"no blame, no shame"* approach is critical to a good working partnership. Although anxiety does run in families, not all parents are overanxious. Even parents who are typically non-anxious may present as highly anxious because of the crisis elicited by their child's symptoms. For example, Casey's parents, normally calm and collected, are driven to distraction with his incessant reassurance seeking. To the naïve observer, they appear to be easily flustered, highly reactive and impatient with Casey. Strategies for smoothing out rocky partnerships are presented in Chapter 14.

If it is anticipated that extensive or intensive therapy is imminent, consultation and partnership with a CBT therapist in the community may be sought. If medications are indicated, a child psychiatrist may become part of the partnership. Parents may initiate these contacts, either at the recommendation of the school, or of their own choosing.

CONDUCT SYSTEMATIC ASSESSMENT

An accurate understanding of the child involves understanding him as a person, not as a problem. It is necessary to recognize the child's strengths, talents, interests, and personality, as well as his difficulties. It is equally important to appreciate the needs and strengths of the family and class environment because these are significant influences in the child's life.

There are several methods of assessment. The most common are behavioral observations, interviews, rating scales, questionnaires and psychological tests. The Case Manager, in consultation with the Pupil Services Team, determines what methods of assessment to pursue. A multidisciplinary team assessment by relevant teachers, counselors, parents, the psychologist and other involved staff provides a more comprehensive picture of the child's strengths and difficulties in different contexts. The assessment continues during and after the intervention process in order to track changes in the child's behavior.

≈   **Questions to be Addressed by School Assessment**   ≈

- ❑ What is the specific behavior that is problematic?
- ❑ When did it begin?
- ❑ When does the behavior occur and in what circumstances?
- ❑ What is the frequency and duration of the behavior?
- ❑ Is the level of the behavior excessive for the situation?
- ❑ How distressed is the child?
- ❑ What is the child's developmental level?
- ❑ Is the behavior normal and expected for the child's age?
- ❑ What factors in the classroom, school or home environments appear to contribute to the child's behavior?
- ❑ How is the child's academic and social functioning affected?
- ❑ How do peers, teachers and parents respond to the child's behavior?
- ❑ What seems to calm the child, and what seems to escalate anxiety?
- ❑ What are the child's coping skills?
- ❑ What are his resources and personal strengths?
- ❑ Does the child seem to be improving without intervention?
- ❑ What are the risks and side effects of different types of treatment?
- ❑ How do the parents and child feel about treatment?
- ❑ Are the child's needs within the purview of school personnel?
- ❑ Is there access to a community professional who treats anxiety?

Behavioral observations

Teachers and parents can carefully observe and record the child's behaviors in different contexts. An accurate assessment will require observations of the situations, triggers, frequency, severity, duration, interference, and peer and parent/teacher responses related to the problem behaviors. Observations may occur at school, home and other settings, at different times of day and in different activities. A more complete picture of the child is generated when there are multiple caregivers making observations.

Interviews

Interviews with the child, parent, teachers and other relevant school staff complement and supplement the information derived from observations. Interviews with the child allow a better understanding of the child's thought process and mood state, for which the child is the best informant. Insight, motivation and readiness to engage in treatment can also be assessed via interviews. The parents provide information about the history, pervasiveness and persistence of the child's behaviors. Parents and teachers share their observations and interactions with the child, and offer their own perspectives on the problem behaviors. Classroom and home practices that might exacerbate or calm the child's anxiety are also assessed in interviews with parents and teachers.

Psychoeducational testing

Psycho-educational testing is indicated when a child's academic performance is falling below expectations. For some children, anxiety, frustration, resistance and explosiveness develop due to learning or language difficulties. For others, anxiety may impede the acquisition of academic skills. IQ and achievement testing may be conducted to assess for learning disabilities, speech and language impairments.

Self-report questionnaires

Self-report questionnaires allow children to describe their thoughts and feelings. These measures usually have statements describing specific aspects of anxiety, depression, fears and other thoughts or feelings. The child answers "Yes" or "No," or rates himself on a scale according to the extent to which the statements pertain to him. Children usually find these questions easier to answer and less intimidating than answering questions in interviews.

Rating scales

Rating scales allow parents and teachers to rate the child on a wide range of behaviors at home and at school. Commonly used self-report questionnaires and rating scales along with their specific uses are listed in Table 9.

Table 9: Assessment Instruments for Children and Adolescents

SELF-REPORT MEASURES*

Measure	Ages	Content	Assesses	Domains
Fear Survey Schedule-Revised (FSSC-R) Ollendick, 1983	7-18	80 items 3-point scale	General fearfulness	Failure and criticism, the unknown, injury, small animals, danger and death, medical procedures
Leyton Obsessional Inventory-Child Version (LOI-CV) Berg, Whitaker & Davies, 1988	10-18	20 items Yes/No	Obsessive thoughts	General obsessive, dirt-contamination, numbers-luck, school-related symptoms.
Multidimensional Anxiety Scale for Children (MASC) March, 1997	8-16	39 items 4-point scale	Symptoms of anxiety	Physical symptoms, social anxiety, harm avoidance, separation anxiety
Revised Children's Manifest Anxiety Scale (RCMAS) Reynolds & Richmond, 1978	5-19	37 items, Yes/No	Chronic anxiety	Physiological anxiety, worry/oversensitivity, social concerns
Screen for Child Anxiety Related Emotional Disorders (SCARED) Birmaher et al., 1997	9-18	38 items 3-point scale	Symptoms of anxiety	Somatic/panic, general anxiety, separation/school anxiety, social anxiety
Social Anxiety Scale for Children (SASC) La Greca & Stone, 1993	8-12	22 items	Social anxiety	Negative evaluation, social avoidance, distress
Social Phobia and Anxiety Inventory for Children (SPAI-C) Beidel, Turner & Morris, 1995	8-17	44 items 4-point scale	Social anxiety	Assertiveness, social encounters, public performance
State-Trait Anxiety Inventory for Children (STAIC) Spielberger, 1973	9-12	40 items 3-point scale	Chronic anxiety	Trait anxiety State anxiety
Youth Self-Report (YSR) Achenbach, 1991c	11-18	120 items 3-point scale	Social competence, behavior problems	Internalizing (withdrawn, somatic, anxious/depressed), externalizing (social, thought, attention problems, aggression)

PARENT AND TEACHER RATING SCALES*

Child Behavior Checklist (CBCL) Achenbach, 1991a	4-16	120 items 3-point scale	Social competence, behavior problems	Internalizing (withdrawn, somatic, anxious/depressed), externalizing (social, thought, attention problems, aggression)
Child Behavior Checklist-Teacher Report Form (TRF) Achenbach, 1991b	4-18	123 items 3-point scale		
Conners Parent Rating Scale-Revised (CPRS-R) Long form Conners, 1997	3-17	80 items 4-point scale	Problem behaviors	Oppositional, social problems, cognitive/inattention, psychosomatic, hyperactivity, DSM-IV symptom subscales, anxious-shy, ADHD index, perfectionism, Conner's Global Index
Conners Teacher Rating Scale-Revised (CTRS-R) Long form Conners, 1989	3-17	59 items 4-point scale		

*The listed psychological measures must only be administered and interpreted by professionals who are qualified to do so by virtue of their training and experience in psychological assessment of children.

CONSULT AND/OR REFER

When the assessment is completed, the Case Manager meets with all members of the partnership to present and discuss the findings, draw conclusions and develop a prospective intervention plan. It is important to align all parties with regard to perceptions of the child's difficulties and to come to agreement on a path of intervention. This is an opportune time to identify and problem-solve potential concerns and obstacles to a treatment plan. If indicated, referral to a community provider should be pursued. School staff may help parents identify appropriate community resources such as a child psychologist who provides CBT or a psychiatrist for medication. Chapter 14 provides specific information on how to locate appropriate professionals to treat anxious children and adolescents.

DEFINE GOALS AND PRIORITIZE TARGET BEHAVIORS

CBT techniques are directed at specific symptoms and behaviors, not at diagnoses. For example, perfectionism, which may be a symptom of OCD or GAD, is treated with realistic thinking strategies and exposure, regardless of the child's diagnosis. "Target" behaviors, which are the specific behaviors that are identified for change, must be recognized, described and rank ordered according to priority. Concrete, achievable goals and outcomes must be clearly defined. Treatment must then be applied systematically to selected targets in order of priority. Each child is unique and different in her needs, and treatment goals and interventions must be tailored to each child's specific needs.

Pressure to "fix" all the child's difficulties as soon as possible can come from many directions. Parents, teachers, other school staff, and perhaps even the child herself may be impatient for results. The sense of urgency can blur clarity and actually set back treatment. Effective treatment is conducted in small, systematic and manageable steps. Treatment should therefore not be rushed into overzealously (see more on *Treatment Readiness* in Chapter 9 and later in this chapter).

DESIGN PROBLEM-FOCUSED INTERVENTIONS

At this stage, the team focuses on outlining specific stabilization and intervention strategies, as discussed in Chapter 12. These may include classroom adaptations and accommodations.

≈ *Focus of CBT Interventions at School* ≈
❑ Identify fears, worries and anxieties
❑ Identify body changes connected with anxiety
❑ Link thoughts, feelings and physical symptoms
❑ Identify specific triggers for anxiety
❑ Identify and correct sources of anxiety when possible
❑ Take charge of feelings and behaviors
❑ Develop realistic self-talk
❑ Learn to self-soothe, take space
❑ Confront fears via gradual exposure
❑ Use problem-solving skills
❑ Build confidence and optimism
❑ Utilize appropriate assertiveness and social skills
❑ Develop self-reliance

CBT strategies such as realistic thinking, self-instruction training, problem-solving skills and exposure are selected and applied as suitable to help the child overcome and manage anxiety. Some children may also benefit from social skills training. Interventions should capitalize on the child's strengths to boost self-confidence and increase self-efficacy. Many children will benefit from parents and teachers using management strategies that foster non-anxious behavior (see Chapter 11). Most importantly, parents and teachers need to be consistent in handling anxious behavior.

It is often useful to archive a "library" of strategies that seem to help children with given difficulties. Techniques that have worked for other children in similar situations may reduce the amount of time spent in "trial and error." Chapter 15 presents such a collection of strategies. Strategies that are effective for a given child should be recorded in a *"Skill Diary"* or notebook in which successful techniques are documented. The Skill Diary should be easily accessible to the child and parents, to allow quick referencing when the need arises.

Some children with anxiety may qualify for an Individualized Education Plan (IEP), in accordance with the Individuals with Disabilities Education Act due to the severity of their condition and the magnitude of its impact on academic functioning. The pupil services team, in conjunction with parents, implements relevant steps to procure the necessary services for the child. For children whose disability is not as severe, a 504 Plan, which is broader and less formal than an IEP, may suffice. For more information on IEP's and 504 plans, see the *Resources* at the end of this book.

CULTIVATE TREATMENT-READINESS

As discussed in Chapter 9, the child's readiness to change and active participation are very influential factors in treatment success. Yet, many children are not motivated or ready, because confronting anxiety is initially both counter-intuitive and daunting. A child who is afraid does not exactly want to hear that she must face her fear to overcome it. Cultivating the child's treatment readiness is necessary because the chances of success are greatly enhanced by good preparation, and jeopardized by lack thereof.

The four steps involved in building treatment readiness in an anxious child are discussed in depth in Chapter 9: First, the child's level of distress must be stabilized. A child who is distraught and struggling to get through the basics each day cannot really engage in treatment. Accommodations may be necessary to decrease stress and help the child stabilize.

Second, effective communication is one of the necessary keys to readiness. Helping the child understand the process whereby fears are conquered is important. Thoughtful, purposeful communication allows the child to understand CBT, particularly exposure, clearly, simply and accurately, at his level of comprehension. It will also dispel misconceptions and fears, and prepare him for treatment. When children don't understand CBT well, they are unnecessarily apprehensive, unwilling or ambivalent. They are reluctant to take the risks that CBT requires and quick to withdraw before habituation can take place. Metaphors and analogies such as the *Worry Hill* (see *Resources*) and the *Noise at the Window* are useful for anxious children.

Third, effective persuasion helps children see the *necessity* for change, the *possibility* for change, and the *power* to change. Helping the child see the benefits of overcoming anxiety convinces him of the necessity for change. The child needs to know that anxiety can be successfully overcome, which lets him know there is the possibility for change. Finally, the child must understand that he has the power to overcome anxiety by making a change in behavior. The recognition that he has the power to change is a liberating experience for the child. It is a major step in the preparation for recovery. See *Engaging Reluctant Children* in Chapter 14 for strategies to approach children who resist participation in their own recovery.

Finally, there must be collaboration with the child and family. It is important to build rapport, and remove any sense of blame or shame. It is also essential to convey hope, confidence and optimism. The child must view the relationship with parents and school staff as a helping relationship, not a punitive or critical one.

APPLY INTERVENTIONS

Once the interventions have been designed, and treatment readiness optimized, the process of implementation begins. Before applying the plan, it is necessary to have the following issues clarified, agreed upon, and communicated among all members of the team.

≈ **Issues to be Clarified before Intervention** ≈

- ❏ What precise steps are involved in each intervention?
- ❏ What resources will be needed to put the plans into action?
- ❏ What specific roles are to be played by the child, parent, teacher, other school staff or other provider?
- ❏ Who is responsible for implementing and monitoring each intervention?
- ❏ Do staff or parents need to be trained before proceeding?
- ❏ Has the child been prepared adequately for each intervention?
- ❏ Where and when will each intervention occur?
- ❏ What exactly will happen when the intervention is carried out?
- ❏ How will the child's response to each treatment be recorded?
- ❏ How will the plan be evaluated?
- ❏ How will the need for modifications be determined?
- ❏ How will changes be incorporated and executed?

EVALUATE AND MODIFY

Finally, the plan that has been put in place must be evaluated systematically to determine if it is meeting its goals. The treatment plan should be examined after a predetermined amount of time, such as a given number of days or sessions. The most important aspect of evaluation is the child's response to the intervention.

The child's progress is systematically measured using the same methods that were used to obtain baseline or pre-treatment functioning. Approximately 75% improvement is a good indicator of treatment success, and less than 30% may be indication for serious revisiting of the plan or involvement of a community provider. These are rough guidelines for determining success. Each child's needs and circumstances are unique and different; indicators of improvement must therefore be individually considered for each child. For some, 40% improvement may be considered substantial, for others 90% may be ideal.

≈   *Questions for Evaluation*   ≈

- ❑ Have the goals been reached?
- ❑ Were interventions implemented as agreed and written?
  - o If not, what needs to be corrected?
- ❑ Have there been obstacles to the application of the plan?
  - o If yes, what changes need to be made to eliminate the problem?
- ❑ If progress is in the right direction, what is the next step?
- ❑ For how long should treatment be continued?
- ❑ When is the intervention to be tapered and stopped to allow the child to utilize the skills he has acquired?
- ❑ What is the follow-up plan?
- ❑ When and how often will booster sessions be provided?

Once the goals have been reached, a follow-up plan should include periodic monitoring of the child's progress. Periodic booster sessions should be provided to reinforce and support the child's efforts to manage anxiety successfully. If success is limited or slower than expected, the team must examine the plan and identify obstacles. Plans must be modified or fine-tuned as necessary and impediments must be remedied. Each participant's motivation, investment and actual participation must be evaluated and shored up with resources if needed. If there is less than expected improvement after two weeks, a community provider's input must be actively sought.

The application of the action plan is illustrated below, using the case of Sarah (see Chapter 2 for a refresher). All the forms referenced in the plan are available in *Forms and Tools* at the end of this book.

AN ACTION PLAN FOR SCHOOL REFUSAL/SEPARATION ANXIETY

Sarah is in second grade and has difficulty attending school. Sarah's mother transports her to school every day because she refuses to ride the school bus. She has often arrived late, and recently has stopped attending school altogether. When Sarah is in school, she is tearful, jittery, preoccupied and unable to focus on her work. She begs to go to the nurse's office and calls her mother to take her home.

Identify specific concerns

Sarah has been at least one hour late for class for 4 out of 5 days in the past 2 weeks. This week, she has attended school for only 2 days out of 5. When in class, Sarah is distraught and cannot concentrate. She completes about 40% of her work on time. She leaves the classroom at least three times a day. Her academic performance, which was above average, is in danger of dropping to below average.

Develop helping partnerships

Sarah's teacher, Mrs. Francis, sets up a meeting with Sarah's mother, Mrs. Reed. They have talked on the phone and exchanged emails frequently to discuss Sarah's difficulties. Mrs. Francis and Mrs. Reed agree that Sarah needs some help on both at home and on the school front. They agree that collaboration is essential, and that Sarah should be referred to the Pupil Services Team (PST) for more comprehensive assessment and interventions.

Mr. and Mrs. Reed meet with the PST. The PST designates the school psychologist, Mr. Lewis, as the Case Manager who will develop and oversee the implementation of an assessment and intervention plan at school. He will act as the point person for communication with the Reeds and the school staff. Mr. Lewis and Mrs. Reed will initially have daily phone contact to discuss concerns and provide updates. Mrs. Reed and Mrs. Francis, the teacher, will also communicate about Sarah's progress at school and at home, and discuss concerns or questions via a *Parent/Teacher Log* (see Figure 7). Sarah will carry the log in her book bag and give it to her teacher in the morning and her mother each evening. Sarah's parents and the PST agree that Sarah may need to be referred to a CBT therapist in the community if Sarah does not show improvement within two weeks.

Figure 7: Parent-Teacher Log

PARENT-TEACHER LOG

Child's Name: **Sarah**   Parent/Teacher: **Mrs. Francis**   Date: **Nov 13**

0	1	2	3	4	5	6	7	8	9	10
No problems			Mild		Moderate		Strong			Extreme

What went well for the child today? In what situations did he/she experience success?
Math homework on time, 100% accuracy

Overall mood/anxiety for the day (0-10): 7

Were there any situations in which the child was upset? If yes, please describe the situation: Second period, Class was reading a book about a family trip to the zoo.

Child's mood and distress in this situation (0-10): 9

Describe child's specific behaviors (yelling, crying): Crying, pleading to call her mother, saying she didn't want to hear the story

Describe child's feelings (sad, afraid): Sad, upset, worried about mother

What was the impact of the behavior? Not able to finish story, class disrupted

How did you handle this situation? Asked her to take space, look at calming pictures, so that class could complete the rest of the story
How did the child react to your handling? Stopped momentarily, but resumed soon

How long did the episode last? 45 minutes

What was the child's overall effort in the situation?   Moderate
How did you reward the child's effort? Praised her for trying

Other comments/questions: Seems like the story reminded her of her mother

---

Conduct systematic assessment

Mr. Lewis develops an assessment plan for Sarah. It includes behavioral observations, self-report measures, rating scales and interviews with Sarah, her parents, and relevant teachers.

Behavioral observations are conducted at home and in different settings at school. The Reeds complete the *Home Behavior Observations* of Sarah (Figure 8) in the following situations: when she wakes up, gets ready for school, gets on the bus, returns home, does homework, and goes to bed. School staff record *School Behavior Observations* (Figure 9) when Sarah arrives at school, during different class periods, and in different activities and settings such as gym, art, and the playground. They record Sarah's mood, behaviors, triggers, the effects of her behavior on herself and others, and what seems to calm her.

Figure 8: Home Behavior Observations

HOME BEHAVIOR OBSERVATIONS
Child's Name: Sarah   **Parent:** Mrs. Reed   **Date/Time:** Nov 15, 7am
Situation and triggers: Sarah has to wake up and get ready for school
Specific behaviors and duration: Crying, refusing to get out of bed, saying she did not want to go to school for 45 minutes
0   1   2   3   4   5   6   7   8   9   10 No problems   Mild   Moderate   Strong   Extreme
Rate the following (0-10): Distress: 8   Disruption: 5
Impact/consequences of behavior: Misses bus, has to be carried out of bed, driven to school, arrives 2 hours late

Figure 9: School Behavior Observations

SCHOOL BEHAVIOR OBSERVATIONS
Child's Name: Sarah   **Teacher**: Mrs. Francis   **Date/Time**: Nov 15, 11am
Situation and triggers: Math class. Sarah gets all problems correct
Specific behaviors and duration: Happy, pleased with herself
0   1   2   3   4   5   6   7   8   9   10 No problems   Mild   Moderate   Strong   Extreme
Rate the following (0-10): Distress: 1   Disruption: 0
Impact/consequences of behavior: Sarah is happy and confident

Mr. Lewis talks to Sarah to learn about her thoughts and feelings, and her reluctance to go to school. He assesses her level of distress, insight into the impact and consequences of her actions, and motivation and readiness to overcome fear. In an interview with Sarah's parents, Mr. Lewis obtains their perspectives on Sarah's behaviors. He also learns about Sarah's childhood development, the history of her anxiety, her strengths and resources, and family factors as pertinent to Sarah's difficulties. He learns how Mr. and Mrs. Reed individually and jointly react and respond to Sarah's school refusal. In an interview with Mrs. Francis, Mr. Lewis obtains the teacher's perspective on Sarah's anxiety, the consequences to her academic, social and psychological competence, and the impact of her behaviors on peers and the classroom environment.

Mr. Lewis asks Sarah to complete self-report measures of anxiety and depression such as the Multidimensional Anxiety Scale for Children and the Fear Survey Schedule (see *Assessment Instruments* in Table 9). The Reed's rate Sarah's behaviors at home on the Child Behavior Checklist, and Mrs. Francis rates Sarah's classroom behaviors on the Child Behavior Checklist-Teacher Form. Mr. Lewis decides that IQ and achievement testing is not indicated at this time, because Sarah has been an above average student, and there are no questions regarding her learning potential.

Mr. Lewis consolidates all the information received from Sarah, her parents and teachers. He determines the nature of the problem, its frequency and severity, the contexts in which it occurs and potential triggers. He examines school and classroom practices and family factors that might be contributing to Sarah's anxiety. He establishes baselines for the frequency, severity, distress and length of episodes of anxiety. He identifies Sarah's strengths and coping resources that can be utilized to build her competence and self-esteem. He evaluates her motivation and readiness to master anxiety. He assesses whether intervention is within the scope of school, and determines the need for partnership with a community provider. The assessment yields the following picture of Sarah's difficulties:

Sarah reports that she is worried about being at school for fear that "something bad" will happen to her family while she is away. She rates her fear at 9 out of 10 on the *"Fearmometer"* (see Figure 2). No particular school-related stressors are found to be contributing to her fear. Sarah's family is under some stress lately due to her father's loss of employment. The Reed's are aware that they have allowed Sarah to stay close to them for fear of provoking her fear and distress. Parents and teachers acknowledge that they have been reassuring Sarah excessively but ineffectively. Sarah's strengths include good social skills, the fact that she is a friendly, caring and helpful child and a natural leader when not anxious. She is a skilled artist and enjoys reading and crafts. Sarah says she is read to "be happy again."

Consult and refer

Mr. Lewis meets with Sarah's parents and the PST to present and discuss the results of the assessment and to obtain consensus agreement on his conclusions. The PST and Sarah's parents agree that the school can provide assistance to Sarah to enable her to attend school without disruption. A 504 Plan is initiated to formalize and ensure services for Sarah, and to secure appropriate resources for school staff to provide the services. The PST team and Sarah's parents agree to continue to work collaboratively to help Sarah make an effective return to school.

The intervention plan will include classroom accommodations, gradual exposure, reality testing and improved child management. The Reeds also agree to seek treatment with a community mental health provider who specializes in CBT for anxiety to help with issues at home. The PST team decides to begin interventions while awaiting collaboration with a CBT therapist. Mr. Lewis discusses the findings and recommendations with Sarah. Sarah is motivated to overcome anxiety and willing to accept help.

Define and prioritize target behaviors and goals

The PST team, Sarah and her parents participate in identifying specific target behaviors, goals, and indicators of improvement. Of several identified concerns, the two most important are selected:

Goals:

1. Sarah will learn skills to overcome anxiety that prevents her from attending school.
2. Sarah will build self-reliance in coping.

Target behaviors:

1. Sarah will get ready for school and get on the bus on time.
2. Sarah will stay in school all day, with one visit to the nurse if needed.

<u>Indicators of treatment success:</u>

1. Sarah will remain in school all day (with no more than one visit to the nurse's office each day) for at least two weeks.
2. Sarah will ride the school bus for at least two weeks.
3. Sarah's fear temperature about being at school will be no more than 4 for at least two weeks.
4. Parents and teachers will report at least 75% improvement in target behaviors.

Design problem-focused interventions

The PST and Sarah's parents meet to brainstorm and select interventions for addressing target behaviors. The most relevant and appropriate solutions are selected, based on evidence of their effectiveness, feasibility and acceptability. The team shares its plan with Sarah and invites her input.

<u>Phase I</u>

The PST and Sarah's parents meet to brainstorm and select interventions for addressing target behaviors. The most relevant and appropriate solutions are selected, based on evidence of their effectiveness, feasibility and acceptability. The team shares its plan with Sarah and invites her input.

1. Sarah will not be penalized for coming to school late, for having to leave the classroom, or for calling her mother.
2. Sarah will receive a reduced workload of shorter assignments and less homework.
3. Sarah will not be required to complete unfinished school assignments at home.
4. Sarah will be assigned a "peer buddy" to help stay on task in class.
5. Sarah will signal the teacher with a blue card if she has to take space.
6. Sarah will take space at a corner desk until she is calm.
7. A classroom aide will assist the teacher in working with Sarah.

<u>Phase II</u>

Once the crisis has abated, the following interventions will be implemented to address cognitive, behavioral and physiological aspects of anxiety.

1. Realistic thinking to modify Sarah's fearful thoughts about her mother getting hurt while she is at school.

2. Exposure to help Sarah confront fears of being in school without her mother.
3. Relaxation and deep breathing exercises to help Sarah reduce physical tension.
4. Management strategies for caregivers adopt consistent limits, foster self-reliance, attend to and reward non-anxious behaviors.

Cultivate treatment readiness

Mr. Lewis meets with Sarah to invite her input into the treatment plan and let her know that school staff and her parents are committed to helping her. He seeks to foster motivation, active participation and compliance. He explains the metaphor of the *Worry Hill* to describe exposure and habituation, and the *Noise at the Window* analogy (see Chapter 9) to describe reality testing and self-talk. He helps Sarah see how fear is keeping her from having fun and enjoying school. Sarah admits that she would rather be playing with her friends than be scared and upset all the time. Mr. Lewis conveys hope, confidence and optimism about conquering fear. He reiterates that Sarah's parents, teachers and school team are rallying for her.

Apply interventions

Mr. Lewis and the team specify each person's role before the plans are implemented. Methods for evaluation, regular feedback, communication, and accountability are detailed. Mr. Lewis will work individually with Sarah to teach her to connect thoughts and feelings using the *My Thoughts and Feelings* form (Figure 10). Mr. Lewis will teach Sarah to rate the severity of her fears using the *Fearmometer*. They will then develop an exposure hierarchy, using the fear temperature ratings to rate difficulty and rank order the tasks. Mr. Lewis will oversee the exposure exercises, some of which will be conducted at school and others at home by Sarah's parents. Mrs. Francis will implement exposures in the classroom with Mr. Lewis's and the aide's assistance. Mr. Lewis instructs each participant in CBT and exposure (see Chapter 9) to prior to beginning the exercises. Mr. Lewis decides when the team is ready to proceed.

Figure 10: My Thoughts and Feelings

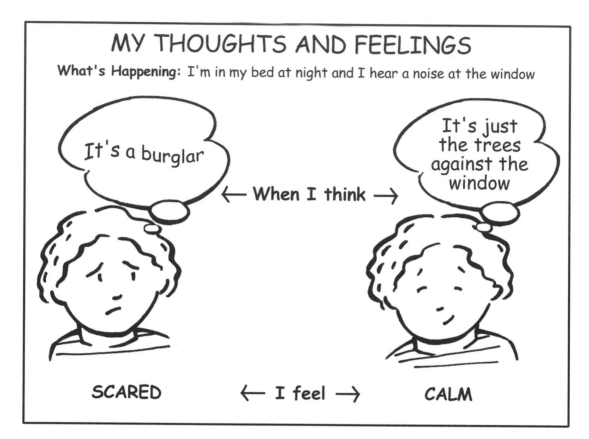

Sarah's exposure hierarchy or *Fear Ladder* is described in Figure 11. Mr. Lewis coaches Sarah on the exposure steps using the RIDE acronym. Sarah is given a *Worry Hill Memory Card* (Figure 12) to help her remember the RIDE steps.

As Sarah achieves success on one task, she moves to the next exercise. Her progress on the exposure exercises is tracked daily using the *Exposure Progress Record*. Sarah's progress at the end of two weeks is described in Figure 13.

Parents and teachers are consistent in encouraging and rewarding Sarah's efforts, no matter how minor they might appear. They give her consistent messages that attending school is necessary. They are kind but firm in setting limits on reassurance seeking. They encourage independent activities and self-reliance. They make opportunities to allow Sarah to use her strengths and talents so that she builds self-confidence.

Figure 11: Exposure Hierarchy for School Refusal/Separation Anxiety

SARAH'S FEAR LADDER	Date: November 30	
Goal: Ride on school bus and stay at school all day without calling Mom.		
Things I am afraid to do		**My fear temperature**
1. Wake up, get dressed and do school work at home on regular school schedule.		2
2. Get in the car, drive to school and return home.		4
3. Stay in the car in the parking lot for 15 minutes.		5
4. Drive to the bus stop and wait for the bus, but not get in.		6
5. Ride the bus to school but return home.		6
6. Enter the building, meet the teacher's aide at the door and pick up assignments to take home.		7
7. Stay in Mr. Lewis's office and do schoolwork for 1 class period.		7
8. Be escorted to class by the aide and stay for one class period.		8
9. Stay in class all morning, with one phone call to Mom.		8
10. Stay in class all morning with no phone calls to Mom.		9
11. Stay in class all day with no phone calls to Mom.		10
12. Stay after school to help Mrs. Francis.		10
13. Stay after school, and Mom is late to pick me up.		10

Figure 12: Worry Hill Memory Card

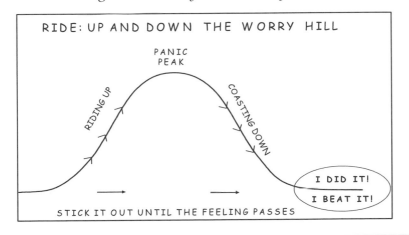

Rename the thought. *"It's simply anxiety, not me."*
Insist that YOU are in charge! *"I'm in charge, not anxiety."*
Defy anxiety, do the OPPOSITE: *"I will go to school and stay until all day. I will ride up the Worry Hill and stick it out until my worry goes away."*
Enjoy your success, reward yourself. *"I did it. I can do it again."*

Figure 13: Exposure Progress Record

My Successes : Sarah	Date: December 16		
Goal: Ride on school bus and stay at school all day without calling Mom.			
Things I was afraid to do	**My fear temperature**		**My reward**
	On start date	**Today**	
1. Wake up, get dressed and do school work at home on regular school schedule.	2	0	Extra bedtime story
2. Get in the car, drive to school and return home.	4	0	Bake cookies with Mom
3. Stay in car in parking lot for 15 minutes.	5	1	New paints
4. Drive to the bus stop and wait for the bus, but not get in.	6	0	New set of paintbrushes
5. Ride the bus to school but return home.	6	1	Help dad clean bicycles
6. Enter building, meet teacher at door and pick up assignments to take home.	7	2	Watch my favorite video
7. Stay in Mr. Lewis's office and do schoolwork for 1 class period.	7	2	Bike ride with Mom
8. Be escorted to class by Mrs. Francis' aide and stay for one class period.	8	2	Ice cream at Jake's Cakes
9. Stay in class all morning, with one phone call to Mom.	8	2	Invite my friend Ashley
10. Stay in class all morning with no phone calls to Mom.	9	3	Sleepover with Ashley
11. Stay in class all day with no phone calls.	10	3	Trip to mall
12. Stay after school to help Mrs. Francis.	10	3	Movie
13. Stay after school, and Mom is late to pick me up.	10	4	Family dinner at restaurant

Mr. Lewis helps Sarah confront anxious thoughts as described in Figure 14.

Figure 14: Facing My Fears

	FACING MY FEARS
Name: **Sarah**	Date: **Nov 30**
Situation:	Riding the school bus.
What am I feeling?	Nervous and jittery
What's my fear temperature 1-10?	8
What am I thinking?	What if I vomit and look stupid? The kids will laugh at me.
What's the proof that it will happen?	I've vomited once before.
What are the chances it will happen?	Pretty small I guess, because I've only vomited once in two years.
So what if it happens?	Well, actually no one laughed last time. The driver helped me get to the nurse's office and change. It wasn't too bad after all.
How can I deal with it?	I'll carry a plastic bag and a change of clothes on the days I feel really queasy.
What can I say and do to help myself?	I can say, "It's no big deal, I can do it."
What's my fear temperature now?	2

Evaluate and review

During the first week, Mr. Lewis conducts a daily review of progress with the Reeds and Mrs. Francis. In the second week, they have telephone contact every alternate day or as needed. The team meets in two weeks to review Sarah's progress and to revisit the plan. In subsequent weeks, there is weekly review of Sarah's progress and the plan. Changes in Sarah's fear temperature, percentage improvement noted by the Reeds and Mrs. Francis, number of hours or days Sarah spends in school, and instances of tardiness are examined.

Sarah responds well to the intervention plan. She is less pressured and tense in response to the accommodations that are made for her, and is able to devote her energy to CBT exercises for overcoming anxiety. Sarah moves rapidly up the exposure hierarchy as she learns that her fears do not come true. Within two weeks, she is at school on time, and stays for the entire day. On some days, she asks to visit the nurse's office, but she seems to be using less frequently. She rates her maximum fear temperature as a four on most days. Sarah is back to being her bright, active self again. She looks like the weight of the world is off her shoulders. The Reeds decide to seek treatment with Dr. Greene, a child psychologist in the community who specializes in CBT for anxiety, to address broader issues of anxiety on the home front. Dr. Greene and the school team consult and collaborate to bolster the progress that Sarah has already made. The collaborative partnership between school staff, Sarah, her parents and Dr. Greene has been successful in helping Sarah "be happy" again.

EXPOSURE HIERARCHIES FOR COMMON ANXIETIES

The following are sample hierarchies for other common anxiety-related problems. The children named below are described in Chapter 2.

Figure 15: Gradual Exposure Hierarchy for Reassurance Seeking

All exposures are to be conducted without Casey apologizing.

CASEY'S FEAR LADDER Date: Dec 12	
Goal: Not ask a "worry question" or apologize more than once.	
Things I am afraid to do	**My fear temperature**
1. Wait for 2 minutes to receive an answer to a worry question	4
2. Wait for 5 minutes to receive an answer to a worry question	5
3. Mom/teacher answer the same question no more than 5 times	6
4. Mom/teacher answer the same question no more than 2 times	6
5. Mom/teacher answer the same question no more than once	7
6. Write the answer on an index card and read it to myself	7
7. Answer the question for myself without the index card	8
8. Say "stupid" out loud on purpose at home without apologizing	9
9. Say "That's rotten" out loud on purpose to my teacher	9
10. Use a paint brush to paint a picture	10
11. Dip my fingers in paint and finger paint a picture	10

Figure 16: Gradual Exposure Hierarchy for Perfectionism

EMILY'S FEAR LADDER Date: Apr 15	
Goal: Stop worrying about making mistakes in my school work.	
Things I am afraid to do	**My fear temperature**
1. Draw a doodle while the math teacher is explaining a problem	3
2. Look out the window while the teacher is giving an assignment	4
3. Have no erasers in my book bag and desk	5
4. Hand in math homework with a problem untidily crossed out	6
5. Write down an answer that I am not sure is right	6
6. Hand in an assignment with a mistake, without correcting it	7
7. Deliberately leave my homework at home	7
8. Deliberately not study half the list of spelling words	8
9. Spell two words wrong on purpose for the spelling test	9
10. Bring the wrong textbooks to school	9
11. Answer a question in class wrong on purpose	10
12. Get a B on a test and say, "Good for me!"	10

Figure 17: Gradual Exposure Hierarchy for Contamination Fears

All exposure exercises to be completed without Alex washing his hands.

ALEX'S FEAR LADDER Date: Jan 10	
Goal: To be around other kids and not worry about being touched.	
Things I am afraid to do	**My fear temperature**
1. Have a kid pass by my desk but not touch it or me	2
2. Have a kid brush my desk with his clothes as he passes by	4
3. Let my parents touch me with unwashed hands	5
4. Have the kid next to me borrow my books	6
5. Let a kid put a book into my book bag	6
6. Pat two kids on the back	8
7. Stand in the middle of the cafeteria line, not at the end	9
8. Hold hands with other kids to make a circle in gym	9
9. Shake hands with 5 kids before lunch	10
10. Eat lunch after shaking hands, without washing my hands	10

Figure 18: Gradual Exposure Hierarchy for Social Anxiety

JOSEPH'S FEAR LADDER	Date: Sept 30	
Goal: To sit with kids I don't know in the cafeteria and start a conversation.		
Things I am afraid to do		**My fear temperature**
1. Say hi to the guy who sits next to me in class		2
2. Ask him how he's doing and talk to him for 2 minutes		4
3. Ask if I can borrow a pencil		4
4. Ask two kids in my class what they did over the weekend		5
5. Tell two kids in my class about a new book I read		6
6. Walk in the middle of the cafeteria line, not at the end		7
7. Say hi to the person in front of me and behind me		8
8. Start a conversation about the food with the kid next to me		8
9. Pick up my food and sit at a table with at least 2 kids at it		9
10. Converse with the kids at the table for at least 5 minutes		9
11. Sit at a table with 5 or more kids		10
12. Say hi and introduce myself to each kid at the table		10
13. Converse with the kids at the table for at least 5 minutes		10

Chapter 14

Challenges on the Road to Recovery

There are several challenges that may present themselves to parents and schools in helping children gain mastery over anxiety. This chapter discusses some of the most common, along with suggestions for negotiating these challenges.

FINDING THE RIGHT THERAPIST

Scientific data supports CBT as a highly effective intervention for anxiety in children and adolescents (see Chapter 9). Finding an expert in CBT for anxiety is therefore paramount to a successful plan for recovery. However, there are many different approaches to therapy, and many mental health professionals do not have expertise in using CBT to treat anxiety. There is a shortage of therapists who have the training or experience to treat children or adolescents using CBT. This chapter provides guidelines for finding the right professionals to treat anxious children. Table 10 at the end of the chapter provides suggested questions for selecting a CBT therapist.

The two most important attributes to look for in a therapist are the *right expertise* and the *right clinical style*, as described below.

Expertise

Many professionals such as psychiatrists, psychologists, social workers and marriage and family counselors are licensed to provide therapy for mental health conditions. However, these professionals have different training backgrounds, and therefore have diverse skills and expertise to offer. Neither the degree they hold nor their years of experience are sufficient to make them the right therapist.

Among mental health professionals, *clinical psychologists* are most likely to have the required training and expertise in CBT for anxiety. They may have a Ph.D. (Doctor of Philosophy) degree that involves 6-7 years of graduate training in psychology, research, statistics, assessment and therapy, or a Psy.D. (Doctor of Psychology) degree that involves 4-5 years of clinically focused graduate training. Psychologists complete clinical internships that give them intensive experience in assessing and treating mental disorders. Nonetheless, being a psychologist does not guarantee expertise in CBT.

Psychiatrists are physicians and have an MD degree. After completing medical school, they complete a residency in psychiatry, during which they receive specialized clinical training in diagnosing and treating mental disorders. Some psychiatrists undergo further training to become child psychiatrists, and may take examinations to become board-certified. Psychiatrists are trained and licensed to prescribe medications. A board-certified child psychiatrist is most likely to have the right expertise in prescribing medications for anxiety. Some child psychiatrists focus their practices primarily on medication treatment, whereas others also provide psychotherapy. Some psychiatrists have training and experience in CBT.

Behavioral pediatricians are pediatricians who provide diagnosis, consultation and some treatment of children with mental health issues in addition to medical illnesses. They may prescribe psychiatric medications and be able to provide guidance on behavioral interventions. Pediatricians treat children with a wide variety of illnesses, both physical and emotional, and need to spread their expertise over a wide array of conditions. Like psychologists and psychiatrists, behavioral pediatricians may not have expertise in CBT.

Social workers have an MSW (Masters in Social Work) degree that involves 2-3 years graduate training in psychotherapy and social work. They may often have other state and national certifications such as ACSW, CSW or LICSW after their names. Their training emphasis is typically in family therapy. They are generally quite knowledgeable about navigating the social service system and accessing appropriate services. Social workers and other professionals who have master's level training such as marriage and family therapists, psychiatric nurses, and counselors are sometimes also trained to provide CBT.

Clinical style

The "bedside manner" of the therapist is important because CBT involves confronting fears, which is exactly what a child with anxiety does *not* want to do! Exposure exercises involve taking risk; risk involves trust in the therapist. The therapist should be an expert in treating children and adolescents and should have the skill to adapt CBT for a child. He or she must be able to engage the anxious child and cultivate his readiness for treatment (see Chapter 9) in a straightforward, clear, kind and firm manner. Good rapport and a trusting relationship are necessary because the child will have to work intensively with the therapist for several weeks or months. The therapist will gear the treatment to the age and maturity level of the child, and use metaphors and analogies to communicate important concepts with the child. It is as important for the therapist to involve the *parents* actively in treatment.

Good therapists convey a sense of warmth, genuine compassion and empathy, and are good listeners. They put children and parents at ease. They welcome thoughts, comments and questions, and share information readily. They appear comfortable in their knowledge and experience. They instill a sense of confidence and hope. They also engage the child with understanding, and show skill in eliciting their cooperation and motivation. Good therapists are also balanced and open in their views regarding CBT, medications, and other adjunctive supportive treatments. A therapist who is dogmatic about specific treatments may not be able to help parents make well-informed treatment decisions.

The *Suggested Questions for Selecting a Therapist* in Table 10 may help the search for the right therapist remain focused and fruitful. The questions are only guidelines to help narrow the search, and should be selected according to their relevance. The quality of the interactions that parents have with a potential therapist when they ask these questions may be an indication of the therapists' clinical style. Support organizations such as the AABT, ADAA and OCF listed at the end of this book are a good starting point for locating CBT therapists.

BARRIERS IN PARTNERSHIPS

Although working together in partnership is ideal for optimizing resources, many challenges can arise because parents, schools and clinicians often have different goals, expectations and means. There are many instances in which partnerships between schools and parents are weak or nonexistent. There are two sides to this picture: Schools who perceive parents of a given child as unwilling to cooperate, and parents who perceive school professionals as uninformed or uninvested. Barriers can also arise in partnerships between the school and community providers.

Table 10: Suggested Questions for Selecting a CBT Therapist

≈   *Suggested Questions for Selecting a Therapist*   ≈
❑ Do you use cognitive-behavioral therapy (CBT) to treat anxiety?
❑ Please explain how CBT works and what it involves.
❑ How many children have you treated successfully with CBT?
❑ What specific techniques would you use for my child's symptoms?
❑ How do you get a child ready for treatment?
❑ How long is each session and how frequent are the sessions?
❑ How long is the treatment, and what affects the length of treatment?
❑ At what point can we expect to see results?
❑ What signs do you look for to know if treatment is working?
❑ What do you suggest if no improvement is seen at that point?
❑ What is your approach to working with parents and families?
❑ Can we meet with you alone, without our child present, if needed?
❑ How do you involve parents in making treatment decisions?
❑ Will you be able to help us with day-to-day parenting issues?
❑ Are you available if we have questions or a crisis between sessions?
❑ What is your opinion about medication for children with anxiety?
❑ If you do not prescribe medications, can you refer us to a child psychiatrist with whom you would collaborate in treating our child?
❑ Would you consult or meet with my child's school staff if required?
❑ What is the cost of treatment?

Barriers between parents and schools

Parents may have many reasons to be reluctant to work with the school, even when they are caring and involved parents. They may have many misgivings about letting the school know about the child's difficulties, due to concerns about the implications. They may be afraid to have their child labeled because they do not know the immediate and long-term repercussions of the label. They do not want their child to be treated as different or "inferior," or to incur peer ridicule. Will the label and record follow their child to college and to the workplace? Parents may be struggling to decide what course of action is best for their child at the moment and in the future. Parents may also be hesitant if rapport with the teacher or other school staff is weak. They may believe that the child's teacher may not understand, be punitive or downplay their concerns. Many parents are concerned that if they inform the school of their child's difficulties, there will be an immediate push to place the child on medication. Parents may view this as schools opting for the "easy way out." Many parents are very reluctant to place their kids on medication, and don't want the school to influence their decision.

The issue of confidentiality is one that makes many parents reluctant to divulge sensitive information about their child to the school. "School" is a lot of people, most of whom the parents may not ever encounter directly. There is a great deal of variability among school staff in adherence to laws of confidentiality. What are the limits of confidentiality within the school system? What are the safeguards against information being accessible to staff who have no need to be informed? What is the guarantee that peers will not find out? Some parents and children have found out the hard way that confidentiality can sometimes be very loosely defined or loosely guarded in the vast hallways of the schools.

Partnerships that originally started out on the right foot may go sour along the way, often due to a breakdown in communication or failure to implement agreed-to accommodations or interventions. For example, parents may be disillusioned because a plan for accommodations was not put into action as agreed to by all parties, and the child was penalized. Such situations may reflect gaps and mishaps in communication within the school's internal system of communication.

Differences in viewpoint can evolve into power struggles when parents and schools lock heads about the child's needs and requisite services in school.

Parents are more educated than ever about their children's conditions and needs, and more actively involved in advocating for their children in school. They are more likely to propose their own views and to challenge the recommendations of the school if they do not see them fitting. They are less likely to just accept what they hear from school staff.

There are also many reasons why schools may sometimes be less than ideally helpful to an anxious child. Their inability to mobilize or organize to help the anxious child may not be willful. Instead, it may merely reflect lack of knowledge and understanding about anxiety. School staff may simply not understand the anxious child's needs. In addition, many schools may not have adequate resources to help children with special needs, even though the law requires that they do. Teachers may be overwhelmed trying to meet the needs of all the children in the class. Anxious children may therefore be the *children in the shadow*, taking back seat to children whose difficulties demand more immediate attention. Teachers may not have additional backup assistance when crises arise. They may be frustrated and isolated in dealing with an anxious child. Mental health professionals in schools may be overburdened. Some schools have school psychologist to student ratios of 1:2500, counselor to student ratios of 1:550 (the recommended ratio is 1:250) and social worker to student ratios much higher than the recommended 1:800.

School professionals who intend to help may sometimes get caught in administrative and political tangles regarding supply and demand of resources. A disproportionate number of special-needs children within a classroom or given school can severely tax resources because the demand exceeds the supply. There is great variability both across and within schools with regard to level of understanding, support and assistance for anxious children. Some school professionals subscribe to the philosophy that schools should attend to children's academic needs only. Others may see the child's emotional well being as inextricable from the child's academic functioning. Some staff may believe that an anxious child needs to be reassured, comforted or removed from a distressing situation, whereas others might insist that staff are being easily manipulated by the child's anxiety and needs only firm discipline. Sometimes, there may be a mismatch in styles between a teacher and child or parent. Some educators may be strict, rule-bound and less flexible in accommodating the anxious child. Others may be warm, empathic and willing to do the extra hard work of helping a child.

Schools and parents may differ in their assessment of the child's needs. Discrepancies may arise particularly in situations where children may need to be formally classified to receive necessary services. There is controversy and debate about whether anxious children are appropriately classified. Like most states in the U.S., the state of New York has two categories within which anxiety disorders may be classified: *Emotionally Disturbed* (ED) and *Other Health Impaired* (OHI). The ED label has developed a disparaging connotation, and parents cringe at having their child labeled as "disturbed." They are concerned about the label following their child through high school, college and perhaps even into the workplace. Stigmas, incorrect classification, lack of instructional relevance and exclusion of children from regular education have added to these problems.

In recent years, children with Tourette Syndrome and OCD have sometimes been classified as OHI because these disorders have been shown to have a neurobiological basis. Some parents and professionals believe that anxious children should also be classified as OHI. Those who stand by the ED label argue that exceptions can set an unsustainable precedent because every psychiatric disorder potentially has a neurobiological component; therefore, a child with any psychiatric condition could potentially be classified as OHI. There are larger political, policy and funding ramifications to these labels that are beyond the scope of this book.

Barriers with community providers

Many barriers may also be evident in the partnership with community providers. Most commonly, community providers may not recognize the potential of schools and parents to be powerful contributors and agents of change in the child's recovery. They may not know how schools operate with regard to structure, services and procedures for children with mental health needs. Community providers may make recommendations for the child to receive services in school that are not consistent with the legal guidelines or resources to which the school is bound.

A common point of contention is the definition of *Learning Disability* (LD). Community providers may label a child as "Learning Disabled" based on psychiatric criteria, and recommend that the school classify the child accordingly and provide appropriate services. The psychiatric criteria for learning disability are broad and open to interpretation as they only require the child's functioning to be "substantially below" expected levels. Parents approach the school, label in hand, requesting services for the child. The school is bound to a *different* definition of LD, which is more precise. For example, the state of New York's Special Education definitions require a child's functioning to be "50% below their expected level" to be classified as LD. Schools cannot merely follow the provider's recommendations, without doing their own assessment and classification. Parents may then perceive the school as unresponsive to their needs and rejecting of the clinician's expertise. A similar example of conflict in the partnership occurs when a community provider recommends "home tutoring" for the child without first consulting the school. There are many psychological, academic, social, financial and staffing issues that must be considered before a child is placed on home tutoring.

Another obstacle arises when community providers do not see collaboration with the school as feasible as a result of their workloads. Some providers may not initiate contact with the school because they think the school is not interested or involved in the child's mental health issues. School professionals may vary in their interest and willingness to build partnerships with community providers. Some actively initiate contact to develop partnerships whereas others may be less involved.

WORKING THROUGH THE OBSTACLES

A proactive, positive and preventive approach can preempt many obstacles from arising. Many crises can be averted when good partnerships are in place ahead of time. Schools that proactively foster a culture of partnership with parents in every area of a child's functioning will encounter fewer problems in working with parents when a child has difficulty. Schools can initiate meetings with parents before the school year begins, provide a welcoming environment, and send the message that parental involvement is valued. Parent participation increases when it is invited and promoted, rather than passively accepted. Schools may foster open dialogue and provide opportunities for parents to have decision-making roles in school issues. In an environment of collaboration, a child's problems become a shared responsibility that is addressed jointly by parents and school staff.

Teachers, who are on the front-line of teamwork with parents, may need a range of resources to facilitate optimal alliances. Schools may need to release time for teachers to meet with parents in order to build better collaborations. It's a process that takes time and needs to be started well before a crisis arises. Teachers may also need support and consultation on how to handle anxious children. Although many teachers now have training and experience in working with special-needs children due to mainstreaming, they are primarily educators, not mental health personnel. They may need specific resources such as "how-to" strategies and an aide to provide an extra pair of hands, eyes and ears. Teachers may also benefit from peer social support to relieve the sense of frustration and isolation they might experience.

Parents must also have an accurate understanding of the school's capabilities and constraints. Schools can educate parents in order to allay concerns pertaining to confidentiality and labeling. Schools must adhere strictly to laws and guidelines regarding confidentiality. A militant attitude on either side of the partnership is detrimental. Parents who are just waiting for the school to make a mistake to prove their incompetence are unlikely to be able to work with the school. It is important that parents not get overly focused on procedural errors that were accidental.

Parents who have concerns about labeling may want to learn more about the *Rights without Labels* movement (see *Educational Resources* at the end of this book). The concept of Rights Without Labels grew out of the need to remedy problems related to labeling children as "emotionally disturbed" or "handicapped." The thrust of the movement is to meet the special needs of children without labeling them or removing them from mainstream classes. Educational programs are tailored to curriculum and instructional deficits and strengths that are pertinent to the child's unique needs.

Schools and parents must be willing to take an honest look at problems on *both* sides of the fence. Parents may need to acknowledge and change parenting practices that are detrimental to the child's development. Schools may need to examine disciplinary practices, classroom atmospheres and school policies that adversely affect the child. All said and done, parents who believe that schools are not responding to their child's needs despite efforts to remedy obstacles may seek due process. information on due process may be found in the *Educational Resources* at the end of this book.

With regard to partnerships with community providers, schools and parents are encouraged to initiate contact with community providers to seek collaboration. Schools may educate community providers on special education classifications and procedures, and other relevant information when possible via brief summary sheets. It may also benefit schools to maintain a master list of community providers with whom there have been successful partnerships.

ENGAGING RELUCTANT CHILDREN

Parents, schools and clinicians may encounter situations in which children or adolescents are not ready to participate in an intervention plan. Plowing ahead with the scheduled treatment in the face of the child's reluctance will most likely result in a futile power struggle. Instead, it is time to stop, step back, and start afresh. Most children who are initially unwilling to engage in therapy will be amenable to participation if their reluctance is understood and addressed properly.

As discussed in Chapter 9, it is important to recognize that *motivation* and *readiness* are not synonymous. Many children have a desire to get well, and are therefore motivated, but may still not be *ready* to participate. Reluctance is often preempted by proper preparation for treatment which is discussed in Chapter 9.

Going through the *PACES*, as outlined below, will help clarify and reduce treatment reluctance in children and adolescents.

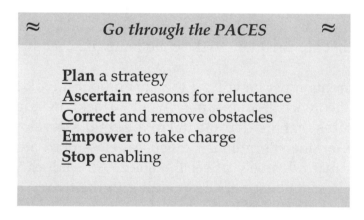

≈   **Go through the PACES**   ≈

Plan a strategy
Ascertain reasons for reluctance
Correct and remove obstacles
Empower to take charge
Stop enabling

Plan a strategy

Parents and school staff may lose patience with a hesitant child. A thoughtful, planned approach may take a little longer to execute, but will be far more effective than one that emerges in the heat of the moment. Impulsive reactions of anger, frustration, ultimatums or coercion are unlikely to charm a child into participation.

Ascertain reasons for reluctance

Reluctance to participate in treatment is generally due to misinformation, misunderstanding, and misconceptions about anxiety and its treatment. It may take considerable patience and creative inquiry to unearth the barriers to treatment. It is not uncommon for a child to say, *"I don't know, I don't care, I just don't want to,"* than to offer some clearly conceptualized and articulated answer. Others may protest, *"I don't need therapy. I can do it myself. There's nothing wrong with me."* Bravado often reflects fear, misunderstanding or embarrassment.

There are many reasons for treatment reluctance. Some children may be embarrassed and angry about being identified and being in the spotlight. Others may feel that treatment forces them to admit their worst fears and to acknowledge that they are indeed "defective." They may believe that anxiety is their destiny and that they have no control or choice in the matter. They resist the social stigma of going to "the counselor's office." Many teens and preteens may actually prefer to suffer in secrecy than to allow their peers to have any inkling that they are "crazy." Resistance in teens may be an expression of the need to assert independence. Resistance may also be a sign of a tenuous alliance between child and parent or child and school staff. If the child does not have adequate trust, she is likely to be cautious about engaging in treatment.

Strange as it may sound, some children and adolescents may even be afraid to get well and face the challenges of the world from which they have retreated. Despite the burdens of anxiety, they may find comfort in the familiarity of their lives and the fear of the unknown may overshadow the fear of the present. For some children who are accustomed to depending on adults to rescue them, anxiety may just not be bothersome or cumbersome enough to warrant the effort required in therapy.

If children have not understood how exposure and habituation work, they may be afraid that they will be forced into confronting their fears against their will and that they will not be able to survive the ensuing anxiety. For other children, there might be a sense of futility, hopelessness and helplessness about recovery. Children who are depressed or highly anxious may be overwhelmed and lack the energy, organization or focus to comprehend or accept CBT.

Finally, parents and schools must consider the messages they are conveying to the child, either consciously or inadvertently. Children can often read adults' emotions and subtle nonverbal cues. Is there clear and consistent conviction among parents and school staff about the need for and the importance of CBT? Is there hope and optimism about the outcome? Is there ambivalence and lack of confidence in the process and the players involved? Is there a weak partnership between parents and school?

Correct and eliminate the obstacles

If the reasons behind the reluctance are uncovered, the huge "unknown" becomes manageable. Misunderstandings about anxiety and CBT can be corrected with carefully constructed explanations at the child's level of comprehension. Metaphors and analogies such as the *Worry Hill* and the *Noise at the Window* (see Chapter 9) to describe CBT are understandable to most children. Feeble alliances and partnerships should be addressed and remedied. Children may also benefit from talking to other children with anxiety who have been through treatment and overcome anxiety successfully. Sometimes, children just need a little nudge or boost of confidence to get through the anticipatory anxiety.

Empower

CBT is a process of changing the way of thinking and behaving, and works best when it is an internal process. A child has to participate actively in CBT for the best results. Parents and school personnel are in charge of deciding what is best for the child, and conveying that clearly and firmly, with encouragement, hope and enthusiasm. Rather than coerce an unwilling child, it is more worthwhile to put the effort into helping the child see why and how she needs to overcome anxiety. The child must be persuaded about the *need for change*, the *possibility for change* and the *power to change*.

Provoking the child's desire to get better fosters the need for change. The child loses perspective of reality when caught up in anxiety. Instilling and cultivating the desire to be well again and to have a chance to enjoy life will enhance readiness. The child must consciously recognize and acknowledge the ways in which anxiety steals the pleasures of his life away. *"Yes, I'd rather spend 3 hours playing soccer than 3 hours washing my hands."* The child must see how life can be different without anxiety. Listing all the pros and cons of going through CBT versus remaining anxious can be helpful. *"Even if you could get 1% better, isn't that better than nothing? Why would you not want to get better?"* Giving the child as much tangible evidence as possible regarding the effectiveness of treatment allows him to see the possibility for change. A powerful way to do this is for the child to interact with other children who have been through treatment successfully (with informed consent from both sets of children and parents). Finally, the child must know that he is trusted and given the space and the time to think, and the power to make the choice. Rewards can be helpful motivators for children.

Stop enabling

If the reasons for reluctance are still unclear or if the child is still unwilling to participate, parents and school professionals will need to stop "enabling" the child's anxiety. Enabling or accommodating includes assisting the child with rituals, providing continuous reassurance, complying with demands and rules, or going out of the way to shield the child from anxiety triggers.

Some children may need to experience the full impact of their anxiety without being protected or rescued. Enabling behaviors should be withdrawn gradually, with calm, purposeful resolve. The child will begin to see how unpleasant anxiety can make his life when he is not continually rescued. The goal of this intervention is not to punish the child, but to help him realize exactly how debilitating anxiety can be. This step can be very hard on parents because the child may vociferously resist the parents' efforts to stop enabling. Parents may feel guilty about being "the meanest parent in the world," and may be beleaguered by the child's pleas and meltdowns. It is *only* when parents are firm in their commitment to help the child learn the right behaviors that the child will begin to make the effort. Buckling under pressure merely reinforces and rewards the child for his resistance. (See Chapter 11 for other effective parenting strategies).

If the child is still reluctant, referral to a community mental health professional may be an appropriate step. Even if the child won't participate, parents and other family members may attend therapy and benefit from learning how to cope with the child's anxiety and to provide support without enabling.

Meltdowns, Panic and Explosiveness

Anxious children may have "meltdowns" when they encounter fear triggers. These abrupt, intense and often unpredictable episodes of panic, distress, frustration, anger or aggression reflect a coping failure when the child is caught off guard, feels trapped, or sees no way out of a difficult situation. Some children who have meltdowns can be noncompliant, aggressive or destructive. Anxious children are usually filled with remorse after these episodes because they typically do not intend to be difficult.

Parents and other caregivers typically react in three ways, for lack of a better way to calm down the child: They either attempt to talk down the child in the midst of the meltdown, become rigid and punish the "misbehavior" or become so angry that they have a meltdown of their own. Sometimes, they do all three in sequence. Parents who have resorted to these approaches know only too well that none of them really seem to stop the meltdowns.

Why doesn't talking down work? As discussed in Chapter 11 emotion and logic are mutually exclusive. Any child or adult who is very aroused and distraught is not able to think rationally because their energy is diverted completely to handling the over-arousal. Although the intention is to try to calm down the distraught person, trying to reason with him actually has the *opposite* effect—it creates over-stimulation for the person who is already unable to cope with the level of stimulation.

Simply meting out punishment to anxious children does not do much to help either. It might alienate the child even further. Consider Alex, the child with OCD who "lost it" because he was touched by a peer in the cafeteria line. The touch triggered his fear of dying from hepatitis. No wonder he was so agitated. His belligerence was a gut reaction of protecting himself from a threat that was very real to him. Although aggressive behavior is not acceptable, merely punishing Alex with detention did not teach him a thing about how to avert similar situations in the future.

It is necessary for children to learn how to live in and participate in the rules and norms of family, school, community and society. Yet, children don't necessarily learn those lessons from punishment. In fact, many children who are punished repeatedly and severely don't seem to make any headway in learning those lessons. This does not imply that a child should be allowed to engage in misbehavior with no consequences. Consequences are necessary; however, the goal of consequences should be not merely to punish, but to help the child learn what to do differently next time.

There are two problems with traditional punishment. Typically, punishment tells the child what is *not* acceptable, but neglects to tell the child what *is* acceptable instead. We assume that because, as adults, the appropriate action is obvious to us, it is similarly evident to a child. The child is well aware that he will be punished, but he still doesn't have an alternative way of handling his frustration. When the child repeatedly does the same thing, the parent says, *"How many times have I told you not to do this?"* which implies that he is doing it willfully, knowingly and in defiance. When kids are young or immature, it takes maturity and repeated training to learn seemingly simple things. Another problem with punishment is that it is often meted out in anger and in haste. Its intent may be to make the child feel the pain of his actions or to make the punisher feel good. Often, it may be excessive and harsh, because the adult is reacting with anger, not with reason. None of these are helpful to the child. Fear of punishment leads children to become surreptitious and to lie to escape the consequences.

> *It is intuitive for adults to tell children what not to do, but to forget to tell them what they should be doing instead.*

So how should adults handle meltdowns? The most important thing to know is that once a meltdown is in progress, trying to reverse the situation is a *lost cause*. The only thing is useful in the situation is for adults to allow the meltdown to run its course while remaining calm and ensuring the safety of the child and others. Parents and teachers must do whatever is necessary to maintain safety, but otherwise not try to reason with the child. If there is no threat to safety, it is best to simply walk away until the storm has passed.

Corrective Learning Experiences

I use the term *Corrective Learning Experiences* (CLE's) to describe the process of converting a child's unacceptable behaviors into *teachable moments*. CLE's are grounded the 3 P's framework—proactive, positive and preventive—to teach children how to develop self-control and responsible behavior. The most productive way to handle a meltdown is to intervene proactively rather than reactively to prevent future meltdowns. It is best to be familiar with the concepts in Chapter 11, *What Parents Can Do to Help*, before reading this section.

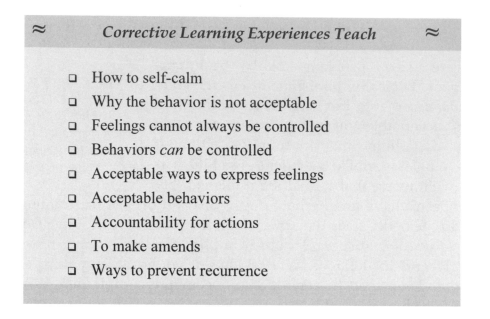

≈   ***Corrective Learning Experiences Teach***   ≈

- ❑ How to self-calm
- ❑ Why the behavior is not acceptable
- ❑ Feelings cannot always be controlled
- ❑ Behaviors *can* be controlled
- ❑ Acceptable ways to express feelings
- ❑ Acceptable behaviors
- ❑ Accountability for actions
- ❑ To make amends
- ❑ Ways to prevent recurrence

Corrective Learning Experiences involve the steps described in Table 11. The entire sequence should be carefully planned and discussed with the child before it is implemented. The child should be informed and aware of the steps ahead of time, as he will not respond favorably to surprises. The Feeling Thermometer (see Chapter 9) is used throughout the CLE process. Figure 19 illustrates the use of CLE's with Alex. (A *CLE Worksheet* is provided in *Forms and Tools* at the end of this book).

Table 11: Steps in Corrective Learning Experiences

Steps in Corrective Learning Experiences
1. Identify triggers
2. Anticipate and dissipate
3. Offer choices
4. Foster self-calming
5. Disengage
6. Reengage
7. Reduce recurrences
8. Require accountability
9. Insist on amends

1. Identify triggers

Misbehavior may occur for a host of different reasons. It is important to try and understand the basis for the behavior rather than make assumptions. "Bad" behavior is not necessarily deliberate, voluntary, or malicious in intent, even though it might appear that way. For instance, teachers assumed that Alex was belligerent and aggressive for no good reason. They did not realize or take the time to learn that Alex was petrified of contracting a fatal disease because he was touched in the cafeteria line by a peer. School personnel might have had a different response to Alex had they known that intense panic was fueling his aggression.

2. Anticipate and dissipate

The best preventive step to imminent misbehavior is to nip it in the bud. This calls for close observation and recognition of typical triggers and early cues that may precede the behavior. Common triggers that can be anticipated and removed include irritants such as hunger, fatigue, the need for down time to decompress, and time to adjust to transitions. Some common cues are becoming quiet, sullen, irritable or flustered. When early cues are evident, parents and teachers can ask the child if they are okay, if something is bothering them, and if they would like to talk about it or need some help. The child is coached in rating his level of distress on the "*Feeling Thermometer*" (see Figure 2 in Chapter 9). Unnecessary crises can also be warded off when parents are consistent and predictable in their behaviors, and prepare children for what to expect ahead of time.

Alex's teacher notices that he is irritable when he files out of the room. By asking him if he is okay, she learns that he would rather not go to the cafeteria when it is crowded. She helps avert an aggressive encounter by permitting him to walk at the end of the line. Although this intervention might appear to be fostering avoidance, it is an *accommodation* until Alex learns to manage his distress (see *Management of Anxiety* in Chapter 12).

3. Offer choices

If the child continues to show signs of escalation, it is time to speak the language of choice. Children cannot see the early warning signs of a meltdown as quickly as adults might see them. Therefore, when the adult sees the early signs, it may help defuse situation to step in and offer the child simple face-saving choices. *"You can choose to walk away and calm down or you can choose to head for a meltdown. You can choose to use words to explain why you are upset or you can scream and hit. Remember that whatever you choose will have consequences. Which one do you choose?* The child can be given the option of leaving the situation and venting in a safe place. Parents and teachers can add fuel to the fire by becoming rigid and inflexible around relatively trivial issues. Power struggles, arguments and negotiation should be avoided when the child is upset.

4. Foster self-calming

Anxious children often depend on adults to help them calm down when distraught or overwhelmed. A CLE approach shifts this responsibility back on the child, and teaches self-reliance in calming. The first step in self-calming is to remove oneself from the situation in order to reduce over-stimulation and regain self-control. Parents teach the distraught child to *take space* in a designated quiet place away from the distressing context. Safe spaces may include the child's room, the counselor's office or a carrel in the classroom or hallway where the child can be alone until he calms down. Taking space allows the intensity of the child's emotions to abate without any further irritation from the environment. The child is offered deep breathing or other calming activities such as music or physical exertion to hasten the process of calming down. Over time, the child is encouraged to initiate taking space on his own. When the child seeks taking space on his own, he begins to take control of terminating his own escalation. Gradually, he learns to recognize early warning cues and to avert them before they accelerate into a crisis. The child is rewarded for efforts to self-calm.

5. Timely disengagement

If the child does not move into a self-calming mode, parents need to recognize the "point of no return" at which to disengage from interaction with the upset child. As discussed earlier, it is futile to reason with an overly distraught child. Trying to placate or persuade an over aroused child only adds fuel to the fire. Even if the same issue has been discussed with the child several times, he will not necessarily remember how to handle it when he's upset. Parents may also become frustrated when their child is unresponsive and unreceptive to reason. Unproductive "dead-end" interactions can be terminated by calmly exiting the situation, saying, *"We will talk when you are calm. We can't help you until you calm down."* A *"Feeling Temperature"* of 7 or 8 is usually a good indicator for timely disengagement. At this point, parents may need to self-calm as much as the child. They can leave the room and take space in the same way as the child.

6. Timely reengagement

When the storm has passed, it is critical to get back to business and reengage the child in a review of the upsetting situation. Parent and child need to understand and identify feelings and triggers in the situation. The *Feeling Thermometer* is again a very handy tool to help the child quantify the severity of his emotions and of the triggers. The parent validates the child's feelings but helps the child understand why the behavior was not acceptable. The child also learns that whereas feelings cannot always be held back, actions can be controlled. Regardless of the reasons behind the behavior, the child must learn to channel emotions in an acceptable way. Parent and child review what could have been done differently and evaluate the potential effectiveness of alternative solutions. In Alex's case, parents and teachers help him problem-solve alternatives to hitting his peer when upset. Alternatives may include informing the teachers of triggers ahead of time, making arrangements to exit the situation after giving an established signal, or having Alex be last in the cafeteria line, so that he is not touched by a peer.

7. Reduce recurrences

Triggers and disappointments will always abound and cannot and should not be eliminated altogether. Children must learn ways to cope with this reality. Parents and child join together to brainstorm ways to prevent future recurrences. An "EWS" or *early warning system* is one example of a preventive measure. The child and parent (or teacher) agree on cue words or phrases to signal the need for an exit from the situation. The *Feeling Thermometer* may be used to identify a number that warns of an impending meltdown. *"I'm a 5, don't talk to me now, I need to be alone."* Young children can use pictures of different feelings that they might have drawn earlier, when they were calm. Colors may also be used as signals. Red represents *"Stop, leave me alone,"* yellow means *"Slow down,"* and green reflects, *"I could use your help."* Alex can pull a red card out of his pocket instead of having to verbally communicate with the teacher. The teacher knows the red card means that Alex is upset and needs to leave. It is also helpful for children and parents or school staff to proactively make a list of known triggers, and brainstorm ways to handle them. Other potential options are to leave the scene, take deep breaths or count to 10 before responding.

8. Require accountability

Children, like the rest of us, need to learn to be accountable and responsible for their actions. They need to accept and acknowledge the impact of their behaviors. Some situations result in natural consequences, which are the obvious outcome of their actions. For instance, if Alex was having a meltdown at the same time that he should have been on his way to the gym, he endures the natural consequence of missing gym class. Parents can also impose logical consequences. If Casey destroys his toys in anger, the "*Abuse it, lose it*" principle applies. The toys are not replaced. When Alex kicks a hole in the door, he pays for the repairs out of his allowance. With older children and adolescents, curfews or the removal of privileges such as use of the computer or car are usually effective. The penalty should be proportionate to the magnitude of the misbehavior. Consequences are more effective if parents *say it, mean it and do it*. Empty threats undermine parental credibility.

> *Abuse it, lose it*

9. Insist on amends

The child must make restitution for damage done, apologize, recognize how his behavior might have offended or hurt someone, and make reparation for his behavior. Alex must seek out and apologize to the peer he hit. When a child destroys something, he needs to clean up the mess or repair the damage in some appropriate fashion or make up in some other way for inconvenience done. The child is rewarded for going through the CLE process with praise and recognition.

Parents and teachers who handle frequent or intense meltdowns and explosiveness in children are referred to an excellent book entitled *The Explosive Child* by psychologist Ross Greene. Dr. Greene presents a sensitive, insightful and practical method for working effectively with children who are frequently explosive.

Figure 19: Corrective Learning Experiences Worksheet

Child's Name: **Alex**   Parent/Teacher: **Mr. Logan**   Date: **Alex**

SITUATION: Commotion in cafeteria line; Ryan jostled Alex.

CHILD'S BEHAVIOR: Alex punched Ryan, swore at staff who intervened.

1. **TRIGGERS** Crowded hallway, heat, provoked fear of contracting hepatitis.

2. **ANTICIPATE/DISSIPATE**
    Early cues: Alex was mildly irritable in the line. No other signs observed.
    Strategies: Ask Alex if he's okay. Be vigilant for other signs of distress.

3. **CHOICES:** Take control, use words.

4. **SELF-CALMING**   **Feeling temperature: 6**
    Cues for need to self-calm: Irritable, raised voice, fidgety
    Take space: Leave the room and take space in hallway or library.

5. **TIMELY DISENGAGEMENT**   **Feeling temperature: 8**
    Cues: Agitated, not listening, argumentative, defiant.
    How: Stop talking, arguing or reasoning. Leave scene, ask Alex to take space.

6. **TIMELY REENGAGEMENT Discuss:**
    ❖ **What happened?** Alex hit a peer.   **Why?** Didn't like being touched.
    ❖ **What feelings?** Fear and anger.   **Feeling temperature?** 10
    ❖ **Were feelings okay?** Yes.   **Were actions okay?** No.
    ❖ **If not, why not?** Peer was unaware he was provoking; aggression is not acceptable.
    ❖ **How could feelings be expressed appropriately?** Verbalize, tell peer.
    ❖ **How could actions be different?** Walk away, find another spot, ask staff permission to come back later.
    ❖

7. **WAYS TO REDUCE RECURRENCE**
    Early warning signals: Restless, Fear temperature of 6.
    Trigger: Touch   **Solution:** Keep distance. Alex last in line.

8. **ACCOUNTABILITY:** Peer injured, chaos in cafeteria, rudeness to staff.

9. **WAYS TO MAKE AMENDS:** Apologize to peer and staff.

Chapter 15

Strategies at a Glance

This chapter provides a library of strategies for parents, school professionals and clinicians to use to help children cope with a variety of anxiety-related behaviors. These strategies are grounded in the 3 P's of parenting, and are proactive, positive and preventive by design. It is necessary to have read all the preceding chapters in this book before reading or utilizing the strategies listed here. Strategies for a given child are selected as relevant to the child's unique circumstances and needs.

≈   *Skills for Overcoming Anxiety*   ≈

- ❏ Identify and label fears, worries and anxieties
- ❏ Recognize body changes indicative of anxiety
- ❏ Recognize and label thoughts that accompany anxiety
- ❏ Link thoughts, feelings and physical symptoms
- ❏ Identify specific triggers for anxiety
- ❏ Build readiness to overcome anxiety
- ❏ Develop realistic self-talk
- ❏ Acquire and use relaxation skills
- ❏ Confront fears via gradual exposure
- ❏ Expand repertoire of problem-solving skills
- ❏ Build confidence, optimism and self-esteem
- ❏ Utilize appropriate social skills and assertiveness
- ❏ Develop independence and self-reliance

NORMAL STRESS AND ANXIETY

There are many day-to-day situations, tasks and demands that provoke anxiety (see Chapter 3). Novel, unfamiliar or performance-oriented situations such as meeting new children, going to camp or playing in a soccer match commonly arouse apprehension or fear in children. In general, intuitive and common sense approaches are effective for managing normal levels or expressions of anxiety. In most cases, no undue intervention beyond the following suggestions is necessary.

- Normalize the experience. Let the child know that he is not alone and that other children and adults have similar experiences.
- Provide reasonable reassurance and comfort.
- Dispel myths and misconceptions about the feared situation.
- Reduce "over-scheduling" for child and family.
- Explain anticipatory anxiety—"You worry about it more <u>before</u> it happens and less once it actually happens."
- Explain that anxiety will decrease with time and familiarity.
- Use the *Feeling Thermometer* as an index of intensity and change in emotions.
- Set a positive example; role model the behavior the child is expected to learn.
- Make *You and Me Alone* (YAMA) time (see Chapter 11).
- Provide accurate information to remove uncertainty and "unknowns."
- Encourage the child to prepare for the situation, e.g., practice the speech, role-play conversing with a peer, or rehearse the moves in the game.
- Normalize mistakes and imperfections.
- Coach how to respond to mistakes. *"The show must go on."*
- Help the child recall past instances of anxiety he has successfully overcome.
- Coach the child in coping self-talk. Instill optimism, hope and confidence about overcoming anxiety. *"I've done it before, I can do it again."*
- Provide opportunities for repetition of the feared task to increase familiarity.

BACK TO SCHOOL ANXIETY

The prospect of returning to school after a long hiatus is both exciting and anxiety provoking for children. "Back-to-school anxiety" is a universal and ubiquitous experience that can range in severity from "butterflies in the tummy" to panic. Separation fears may resurface for some children. Most children overcome this form of anxiety with reassurance, repetition and familiarity.

How parents can help:

- ❑ Normalize the experience. Let the child know that he is not alone and that other children and adults have similar experiences.
- ❑ Provide reasonable reassurance and nurturing.
- ❑ Remove uncertainty—describe the specifics of what to expect at school.
- ❑ Explain anticipatory anxiety—"You worry about it more <u>before</u> it happens and less once it actually happens."
- ❑ Use the *Feeling Thermometer* as an index of intensity and change in emotions.
- ❑ Explain that anxiety decreases with time and familiarity; each day gets easier.
- ❑ If possible, visit the school, classroom or teacher in advance.
- ❑ Dispel misconceptions about the school, teacher or peers; provide facts.
- ❑ Resume routine of bedtimes, wake up and mealtimes that are consistent with the school routine gradually about two weeks before school starts.
- ❑ Allow the child to take an appropriate "transitional object" such as a small and unobtrusive soft toy to school for comfort, familiarity and security.
- ❑ Use role-play to prepare the child for school-related activities such as riding the school bus, entering the school, finding the locker, greeting teachers and peers.
- ❑ Discuss the positive aspects of school, e.g., seeing friends again, being in band.
- ❑ Set a positive example; role model the behavior the child is expected to learn.

How teachers can help:

- ❑ Provide parents with strategies for preparing the child to return to school.
- ❑ Provide a warm and inviting classroom environment.
- ❑ Have an organized and predictable routine.
- ❑ Allow the child to arrive early to have time to adapt/separate from the parent.
- ❑ Plan for easy, interesting "warm-up" activities to start the day.
- ❑ Prepare the child in advance for what to expect; remove surprises and unknowns.
- ❑ Use the *Feeling Thermometer* as an index of intensity and change in emotions.
- ❑ Designate area in the classroom for *taking space* or quiet time.

- Alternate between energetic and quiet activities, to reduce over- or under-stimulation.
- Define clear areas of the classroom for different types of activities.
- Make classroom arrangements simple for smooth transitions.
- Ease transitions by giving advance notice, explaining the purpose and process of the transition, and describing what is involved in the next activity.
- Provide easy access to incentives, rewards and other positives in the classroom.
- Provide a modified schedule if necessary.
- Encourage inclusive group activities.
- Eliminate pressure-inducing demands and expectations from the classroom.
- Foster acceptance and tolerance; prevent teasing.
- Set a positive example; role model the behavior the child is expected to learn.

COPING WITH TRAUMA, TRAGEDY, WAR AND VIOLENCE

There have been many tragic and traumatic events pertaining to violence, terrorism and war in recent years. Many adults have been deeply troubled by these events and have had difficulty understanding and coping with them. Children are less able, as a rule, to make sense of violent events and to cope with them, than are adults. It is important to keep in mind that reactions to trauma are a *process*, not an event, and may manifest in different ways over time. Parents and school personnel can help children cope in the following ways:

What to Do:

- Stay calm and collected. The child will be looking to you for safety signals.
- Take time to deal with your own reactions; seek support and comfort if needed.
- Ask the child to tell you what he knows of the events; use the child's understanding to steer your response.
- Encourage questions and discussion; let the child's questions be your guide to the content of the conversation.
- Answer questions honestly and accurately; limit answers to necessary details.
- Draw on spiritual or religious beliefs and practices if applicable.
- Speak to the child in terms and language that he understands at his level. Use metaphors and analogies. Young children may benefit from play or drawings.

- Acknowledge and accept the child's fears; let him know that it is normal and natural to feel upset, worried or angry.
- Share your own reactions (within reason), to normalize the child's experience, but not to overburden him.
- Reassure the child that he is safe and protected. Older children and teenagers may benefit from knowing all the measures being taken to ensure their safety, whereas young children merely need to know that they are safe.
- Give children as many valid reasons as possible about why they are unlikely targets, but acknowledge, if necessary, that sometimes, bad things do happen. Some children push for guarantees about safety, and may need to know that absolute safety can neither be predicted nor guaranteed.
- Be physically and emotionally available to provide comfort as needed.
- Make extra *YAMA* time in the mornings, evenings and at bedtime, to allow opportunities for the child to express feelings and ask questions.
- Help the child distinguish between real and imagined fears.
- Teach the child how to communicate distress and to ask for help as needed.
- Use the *Feeling Thermometer* as an index of intensity and change in emotions.
- Limit exposure to graphic replays of the events; turn off the TV if necessary.
- Watch television with the child, to monitor exposure and respond to concerns.
- Avoid detailed adult discussions of the events in front of the child.
- Dispel misinformation and misconceptions; learn and share the facts.
- Model the behavior the child is expected to learn. Be aware of your own feelings and channel them appropriately.
- Teach the child that anger and conflicts are best resolved with words rather than physically or by "lashing out" inappropriately.
- Get "back to business;" resume normal family and school routines quickly.
- Spend time doing enjoyable things with the child; provide distracting activities.
- Maintain regular bedtime schedules, but provide extra comfort if needed such as a nightlight, special toys or sitting with the child until he falls asleep.
- Express faith, hope and optimism about returning to normalcy.
- Help the child (if old enough and so inclined) to show caring and empathy for victims—to donate clothes or toys, collect money, write letters, attend a prayer service or organize a relief effort. Such actions lessen feelings of helplessness.

- ❑ Give the child opportunities to come up with ideas about how to cope or to help the victims. The child's ideas may be very practical and creative.
- ❑ Remember that any behavior is worsened by stress. If the child is prone to anxiety, expect her to be more nervous, tearful and clingy, on edge, distractible, regressed and to have nightmares, (especially if she has seen graphic details).
- ❑ Be vigilant and anticipate signs of excessive or disproportionate distress.
- ❑ If fears or distress are severe, continue for over a month, or start to generalize, seek help from a mental health professional.

What *not* to do:

- ❑ Assume that there is one orderly or predictable way for the child to cope with trauma.
- ❑ Rush the child to "get over" the events; every child responds differently. Allow the child to take his time to figure things out.
- ❑ Volunteer information if the child does not seem to know about the events; instead, remain vigilant for signs of worry or distress.
- ❑ Overload the child with information. Let the child's questions steer the conversation.
- ❑ Discuss worst-case scenarios.
- ❑ Misrepresent, distort or be dishonest about the facts.
- ❑ Burden the child with your feelings. The child may be overwhelmed, interpret your reactions as reason to fear, and feel responsible for taking care of you.
- ❑ Push teenagers or older children to discuss the events. Respect their wishes if they choose not to do so. Let them know you will be available if they need you.
- ❑ Suppress teenage humor as a way of coping, but channel it appropriately.
- ❑ Speculate about perpetrators or motives. Be honest when facts are few.
- ❑ Perpetuate or allow stereotyping of people from different subgroups, cultures or countries; the child may easily generalize these beliefs.
- ❑ Express or condone hatred or inappropriate anger. The child may find it difficult to sort through and manage intense emotions.
- ❑ Allow or condone physical expressions of anger.

SEPARATION ANXIETY

- ❑ Remain calm, matter of fact and firm during routine separations.
- ❑ Limit reassurance to one or two times.
- ❑ Don't hover, question or reassure excessively.
- ❑ Use the *Feeling Thermometer* as an index of intensity and change in emotions.
- ❑ Use the *Parent-Teacher Log* to communicate between home and school.
- ❑ Allow a transitional object for comfort until the child masters anxiety.
- ❑ Limit check-in visits or phone calls when the child is in school.
- ❑ Limit the child's ability to leave school and return home.
- ❑ Use the *Worry Hill* metaphor to explain exposure, habituation and anticipatory anxiety.
- ❑ Remove inadvertent bonuses of staying home or returning home from school.
- ❑ Teach realistic estimation of probabilities of bad outcomes.
- ❑ Teach calming self-talk and behaviors such as taking space when upset.
- ❑ Teach relaxation skills.
- ❑ Begin exposure exercises starting with a few minutes of separation and increasing it in steady increments (see Figure 11).
- ❑ Provide a *Worry Hill Memory Card* for easy recall and practice of exposures.
- ❑ For the child who has been out of school, plan gradual re-entry.
- ❑ Seek opportunities to separate from the child for increasing lengths of time.
- ❑ Create opportunities for repetition and practice.
- ❑ Encourage independent activities and self-reliance.
- ❑ Reward independence and initiative.
- ❑ Set a positive example; role model the behavior the child is expected to learn.
- ❑ Make *You and Me Alone* (YAMA) time to increase positive interactions.
- ❑ Praise any efforts in the direction of separation.
- ❑ Use tangible rewards for any effort in the right direction.
- ❑ Be consistent in the child management approach at home and at school.

SCHOOL REFUSAL/TARDINESS

Homebound instruction should *not* be considered the first choice accommodation for the child who refuses school. Rather, it should be considered as an intervention of last resort, and as a means to an end rather than an end in itself. Plans for homebound instruction should include steps to ensure a gradual return to the school or an alternative environment, and should have a time frame for implementation.

❑ Determine the root cause for school refusal. Don't make assumptions.

❑ Address and remedy legitimate concerns, if possible.

❑ Keep the child in school for as long as possible; avoid sending him home.

❑ Encourage the child to talk to the school psychologist or counselor.

❑ Avoid lengthy arguments or explanations about the necessity of school.

❑ Use the *Parent-Teacher Log* to communicate between home and school.

❑ Be consistent in the child management approach at home and at school.

❑ Remove inadvertent bonuses of staying home such as TV, sleeping or playing.

❑ If the child stays home, simulate school environment at home as closely as possible (follow school schedule, bring work home, sit at desk).

❑ Use the *Worry Hill* metaphor to explain exposure, habituation and anticipatory anxiety.

❑ Use the *Feeling Thermometer* as an index of intensity and change in emotions.

❑ Begin exposure with driving to school, entering in low anxiety area or staying for a short while. Increase time to one class, half day, and eventually full day (Figure 11).

❑ Provide a *Worry Hill Memory Card* for easy recall and practice of exposures.

❑ Develop a signal system to communicate when the child needs to take space.

❑ Designate a place to "take space" periodically or as needed.

❑ Convey confidence, hope and optimism about recovery.

❑ Rehearse and role-play appropriate behaviors.

❑ Set a positive example; role model the behavior the child is expected to learn.

❑ Minimize attention to negative behaviors, maximize to desirable behaviors.

❑ Reward efforts towards attendance and being on time.

REASSURANCE SEEKING

❑ Don't dismiss or belittle the child's questions, e.g., *"That's silly, stop it."*

❑ Don't stop reassurance abruptly or completely.

❑ Make *You and Me Alone* (YAMA) time to increase positive interactions.

- ❏ Use the *Parent-Teacher Log* to communicate between home and school.
- ❏ Be consistent in the child management approach at home and at school.
- ❏ Plan a gradual reduction in the number of reassurances.
- ❏ Prepare the child for the change in intervention; elicit willingness and participation.
- ❏ Use the *Feeling Thermometer* as an index of intensity and change in emotions.
- ❏ Dispel myths and misconceptions about the situation; provide accurate facts.
- ❏ Explain anticipatory anxiety—"The feeling will pass."
- ❏ Use the *Worry Hill* metaphor to explain exposure and habituation.
- ❏ Redirect the child, "Who's asking, you or your anxiety?"
- ❏ Set limits on questions by giving "coupons" that can be redeemed for answers.
- ❏ Remain kind but firm, *"One answer is good enough."*
- ❏ Write the answer on an index card for the child to reference, instead of asking.
- ❏ Encourage the child to answer his questions for himself.
- ❏ Provide a *Worry Hill Memory Card* for easy recall and practice of exposures.
- ❏ Refrain from giving unlimited reassurance, *"We'll have to see what happens."*
- ❏ Build self-reliance.
- ❏ Teach realistic estimation of probabilities of bad outcomes.
- ❏ Teach calming self-talk and behaviors such as taking space when upset.
- ❏ Teach relaxation skills.
- ❏ Provide Corrective Learning Experiences (see Chapter 14).
- ❏ Set a positive example; role model the behavior the child is expected to learn.
- ❏ Reward the child for refraining from questions or answering them himself.

PERFECTIONISM

- ❏ Normalize and model imperfection—"It's good enough. Mistakes are okay."
- ❏ Help the child re-label the thoughts, *"Is this me or is this my anxiety?"*
- ❏ Use the *Parent-Teacher Log* to communicate between home and school.
- ❏ Be consistent in the child management approach at home and at school.
- ❏ Set limits on checking, erasures and revisions by giving fixed number of coupons.
- ❏ Set time limits for completion of assignments.
- ❏ Use the *Feeling Thermometer* as an index of intensity and change in emotions.

- ❑ Teach self-calming and taking space.
- ❑ Teach relaxation skills.
- ❑ Teach estimation of realistic probabilities of bad outcomes.
- ❑ Teach the child to examine worst consequences of imperfection.
- ❑ Teach the child to examine evidence for worst fears.
- ❑ Generate exposure exercises that involve making mistakes deliberately or having less-than-perfect work on purpose, e.g., being late to class, handing in work with obvious errors (see Figure 16).
- ❑ Teach coping skills to manage feared consequences.
- ❑ Provide a *Worry Hill Memory Card* for easy recall and practice of exposures.
- ❑ Set a positive example; role model the behavior the child is expected to learn.
- ❑ Reward efforts at imperfection.
- ❑ Schedule planned relaxing activities with no goal to be achieved other than fun.

OBSESSIONS AND COMPULSIONS

Washing rituals, frequent visits to the bathroom, touching, tapping, rearranging, and fears of being touched may be expressions of various obsessions and compulsions.

Accommodations:

- ❑ Allow the child to arrive 15 minutes late or leave early, or be last in line in the cafeteria (contamination fears).
- ❑ Allow easy and discreet exit from a triggering situation.
- ❑ Reduce expectations that add pressure.

Interventions:

- ❑ Use the *Feeling Thermometer* as an index of intensity and change in emotions.
- ❑ Use the *Parent-Teacher Log* to communicate between home and school.
- ❑ Be consistent in the child management approach at home and at school.
- ❑ Use the *Worry Hill* metaphor to explain exposure, habituation and anticipatory anxiety.
- ❑ Identify triggers for obsessions and rituals.

- ☐ Begin gradual exposure to fears (see Figure 17).
- ☐ Provide a *Worry Hill Memory Card* for easy recall and practice of exposures.
- ☐ Provide specific guidelines regarding when it's okay to wash, e.g., after using bathroom and before eating.
- ☐ Limit trips to the bathroom with prearranged bathroom times.
- ☐ Gradually reduce frequency and length of trips to the bathroom.
- ☐ Set a positive example; role model the behavior the child is expected to learn.
- ☐ Make *You and Me Alone* (YAMA) time to increase positive interactions.
- ☐ Reward effort; don't punish failure.

WRITING AND READING DIFFICULTIES

Accommodations:

- ☐ Allow oral work, tape-recording, books-on-tape or use of the computer.
- ☐ Provide teacher outlines and shorter assignments.
- ☐ Allow printing if cursive is difficult.
- ☐ Allow a peer to be a "helping buddy," providing notes and extra help.
- ☐ Grade on effort or content rather than appearance.
- ☐ Allow multiple-choice format for tests, rather than essay format.
- ☐ Make a copy of the assignment so that the child can cross out text to prevent re-reading.

Interventions:

- ☐ Identify triggers or reasons for reading/writing difficulties.
- ☐ Use the *Feeling Thermometer* as an index of intensity and change in emotions.
- ☐ Begin gradual exposure to thoughts and fears that trigger writing/reading problems.
- ☐ Make *You and Me Alone* (YAMA) time to increase positive interactions.
- ☐ Reward for effort; don't punish failure.
- ☐ Use the *Parent-Teacher Log* to communicate between home and school.
- ☐ Be consistent in the child management approach at home and at school.
- ☐ Foster self-reliance and independence.

INABILITY TO COMPLETE ASSIGNMENTS AND HOMEWORK

Accommodations:

- ❑ Give additional time to complete the work.
- ❑ Assign shorter assignments.
- ❑ Insist that the child has an assignment book.
- ❑ Carefully structure assignment and homework time.
- ❑ Reduce the homework load.
- ❑ Do not send incomplete assignments home for completion.
- ❑ Limit open-ended choices.
- ❑ Allow the child to complete every other problem.
- ❑ Break work into small segments.
- ❑ Allow breaks to take space.
- ❑ Grade and reward for effort, don't penalize for failure.

Interventions:

- ❑ Identify reasons for difficulties.
- ❑ Use the *Feeling Thermometer* as an index of intensity and change in emotions.
- ❑ Generate exposures to triggers.
- ❑ Use the *Parent-Teacher Log* daily to communicate between home and school.
- ❑ Be consistent in the child management approach at home and at school.
- ❑ Avoid power struggles.
- ❑ Make *You and Me Alone* (YAMA) time to increase positive interactions.

SOCIAL ANXIETY/EXCESSIVE SHYNESS

- ❑ Encourage accurate perceptions of self; make positive self-statements daily.
- ❑ Use the *Feeling Thermometer* as an index of intensity and change in emotions.
- ❑ Teach relaxation skills.
- ❑ Model appropriate social skills.
- ❑ Provide social skills training and practice in introducing, conversing, making friends, speaking in class, etc.

❑ Increase participation in daily social and academic activities.

❑ Provide gradual exposure to social situations (see Figure 18).

❑ Explain anticipatory anxiety—"You worry about it more <u>before</u> it happens and less once it actually happens."

❑ Provide the *Worry Hill Memory Card* for easy recall and practice of exposures.

❑ Provide structured social activities; assist initiation of social interactions.

❑ Increase coping behaviors for dealing with potential rejection.

❑ Make *You and Me Alone* (YAMA) time to increase positive interactions.

❑ Give hope and boost confidence.

❑ Use the *Parent-Teacher Log* to communicate between home and school

❑ Be consistent in the child management approach at home and at school.

❑ Reward efforts to initiate social interaction.

❑ Give peers incentives to increase social interactions with the anxious child.

❑ Foster self-reliance and encourage independent activities.

PANIC

❑ Teach proper labels for panic and anxiety.

❑ Teach the child to distinguish between normal anxiety and panic.

❑ Use the *Feeling Thermometer* as an index of intensity and change in emotions.

❑ Use the *Parent-Teacher Log* to communicate between home and school.

❑ Be consistent in the child management approach at home and at school.

❑ Provide a safe place to take space and calm down.

❑ Teach the child to breathe into paper bag to stop hyperventilation.

❑ Develop a signal system to communicate an impending panic attack.

❑ Place the child's desk near door for easy and discreet exit.

❑ Provide reasonable reassurance.

❑ Provide *Corrective Learning Experiences* (CLE's) for meltdowns.

❑ Be kind but firm in setting limits.

❑ Teach relaxation skills.

❑ Teach calming self-talk.

❑ Generate gradual exposure exercises.

❑ Provide the *Worry Hill Memory Card* for easy recall and practice of exposures.

❑ Make *You and Me Alone* (YAMA) time to increase positive interactions.

❑ Set a positive example; role model the behavior the child is expected to learn.

❑ Reward efforts at self-calming.

DIFFICULTY SHIFTING GEARS

❑ Try to understand reasons for the child's behavior.

❑ Accept the child's limitations in flexibility.

❑ Be proactive—plan, anticipate and ease transitions with the "five-minute warning."

❑ Provide early warning of impending transition.

❑ Provide extra time, visual and concrete cues to aid in transitions.

❑ Keep the routine predictable; avoid abrupt changes.

❑ Use the *Feeling Thermometer* as an index of intensity and change in emotions.

❑ Give the child face-saving choices if he is upset.

❑ Make *You and Me Alone* (YAMA) time to increase positive interactions.

❑ Set a positive example; role model the behavior the child is expected to learn.

❑ Reward successful transitions.

❑ Use the *Parent-Teacher Log* to communicate between home and school.

❑ Be consistent in the child management approach at home and at school.

REFUSAL TO SPEAK IN SCHOOL

❑ Use the *Parent-Teacher Log* to communicate between home and school.

❑ Be consistent in the child management approach at home and at school.

❑ Provide gentle and consistent encouragement, support and reassurance.

❑ Praise any effort toward verbal or nonverbal communications.

❑ Provide praise discreetly to avoid embarrassment of being in the limelight.

❑ Use the *Feeling Thermometer* as an index of intensity and change in emotions.

❑ Avoid power struggles around speaking.

❑ Do not pressure, demand, force or trick the child into speaking.

❑ Do not punish or shame the child for not speaking.

❑ Make *You and Me Alone* (YAMA) time to increase positive interactions.

❑ Set a positive example; role model the behavior the child is expected to learn.

PERFORMANCE/TEST ANXIETY

Accommodations:

- ❑ Allow additional time to reduce pressure.
- ❑ Allow untimed tests or shorter tasks to reduce pressure.
- ❑ Allow a different location, breaks or oral tests.
- ❑ Permit writing on the test booklet or checking off answers.
- ❑ Allow ungraded assignments.
- ❑ Focus on correct answers, not errors.

Interventions:

- ❑ Teach proper study habits and skills; replace poor habits.
- ❑ Focus on learning *well*, not on grades and testing.
- ❑ Focus on effort, not outcome.
- ❑ Normalize anxiety about tests and performance.
- ❑ Use the *Feeling Thermometer* as an index of intensity and change in emotions.
- ❑ Teach effective time management skills.
- ❑ Teach effective test-taking strategies.
- ❑ Answer easiest questions first to build success.
- ❑ Review the test before beginning to answer.
- ❑ Discuss realistic probabilities of bad outcomes
- ❑ Explore worst consequences of poor outcomes.
- ❑ Foster acceptance of uncertainty about outcomes.
- ❑ Don't give unrealistic reassurances.
- ❑ Put tests and scores in perspective; normalize imperfection and mistakes.
- ❑ Teach child to recognize and replace anxious self-talk with calming self-talk.
- ❑ Set a positive example; role model the behavior the child is expected to learn.
- ❑ Make *You and Me Alone* (YAMA) time to increase positive interactions.
- ❑ Use the *Worry Hill* to explain exposure, habituation and anticipatory anxiety.
- ❑ Provide a *Worry Hill Memory Card* for easy recall and practice of exposures.
- ❑ Use the *Parent-Teacher Log* to communicate between home and school.
- ❑ Be consistent in the child management approach at home and at school.

TICS

- ❑ Don't ask the child to stop tics.
- ❑ Don't punish or shame the child for uncontrollable behaviors.
- ❑ Ignore and downplay minor tics and misbehaviors.
- ❑ Divert peer attention away from the child's tics.
- ❑ Allow a discrete exit to allow the child to go to another space until tics subside.
- ❑ Place the child's desk near the door for an easy exit when tics are severe.
- ❑ Educate peers to increase sensitivity and acceptance.
- ❑ Excuse the child from routine expectations when tics are severe.
- ❑ Use the *Parent-Teacher Log* to communicate between home and school.
- ❑ Be consistent in the child management approach at home and at school.
- ❑ Make *You and Me Alone* (YAMA) time to increase positive interactions.

MELTDOWNS AND EXPLOSIVENESS

- ❑ Don't try to reason with a child in the midst of a meltdown.
- ❑ Be proactive in preventing future meltdowns.
- ❑ Use the *Parent-Teacher Log* to communicate between home and school.
- ❑ Be consistent in the child management approach at home and at school.
- ❑ Provide Corrective Learning Experiences (CLE's).
- ❑ Anticipate and intervene early; use early warning cues to communicate.
- ❑ Use the *Feeling Thermometer* as an index of intensity and change in emotions.
- ❑ Give the child face-saving choices.
- ❑ Recognize the point of no return.
- ❑ Provide a safe place to take space when the child is upset.
- ❑ Refocus peers to reduce disruption to the class.
- ❑ Don't argue and debate; pick battles and avoid power struggles.
- ❑ Allow a graceful exit, rather than escalation.
- ❑ After the child has calmed, require that he make amends for damage done.
- ❑ Set a positive example; role model the behavior the child is expected to learn.

References

Achenbach, T.M. (1991a). *Child Behavior Checklist.* Burlington, VT: University of Vermont.

Achenbach, T.M. (1991b). *Child Behavior Checklist: Teacher Report Form.* Burlington, VT: University of Vermont.

Achenbach, T.M. (1991c). *Youth Self-Report.* Burlington, VT: University of Vermont.

Barrett, P.M., Dadds, M.R., & Rapee, R.M. (1996). Family treatment of childhood anxiety. *Journal of Consulting and Clinical Psychology, 64,* 333-342.

Beidel, D.C., Turner, S.M., & Morris, T.L. (1995). A new inventory to assess childhood social anxiety and phobia: The social phobia and anxiety inventory for children. *Psychological Assessment, 7,* 73-79.

Berg, C.Z., Whitaker, A., Davies, M., Flament, M.F., & Rapoport, J.L. (1988). The survey form of the Leyton Obsessional Inventory--Child Version: Norms from an epidemiological study. *Journal of the American Academy of Child and Adolescent Psychiatry, 27* (6), 759-763.

Birmaher, B.S., Khetarpal, S., Brent, D., Cully, M., Balach, J., Kaufman, J., & McKenzie-Neer, S. (1997). The screen for child-anxiety-related emotional disorders (SCARED): Scale construction and psychometric characteristics. *Journal of the American Academy of Child and Adolescent Psychiatry, 36,* 545-553.

Conference on Treating Anxiety Disorders in Youth: Current Problems and Future Solutions (1998). Monograph of the Anxiety Disorders Association of America.

Conners, C. K. (1997). *The Conners Rating Scales-Revised.* North Tonawanda, NY: Multi-Health Systems.

Kendall, P. A. (1994). Treating anxiety disorders in children: Results of a randomized clinical trial. *Journal of Consulting and Clinical Psychology, 62,* 100-110.

La Greca, A.M., & Stone, W.L. (1993). Social anxiety scale for children-Revised: Factor structure and concurrent validity. *Journal of Clinical Child Psychology, 22* (1), 17-27.

March, J.S. (1997). *The Multidimensional Anxiety Scale for Children* North Tonawanda, NY: Multi-Health Systems.

Mental Health: A report of the Surgeon General. (1999). U.S. Department of Health & Human Services.

Ollendick, T.H. (1993). Reliability and validity of the Revised Fear Survey Schedule for Children (FSSC-R). *Behaviour Research and Therapy, 4,* 465-467.

Rapee, R.M. (1996). Improved efficiency in the treatment of childhood anxiety disorders. Paper presented at the thirtieth annual convention of the Association for the Advancement of Behavior Therapy, New York.

Rapee, R.M., Wignall, A., Hudson, J.L., & Schniering, C.A. (2000). *Treating anxious children and adolescents: An evidence-based approach.* Oakland, CA: Harbinger

Reynolds, C.R. & Richmond, B.O. (1978). What I think and feel: A revised measure of children's manifest anxiety. *Journal of Abnormal Child Psychology, 6,* 271-280.

Spielberger, C.D. (1993). *Manual for the state-trait anxiety inventory for children.* Palo Alto, CA: Consulting Psychologists Press.

Resources

Baer, L. (2000). *Getting control*. New York: Plume.

Dornbush, M.P., & Pruitt, S.K. (1995). *Teaching the tiger*. Duarte, CA: Hope Press.

Eisen, A.R. & Kearney, C.A. (1995). *Practitioner's guide to treating fear and anxiety in children and adolescents*. New Jersey: Aronson.

Greene, R.W. (1998). *The explosive child*. New York: Harper Collins

Greist, J.H., Jefferson, J.W., Marks, I.M. (1986). *Anxiety and its treatment: Help is available*. Washington, DC: American Psychiatric Press.

Johnston H.F., Fruehling, J.J. (2002). *Obsessive Compulsive Disorder in children and adolescents: A Guide*. Madison, WI: Obsessive Compulsive Information Center, Madison Institute of Medicine.

Kendall, P. A. (1992). *The Coping Cat Workbook*. Ardmore, P. A.: Workbook Publishing.

March, J.S., & Mulle, K. (1998). *OCD in children and adolescents*. New York: Guilford.

Marks, I. (2001). *Living with fear*. London: McGraw-Hill.

Goldstein, A.P. & McGinnis, E. (1997). *Skills-streaming the adolescent: New strategies and perspectives for teaching prosocial skills*. Champaign, IL: Research Press.

McGinnis, E. & Goldstein, A.P. (1997). *Skills-streaming the elementary school child: New strategies and perspectives for teaching prosocial skills*. Champaign, IL: Research Press.

Rapee, R.M., Spence, S.H., Cobham, V., & Wignall, A. (2000). *Helping your anxious child*. Oakland, CA: Harbinger.

Rapoport, J.L. (1989). *The boy who couldn't stop washing*. New York: Penguin Books.

Swedo, S.A. & Leonard, H.L. (1998). *Is it just a phase?* New York: Golden Books.

Wagner, A. P. (2000). *Up and Down the Worry Hill: A children's book about Obsessive-Compulsive Disorder*. Rochester, NY: Lighthouse Press

Wagner, A. P. (2005). *Worried No More: Teaching Tools and Forms on CD*. Rochester, NY: Lighthouse Press

Wagner, A. P. (2002). *What to do when your child has Obsessive Compulsive Disorder: Strategies and solutions*. Rochester, NY: Lighthouse Press

Wagner, A. P. (2003). *Treatment of OCD in Children and Adolescents: A Cognitive-Behavioral Therapy Manual*. Rochester, NY: Lighthouse Press

Wilens, T.E. (1999). *Straight talk about psychiatric medications for kids*. New York: Guilford Press.

Support Organizations

Association for Behavioral and Cognitive Therapies (ABCT)
305 Seventh Avenue, 16th Floor
New York, NY 10001-6008
212-647-1890   www.abct.org

Anxiety Disorders Association of America (ADAA)
8730 Georgia Avenue, Suite 600
Silver Spring, MD 20910   www.adaa.org

National Alliance for the Mentally Ill (NAMI)
Colonial Place Three
2107 Wilson Boulevard Suite 300
Arlington, VA 22201-3042
703-524-7600   www.nami.org

National Association of School Psychologists (NASP)
4340 East West Highway, Suite 402
Bethesda, MD 20814
301-657-0270   www.naspweb.org

Obsessive-Compulsive Foundation (OCF)
P.O. Box 9573
New Haven, CT 06535
203-315-2190   www.ocfoundation.org

Obsessive Compulsive Information Center (OCIC)
Madison Institute of Medicine
7617 Mineral Point Road
Madison, WI 53717
608-827-2470   www.miminc.org

Tourette Syndrome Association (TSA)
42-40 Bell Boulevard
New York, NY 11361
718-224-2999   www.tsa-usa.org

www.seriweb.com   Special Education Resources.
www.wrightslaw.com   Special education issues.

Forms and Tools

FORM 1: THE FEELING THERMOMETER

The _____ Thermometer

10. Out of Control! Ballistic!
9. Can't Handle It.
8. Really Tough.
7. Pretty Tough.
6. Getting Tough.
5. Not too Good.
4. Starting to Bother.
3. Just a Little Uneasy.
2. A Little Twinge.
1. Piece of Cake!

FORM 2: PARENT-TEACHER LOG

PARENT-TEACHER LOG

Child's Name: Parent/Teacher: Date:

0	1	2	3	4	5	6	7	8	9	10
No problems			Mild		Moderate		Strong			Extreme

What went well for the child today? In what situations did he/she experience success?

Overall mood/anxiety for the day (0-10): 7

Were there any situations in which the child was upset? If yes, please describe the situation:

Child's mood and distress in this situation (0-10):

Describe child's specific behaviors (yelling, crying):

Describe child's feelings (sad, afraid):

What was the impact of the behavior?

How did you handle this situation?

How did the child react to your handling?

How long did the episode last?

What was the child's overall effort in the situation?

How did you reward the child's effort?

Other comments/questions:

FORM 3: HOME BEHAVIOR OBSERVATIONS

HOME BEHAVIOR OBSERVATIONS

Child's Name: **Parent:**   **Date/Time:**

Situation and triggers:

Specific behaviors and duration:

0	1	2	3	4	5	6	7	8	9	10
No problems			Mild		Moderate			Strong		Extreme

Rate the following (0-10):   Distress: Disruption:

Impact/consequences of behavior:

Child's Name: **Parent:**   **Date/Time:**

Situation and triggers:

Specific behaviors and duration:

0	1	2	3	4	5	6	7	8	9	10
No problems			Mild		Moderate			Strong		Extreme

Rate the following (0-10):   Distress: Disruption:

Impact/consequences of behavior:

FORM 4: SCHOOL BEHAVIOR OBSERVATIONS

SCHOOL BEHAVIOR OBSERVATIONS

Child's Name: **Teacher:**   **Date/Time:**

Situation and triggers:

Specific behaviors and duration:

0	1	2	3	4	5	6	7	8	9	10
No problems			Mild		Moderate		Strong		Extreme	

Rate the following (0-10):   Distress: Disruption:

Impact/consequences of behavior:

Child's Name: **Teacher:**   **Date/Time:**

Situation and triggers:

Specific behaviors and duration:

0	1	2	3	4	5	6	7	8	9	10
No problems			Mild		Moderate		Strong		Extreme	

Rate the following (0-10):   Distress: Disruption:

Impact/consequences of behavior:

FORM 5: MY THOUGHTS AND FEELINGS

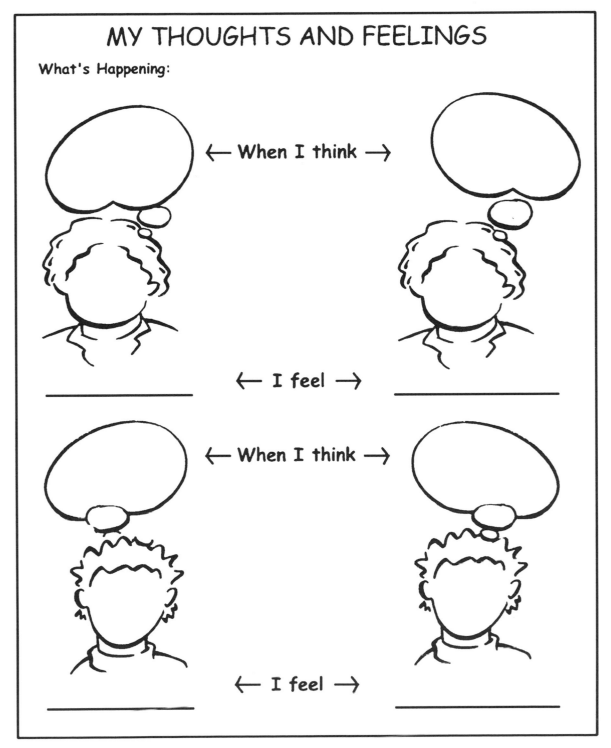

Form 6: My Fear Ladder

Date:	
Goal:	

Things I am afraid to do	**My fear temperature**

FORM 7: EXPOSURE PROGRESS RECORD

My Successes:	Date:		
Goal:			
Things I was afraid to do	**My fear temperature**		**My reward**
	On start date	Today	

FORM 8: THE WORRY HILL MEMORY CARD

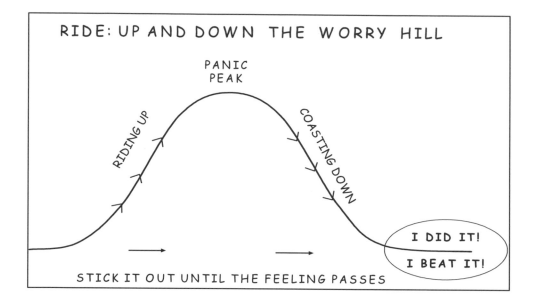

RIDE: UP AND DOWN THE WORRY HILL

PANIC PEAK

RIDING UP

COASTING DOWN

I DID IT!
I BEAT IT!

STICK IT OUT UNTIL THE FEELING PASSES

Rename the thought. ....

Insist that YOU are in charge! ....

Defy anxiety, do the OPPOSITE ....

Enjoy your success, reward yourself. ....

FORM 9: FACING MY FEARS

FACING MY FEARS

Name: Date:

Situation:

What am I feeling?

What's my feeling temperature 1-10?

What am I thinking?

What's the proof that it will happen?

What are the chances it will happen?

What else could happen?

So what if it happens?

How can I deal with it?

What can I say and do to help myself?

What's my fear temperature now?

FORM 10: CORRECTIVE LEARNING EXPERIENCES WORKSHEET

Child's Name: Parent/Teacher: Date

SITUATION:

CHILD'S BEHAVIOR:

1. **TRIGGERS**

2. **ANTICIPATE/DISSIPATE**
    Early cues:
    Strategies:

3. **CHOICES:**

4. **SELF-CALMING**   Feeling temperature: 6
    Cues for need to self-calm:
    Take space:

5. **TIMELY DISENGAGEMENT**   Feeling temperature:
    Cues:
    How:

6. **TIMELY REENGAGEMENT Discuss:**
    ❖ **What happened?**   **Why?**
    ❖ **What feelings?**   **Feeling**
        temperature?
    ❖ **Were feelings okay?**   **Were actions okay?**
    ❖ **If not, why not?**
    ❖ **How could feelings be expressed appropriately?**
    ❖ **How could actions be different?**

7. **WAYS TO REDUCE RECURRENCE**
    Early warning signals:
    Trigger: Solution:

8. **ACCOUNTABILITY:**

9. **WAYS TO MAKE AMENDS:**

INDEX

Worried No More: Teaching Tools and Forms on CD

This companion toolkit helps school professionals and therapists put *Worried No More* into action with children and families

Includes 26 colorful *Teaching Tools* (easy-to-use, 8.5X11 flip cards), ready-to-use Microsoft® Powerpoint® slides (viewer software included), ready-to-print-and-use *Forms on CD* (Adobe® Reader® software included), and *Feeling Thermometers* for school professionals and clinicians to convey key treatment concepts to anxious children and families.

Benefits:
- Powerful visual teaching tools
- Appealing to children and families
- Convenient, easy to use
- Enhances record-keeping
- Increases motivation and compliance
- Improves communication and learning

Sample Forms
- Corrective Learning Experiences
- Parent-Teacher Log
- Home Behavior Observations
- School Behavior Observations
- My Thoughts and Feelings
- The Feeling Thermometer
- My Fear Ladder
- Exposure Progress Record
- The Worry Hill Memory Card
- Facing My Fears

Item Number 4754 $59.95
Software for use with PC's only.

Sample Teaching Tools
- The Anxiety Triad
- The Noise at the Window
- Physical Symptoms of Worry
- The Vicious Cycle of Avoidance
- Lessons to be Learned
- Calm Thinking
- Exposure and Habituation
- Anticipatory Anxiety
- Up and Down the Worry Hill
- The 3 P's of Parenting
- Appropriate Attending
- The *Fearmometer*
- Facts about Exposure and Habituation
- Self-Reliance
- Rewards and Consequences

To Order: Quick Order Form, Toll Free 1.888.749.8768 or www.Lighthouse-Press.com

Up and Down the Worry Hill
A Children's Book about OCD and its Treatment

Item No. 4762 $19.95

This uniquely creative and heart warming book uses a powerful real-life metaphor to help parents and professionals explain OCD clearly and simply through the eyes of a child. Children and adults will identify with Casey's initial struggle with OCD, his relief that neither he nor his parents are to blame, his sense of hope when he learns about treatment, and eventually, his victory over OCD.

"**The best book** available for children with Obsessive-Compulsive Disorder."
Charles Mansueto, Ph.D., Member, Scientific Advisory Board, Obsessive Compulsive Foundation

"**It's a masterpiece**! It captures and conveys the essence of effective behavior therapy for OCD...the metaphors are perfect...Parents, teachers and, most importantly, children will benefit enormously from reading it."
John Greist, M.D., Distinguished Senior Scientist, Madison Institute of Medicine

"**A most helpful book**... carefully motivates the child for treatment."
Michael Jenike, M.D. Professor of Psychiatry, Harvard Medical School

---

The <u>Only</u> Integrated Set of Resources for
Children with OCD, their Parents and their Therapists!
Children: Up and Down the Worry Hill: A Children's Book about OCD
Parents: What to do when your Child has OCD: Strategies and Solutions
Therapists: Treatment of OCD in Children and Adolescents:
Professional's Kit
User friendly, practical and effective!

To Order: Quick Order Form, Toll Free 1.888.749.8768 or www.Lighthouse-Press.com

"The best book available for Children with OCD"

- Charles Mansueto, Ph.D., Scientific Advisory Board, Obsessive-Compulsive Foundation

~ NOW ON AUDIO CD ~

Listen as Aureen Wagner, Ph.D. award winning author and internationally recognized expert in the treatment of childhood OCD reads:

Up and Down the Worry Hill: A Children's Book about Obsessive-Compulsive Disorder and its Treatment.

Audio CD
Aureen P. Wagner, Ph.D.
Up and Down the Worry Hill:
A Children's Book about Obsessive-Compulsive Disorder and its Treatment
Read by the Author

Item Number 4789 $19.95

- Casey's Worries and Habits
- Casey Gets Help
- Note for Parents/Professionals

Appropriate for children with OCD,

siblings and classmates

What to do when your Child has Obsessive Compulsive Disorder: Strategies and Solutions

The Companion Parent Guide to: *Up and Down the Worry Hill*

"<u>Must reading</u> for parents of children with OCD. Clearly the work of a skilled and compassionate clinician. Just as important, it makes interesting reading."
Judith Rapoport, M.D., Chief, Child Psychiatry Branch, National Institute of Mental Health

Using the compelling Worry Hill approach, Dr. Wagner provides families with the blueprint to triumph over OCD.

- Step-by-step practical guidance
- Unlocks the power of the parent-child team to conquer OCD
- Practical, clear and easy-to-understand steps
- The latest scientifically proven advances in recovery

Item No. 4711 $19.95

What the experts say:

❖ "Every parent who has a child with OCD should read this book. I will recommend it from now on." Michael Jenike, M.D., Harvard Medical School

❖ "A "must read," essential book…just the right balance of medical background and practical advice…filled with pearls of wisdom…" Roger Kurlan, M.D., Medical Advisory Board, Tourette Syndrome Association

❖ "A truly remarkable guide for parents, clinicians and school personnel…Expertly written and organized…" John Piacentini, Ph.D., Director, UCLA Child OCD, Anxiety and Tic Disorders Program

To Order: Quick Order Form, Toll Free 1.888.749.8768 or www.Lighthouse-Press.com

Putting the Groundbreaking Worry Hill treatment approach into action!

Treatment of OCD in Children and Adolescents: Professional's Kit

The third part of the integrated Worry Hill Master Set for the Treatment of OCD

This newly revised and expanded popular resource for professionals includes second editions of both the Therapy Manual and Teaching Tools. Dr. Wagner shares her internationally acclaimed Worry Hill protocol for OCD, along with clinical pearls from her many years of experience. She provides expert guidance on special topics including:

- Developing treatment readiness
- Collaborating with parents
- Working with reluctant children
- Overcoming challenges in treatment

The Professional's Kit Includes:

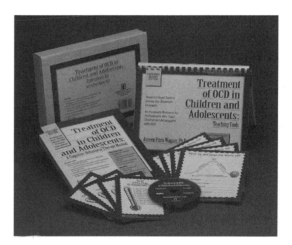

A. Cognitive-Behavioral Therapy Manual (Expanded Second Edition)
B. Complete set of thirty 8.5" x 11" Teaching Tools (Comb bound, Second Edition)
C. Over 35 ready-to-print-and-use forms on CD (PC only)
D. Worry Hill Memory Cards and Feeling Thermometers for use in working with children and families

Item Number 9226 $139.95
For clinicians

Benefits:

- User-friendly and appealing
- Step-by-step protocols
- Easy application and record-keeping
- Clear and self-explanatory
- Detailed case examples

"This manual is the **best available resource for clinicians**...clear, concise and accurate...with a rich supply of clinical insights and practical tips. I highly recommend it to all practitioners, from beginners to seasoned clinicians."

Charles Mansueto, Ph.D., Scientific Advisory Board, Obsessive Compulsive Foundation

"This is a **valuable** treatment manual for youngsters with OCD. I **recommend it with enthusiasm!**"
Judith Rapoport, M.D., Chief, Child Psychiatry, National Institute of Mental Health

Expert Clinician Consultation

Dr. Aureen Wagner provides consultation to school professionals and health care professionals on the assessment and treatment of anxiety problems and disorders in children and adolescents. Consultation is tailored to suit your individual or group needs.

<u>Topics may include but are not limited to:</u>
- Assessment
- Differential diagnosis
- Treatment plans
- Exposure hierarchies
- Cognitive strategies
- Socratic technique
- Treatment reluctance
- Challenges in treatment
- Working with families

Telephone sessions are scheduled at mutually agreeable times.

For information on fees and scheduling, please visit
www.anxietywellness.com

Anxiety and OCD Workshops

For Parents, Schools and Health care Professionals

Dr. Wagner is a nationally sought-after speaker who presents training workshops and seminars

Testimonials from recent workshops:

- "This is the best presentation I have attended in many years. Thank you! I will bring to my district a tremendous wealth of information and specific plans on how to help so <u>many</u> anxious children."

- "Thank you for the wonderful workshop you presented on anxiety… I was extremely pleased with the turnout and the response. Thank you for all your time and effort in tailoring your presentation to meet our needs."

- "This was an excellent workshop on OCD. Information was presented in a thorough, concrete manner to "grip" the attention of a diversely trained audience. I fully appreciated the inclusion of the discussion on adolescents, especially high school age students."

- "This is easily one of the best workshops I have ever attended. Thank you for the wonderful touch and the tremendous knowledge you bring to us."

- "Excellent presentation! Very helpful – warm, articulate and positive. Nice balance of lecture – large/small group."

- "Great presentation – interesting, informative, well prepared, organized. Wonderful overview, clear messages and facts."

- "Very applicable since I work with children – good stuff I can use!"

- Thank you so much! I don't know when I've sat through a presentation that is so practical to what I do in my daily work. I learned a great deal.

- "What a wonderfully informative session. Dr. Wagner's explanation about OCD was easy to grasp and very helpful to me not only as a teacher of an OCD kid, but also the parent of a child with a major anxiety disorder."

- "Dr. Wagner is so articulate; the presentation was effectively and efficiently packed with useful information. Thank you."

For more information, please visit www.Lighthouse-Press.com or call (585) 594-4770

Can't Attend One of Dr. Wagner's Highly Acclaimed Workshops?

Introducing, **Anxiety and OCD at School**. An audio and slide presentation recorded during one of Dr. Wagner's most popular workshops for School Professionals. Just like a real workshop, you'll listen to Dr. Wagner as you view the slides that accompany the presentation, and follow along with the handout. Packed with practical advice, you'll want to listen to this presentation repeatedly. This CD will make a valuable addition to your personal or staff development library.

Dr. Wagner is a highly engaging and sought-after speaker whose workshops consistently receive outstanding reviews. You'll benefit from her many years of working with anxious children, her user-friendly conceptualizations and her practical Worry Hill innovations.

This workshop is ideal for a broad range of school staff, including mainstream and special education teachers, teacher's aides, counselors, social workers, speech and occupational therapists, administrators and school psychologists.

Item Number 4770 $49.95

- For use with personal computers (PC) with a CD-ROM drive.
- Running time approximately 2 hrs., 16 minutes
- Printable 21 page handout

- Introduction
- The Many Faces of Anxiety
- Understanding Anxiety
- Anxiety Disorders
- Differential Diagnosis
- Risk Factors
- CBT
- Child Management
- Medications
- Contributions of School Personnel

To Order: Quick Order Form, Toll Free 1.888.749.8768 or www.Lighthouse-Press.com

Special Offers

The Worry Hill Master Set
for the Treatment of OCD

**Order this set and
save over $29!**
Item No. 9993
Price $149.95

Includes:
1. Up and Down the Worry Hill
2. What to do when your Child has OCD
3. Treatment of OCD in Children and Adolescents:
    Professional's Kit

The Anxiety Treatment Master Set
for the Treatment of Anxiety Problems

**Order this set and
save $10!**
Item No. 9995
Price $74.90

Includes:
1. Worried No More
2. Worried No More: Teaching Tools and Forms on CD

Special Offers

The School Professionals Master Set

Includes:
1. Up and Down the Worry Hill
2. Worried No More
3. Worried No More: Teaching Tools and Forms on CD
4. Anxiety and OCD at School: Live Workshop for School Professionals.
   PC CD-ROM

....

To Order: Quick Order Form, Toll Free 1.888.749.8768 or www.Lighthouse-Press.com

QUICK

Order Form

To place an order:
Call: 1-888-749-8768 (Toll free, USA), OR 1-585-594-0311
FAX your Purchase Order to: 1-585-594-4207 OR
Mail your order to address below

Item	Title	Price*	Qty	Total

* Prices subject to change without notice

SUBTOTAL price of items $_____

Shipping (see chart below) $_____

New York Residents add 8% Sales Tax $_____

TOTAL AMOUNT DUE: $_____

SHIPPING: *Within the U.S.* $5 for the first book, $3 for each additional book
              Orders outside the U.S. $9 for the first book $4 for each additional book

---

PAYMENT:

____ Check or Money Order (payable to *Lighthouse Press* through a U.S. bank in *U.S. dollars*)

____ Purchase Order Attached (Please bill my institution)

____ MasterCard   __Visa   __Discover   __American Express

Card Number_____ Expiration Date_____

Signature (required for Credit Card Orders)_____

SHIP TO:
Name:_____

Street Address_____ _____

City/State/ZIP:_____

Daytime Phone:_____ E-mail (optional):_____

Please mail your completed order form with your check or money order to:
Lighthouse Press Inc., 35 Ryans Run, Rochester, NY 14624-1160

QUICK
Order Form

To place an order:
Call: 1-888-749-8768 (Toll free, USA), OR 1-585-594-0311
FAX your Purchase Order to: 1-585-594-4207 OR
Mail your order to address below

Item	Title	Price*	Qty	Total

* Prices subject to change without notice

SUBTOTAL price of items	$_____
Shipping (see chart below)	$_____
New York Residents add 8% Sales Tax	$_____
TOTAL AMOUNT DUE:	$_____

> *SHIPPING:* *Within the U.S.* $5 for the first book, $3 for each additional book
> *Orders outside the U.S.* $9 for the first book $4 for each additional book

PAYMENT:

_____Check or Money Order (payable to *Lighthouse Press* through a U.S. bank in *U.S. dollars*)

_____ Purchase Order Attached (Please bill my institution)

_____ MasterCard _____Visa _____Discover _____American Express

Card Number_____ Expiration Date_____

Signature (required for Credit Card Orders)_____

SHIP TO:
Name:_____

Street Address_____

City/State/ZIP:_____

Daytime Phone:_____ E-mail (optional):_____

Please mail your completed order form with your check or money order to:
Lighthouse Press Inc., 35 Ryans Run, Rochester, NY 14624-1160